P9-CRB-600

Neurology for the Speech-Language Pathologist

Russell J. Love, Ph.D.
Wanda G. Webb, Ph.D.

Division of Hearing and Speech Sciences
Vanderbilt University School of Medicine
Nashville, Tennessee

Illustrations by Donna B. Halliburton

Butterworths
Boston London Durban Singapore Sydney Toronto Wellington

This book is dedicated to Barbara and Joe

Copyright © 1986 by Butterworth Publishers.
All rights reserved.

No part of this publication may be reproduced, stored in a retrieval system, or transmitted, in any form or by any means, electronic, mechanical, photocopying, recording, or otherwise, without the prior written permission of the publisher.

Every effort has been made to ensure that the drug dosage schedules within this text are accurate and conform to standards accepted at time of publication. However, as treatment recommendations vary in the light of continuing research and clinical experience, the reader is advised to verify drug dosage schedules herein with information found on product information sheets. This is especially true in cases of new or infrequently used drugs.

Library of Congress Cataloging-in-Publication Data

Love, Russell J.
  Neurology for the speech-language pathologist.

  Includes bibliographies and index.
  1. Language disorders.   2. Neurolinguistics.
3. Speech, Disorders of.   4. Neurology.   I. Webb,
Wanda G.   II. Title. [DNLM: 1. Brain—physiology.
2. Brain—physiopathology.   3. Communicative Disorders—
physiopathology.   WL 300 L897n]
RC423.L68   1986   616.85'5   85-23280
ISBN 0-409-95166-8

Butterworth Publishers
80 Montvale Avenue
Stoneham, MA   02180

10 9 8 7 6 5 4

Printed in the United States of America

Contents

Speech Pathology and Neurology: Intersecting Specialties

Howard S. Kirshner, M.D.

NEUROLOGY IS THE study of the effects of disease in the nervous system—brain, spinal cord, cerebellum, nerves, and muscles—on human behavior. The neurologist examines specific functions—higher cortical functions; cranial nerve functions; motor, sensory, and cerebellar functions—all to localize disorders to specific areas of the nervous system. These lesion localizations, along with the clinical history of how the deficit developed and the results of laboratory tests, allow a precise diagnosis of the disease process.

Speech and communication are among the most complicated functions of the human brain, involving a myriad of interactions between personality, cognitive processes, imagination, language, emotion, and lower sensory and motor systems necessary for articulation and comprehension. These functions involve brain pathways and mechanisms, some well understood and others only beginning to be conceptualized. The brain mechanisms underlying higher functions such as language are known largely through neurological studies of human patients with acquired brain lesions. Animal models have shed only limited light on these complex disorders. Stroke has historically been a great source of information, as this "experiment of nature" damages one brain area while leaving the rest of the nervous system intact. For over a century, patients with strokes and other brain diseases have been studied in life, and the clinical syndromes have then been correlated with brain lesions found at autopsy. Recently, new methods of brain imaging have made possible the simultaneous study of a lesion in the brain and a deficit of communication in the same patient. These advances in brain imaging, including computerized axial tomography (CAT scan), magnetic resonance imaging, and positron emission tomography (PET), have brought about a burgeoning of knowledge in this area.

In this book, Drs. Love and Webb have laid the factual groundwork for the understanding of the nervous system in terms of the organization of the brain, descending motor and ascending sensory pathways, and cranial nerves and muscles. Understanding these anatomic systems makes possible the understanding and classification of syndromes of aphasia, alexia, dysarthria, and dysphonia, as well as the effects of specific, localized disease processes on human speech and communication. All these subjects are clearly and accurately reviewed. The speech pathologist who studies this book should have a much improved comprehension of the brain mechanisms disrupted in speech- and language-impaired patients, and, thereby, a greater understanding of the disorders of speech and language themselves.

Perhaps the most important by-product of this book should be a closer interaction between neurologists and speech pathologists. Neurologists understand the anatomic relationships of the brain and its connections, but they often fail to use speech and language to their full limits in assessing the function of specific parts of the nervous system. A careful analysis of speech and language functions can supplement the more cursory portions of the standard neurological examination devoted to these functions. Thus detailed aphasia testing supplements the neurologist's bedside mental-status examination, and close observation of palatal, lingual, and facial motion during articulation supplements the neurologist's cranial nerve examination. The neurologist's diagnosis of the patient's disorder, on the other hand, should aid the speech pathologist in understanding the nature and prognosis of the speech and language disorder. The neurologist and speech pathologist should ideally function as a team, each complementing the efforts of the other. In order for this teamwork to occur, however, each specialist must comprehend the other's language. To this end, Drs. Love and Webb have made the language of the neurologist understandable to speech pathologists. As a neurologist who has worked closely with both of them, I applaud them for this important accomplishment.

Preface

THE SPUR FOR this book was a time-honored one. We found the current crop of textbooks inappropriate to the needs of our students. The senior author in particular has spent considerable effort in recent years attempting to adapt neurology textbooks designed for medical students to the needs of students in speech-language pathology. The results of these efforts often have been frustrating and less than ideal. Therefore, this book is designed as an introduction to neuroanatomy, neurology, and neuropsychology for the student and practicing clinician interested in neurogenic communication disorders. We hope it will be helpful to students without medical training. It is not designed to replace the excellent textbooks now available that have been prepared for courses in adult aphasia, motor speech disorders, and developmental neurologic speech and language problems in children. Rather, it is hoped that this book will serve as a primary textbook for an introductory course in the neurology of speech and language, or as a supplementary source in those usually standard courses in the curriculum that deal with neurogenic communication disorders. This book is aimed at advanced undergraduates and beginning graduate students as well as the working speech-language pathologist.

For authors primarily trained in the field of speech-language pathology rather than neurology, a project like this demands reliance on colleagues in neurology to assist in the development of the work. Howard S. Kirshner, M.D., Department of Neurology, Vanderbilt University School of Medicine, went above and beyond the call of duty in bringing his expertise to bear on this project. He not only read the text for accuracy, but also made important suggestions concerning the organization and clarity of the book. He was extremely patient with our attempts to oversimplify a complex area of knowledge that is rarely grasped completely by the individual who has not had some training in the biological sciences. We are indebted to him for his careful attention to the manuscript, but we wish to indicate that we alone are responsible for errors of fact and flaws in organization and clarity in the text. We are indebted as well to several members of the editorial staff, past and present, of Butterworths. These include David Coen, Arthur Evans, Julie Stillman, and Margaret Quinlin. Finally, no book can be successfully completed without competent secretarial support. We wish to thank Tammy Richardson, Betty Longwith, Sherri Culp, and Solveig Hultgren.

Textbooks grow from seeds of inspiration usually planted by outstanding teachers. We would particularly like to acknowledge Harold Westlake, Ph.D., professor emeritus, School of Speech, Northwestern University, and the late Joseph Wepman, Ph.D., University of Chicago. Both of these scholar-clinicians provided a vision of the role of the speech-language pathologist in the study, diagnosis, and management of neurologic communication disorders. Without their inspiration and contribution as role models, this book probably would not have been written.

R.J.L.
W.G.W.

CHAPTER ONE

Introduction to Speech-Language Neurology

"We must admit that the divine banquet of the brain was, and still is, a feast with dishes that remain elusive in their blending, and with sauces whose ingredients are even now a secret."

—MacDonald Critchley, *The Divine Banquet of the Brain,* 1979

Why Neurology?

Every student of communicative disorders realizes without being taught that the brain is the source of all speech and language behavior. Nevertheless, many students shy away from achieving a basic understanding of the neural mechanisms of speech, language, and hearing because they believe the nervous system is overwhelmingly complex and abstruse. This complexity and obscurity, they fear, will lead only to perplexity and frustration if they attempt serious study of neuroanatomy and neurophysiology.

To compound this attitude, many academic training programs in communicative disorders treat the neurologic aspects of their discipline only superficially, arguing that this aspect of our knowledge is more properly the domain of medicine. In fact, some training programs in communicative disorders would make neurology the exclusive domain of the physician. The arguments generally cited for this point of view are, first, that neurology has little relevance to diagnosis or the day-to-day clinical management of the communicatively disordered client, and, second, that operant/behavioral management principles have been demonstrated to be effective in improving the speech and language of clients. These principles assume no neurologic explanation. This general position is expressed by Starkweather (1983).

Effective as behavioral principles have been in the diagnosis and management of communicative disorders, elevation of operant techniques to a central position in both the theory and practice of speech and language pathology may force the speech-language pathologist into the role of a mere technician, expert at dealing with only one facet of a multifaceted problem. This limited view will never permit a complete understanding of the disorders of speech and language.

There has been an increasing interest in the neurologic aspects of speech and language pathology in the past two decades. Language development and its disorders are being studied in the context of developmental neurology and biological explanation (Lenneberg, 1967). A clearer understanding of the motor disorders of speech has been gained in the last two decades, and the literature on dysarthria and apraxia of speech has been expanded impressively. Interest in the study and treatment of aphasia has so increased that there is now a subspeciality called clinical aphasiology. Research and writing on cerebral speech and language disorders and their mechanisms are no longer solely the province of neurologists, as was almost always the case in the past. Today, the speech-language pathologist, the neuropsychologist, and the neurolinguist are major contributors to the ever-growing abundance of literature on neurologic communication disorders.

In a significant manner this literature reflects the fact that the modern-day speech-language pathologist is playing an expanded and crucial role in the rehabilitation of persons with neurologic disorders. Since World War II, the speech pathology service has become an accepted service in the standard rehabilitation center and many general hospitals. As the role of the speech-language pathologist expands in the rehabilitation of the neurologic patient, the neurologic information and background expected to be part of the academic training will be considerably larger in scope. Future speech-language pathologists will view themselves as important students and contributors to the field of neuroscience. Speech pathology will be one of several specialties contributing to the discipline of behavioral neurology.

It should be emphasized that it is not the responsibility of the clinical speech-language pathologist to diagnose a neurologic disorder. This function is in the realm of the physician. Nevertheless, it is the undeniable responsibility of the speech-language pathologist to assess all relevant aspects of speech and language in those with a known or suspected neurologic disorder. The speech-language pathologist must be accountable for understanding the results of this speech-language assessment in terms of the underlying neurological mechanisms. Further, the clinical speech-language pathologist must be conversant with current methods of neurologic diagnoses and treatment as they apply to persons with communicative disorders. The neurologist's point of view toward speech and language disorders should be familiar to every clinician. In turn, the neurologist must be conversant with assessment methods and therapy procedures of the communication disorders specialist. This is particularly crucial now, since both disciplines have developed relatively independently in the past half century, sometimes to the detriment of both professions and the people they serve.

Historical Roots: Development of a Brain Science of Speech-Language

Speech-language pathology has many of its roots in neurology. In 1861 the French physician, Pierre Paul Broca (1824–1880), studied the brains of two patients who both sustained a language loss and a motor speech disorder. This allowed him to localize the human speech center to a definite circumscribed area of the left hemisphere, and a brain science of speech and language was irrevocably established. Broca's discovery went far beyond the now classic description of an interesting brain disorder called *aphasia*. Possibly foremost among his conclusions was the assertion that the two hemispheres of the brain were asymmetrical in function and that the left cerebral hemisphere contained the speech center in the majority of the population. Important implications of asymmetry of the brain are even now coming to light in neuroscience research some twelve decades later. Asymmetry of function is more pervasive than was thought earlier. It extends well beyond speech to other brain areas and their functions.

Another conclusion that has had everlasting importance for neurology since Broca's death is that specific behavioral functions appear to be associated with clearly localized sites in the brain. The collorary of this observation is that behavioral dysfunction can point to lesions at specific sites in the nervous system. The concept of localization of function in the nervous system has been demonstrated repeatedly by clinical and research methods since Broca first articulated it over a century ago. This observation was so profound that it became a significant historical force in the establishment of the medical discipline of clinical neurology. Much of clinical neurology is dependent on the physician's ability to lateralize and localize a lesion in the nervous system.

Very important for speech-language pathology was the fact that Broca's discovery stimulated a period of intensive search for a workable explanation of the brain mechanisms of speech and language. Probably no period in the history of neurologic science has so advanced the understanding of communication and its disorders as those years between the date of Broca's discovery and World War I.

One of the first and foremost outcomes of this intensive study of speech-language brain mechanisms was the establishment of neurologic substrata for modalities of language deficit other than the expressive oral language described by Broca. In 1867, William Ogle published a case that demonstrated that a cerebral writing center was independent of Broca's center for speech. Carl Wernicke (1848–1905) in 1874 identified an auditory speech center in the temporal lobe; it was associated with comprehension of speech as opposed to Broca's area in the frontal lobe, which was an expressive speech center. Lesions in Broca's area produced a motor aphasia, in Wernicke's area a sensory aphasia. In 1892 Joseph Dejerine identified mechanisms underlying reading disorders. Disorders of cortical sensory recognition, or the *agnosias*, were named by Sigmund Freud in 1891, and in 1900 Hugo Liepmann comprehensively analyzed the *apraxias*—disorders of executing motor acts resulting from brain lesion.

Early Language Models

Of the many neurological models of the cerebral language mechanisms that were generated soon after Broca's great discovery, Wernicke's 1874 model has best withstood the test of time. Wernicke stressed the importance of cortical language centers associated with the various language modalities, but he also emphasized the importance of association fiber tracts connecting areas or centers. Like his teacher Theodore Meynert (1833–1892), he understood that the connections in the brain were just as important as the centers for a complete picture of language performance (Meynert, 1885). In addition, Wernicke organized the symptoms of language disturbance in such a way that they could be used diagnostically to predict the lesion site in either connective pathways or centers in the language system. Ironically, the Wernicke model was eclipsed until the last half of the twentieth century, when it was revitalized and expanded by Norman Geschwind (1926–1984) and his followers (Geschwind, 1974).

Wernicke's model came under criticism by the English neurologist Henry Head (1926). He lumped Wernicke with a cadre of early neurologists he considered the more flagrant of the "diagram makers," implying that they constructed language models that were highly speculative and not supported by empirical evidence. Current methods of neurologic investigation, including electrical cortical stimulation, isotope localization of lesions, computerized tomography, and regional blood flow studies in the brain, have generally vindicated Wernicke's model of language.

Neurologic speech mechanisms, as opposed to language mechanisms, also received attention in the late nineteenth century. In 1871 the famous French neurologist Jean Charcot (1825–1893) described the "scanning speech" that he associated with "disseminated sclerosis," now known as multiple sclerosis (Charcot, 1890). The term *scanning*, probably inappropriate, has also been widely used to describe speech with cerebellar or cerebellar pathway lesions (see Chapter 8). In 1888 an English neurologist, William Gowers (1846–1915) surveyed the neurologic speech disorders, known as *dysarthrias*, in a well-known textbook titled *A Manual of Diseases of the Nervous System*.

World War I

World War I had a profound influence on the study of speech and language mechanisms resulting from neurologic insult. With a large population of head-injured young men with penetrating skull wounds, some neurologists felt an urgency for treatment. A handful of dedicated neurologists provided therapy for these traumatic language disorders because the profession of speech pathology was not yet born. Not until the next decade did the profession really began. Lee Edward Travis has the distinction of being the first individual in the United States to specialize in the field of speech and language disorders at the doctoral level. In 1927 he became the first director of the speech clinic at the University of Iowa. His special interest was in stuttering, and he began to study it in a neurologic context. Influenced by the neuropsychiatrist, Samuel Terry Orton (1879–1948), Travis researched the hypothesis that stuttering was the result of brain dysfunction, specifically an imbalance or competition between the two cerebral hemispheres to control the normal bilateral functioning of the speech musculature. Orton's hypothesis of dysfunctioning neural control of the speech musculature has generally been discredited, but his hemisphere competition theory of stuttering still surfaces from time to time in different guises to explain certain communication disorders.

Although several of the founders of speech pathology in the United States believed that psychological explanations were more rewarding for understanding speech and language problems, there were notable exceptions. In particular, Robert West of the University of Wisconsin; Jon Eisenson, now of California State University; and Joseph Wepman of the University of Chicago were all advocates of neurologic principles in communication disorders.

Modern Times

World War II, bringing in its wake thousands of traumatic aphasic servicemen, utilized neurologists, psychologists, and speech pathologists in treatment programs for the first time. This effort produced a series of books and articles on aphasia rehabilitation, but perhaps the most notable for the neurologically oriented speech-language pathologist was Wepman's *Recovery from Aphasia* (1951). It served as a textbook of language disorders for the growing number of students in the field and often served as their first introduction to a major neurologic communicative disorder.

The study of neurologic speech mechanisms was greatly advanced after World War II by the work of Wilder G. Penfield (1891–1976) and his colleagues in Canada. Penfield, a neurosurgeon, used the technique of electrical cortical stimulation to map cortical areas directly, particularly speech and language centers. In 1950 in *The Cerebral Cortex of Man* and in 1959 in *Speech and Brain Mechanisms*, he documented his observations on cerebral control of speech and language function and wrote on the concepts of subcortical speech mechanisms and infantile cerebral plasticity.

The decades of the 1960s and 1970s were marked by several advances of neurologic concepts in communication and its disorders. Newer linguistic theory, particularly that proposed by Noam Chomsky (1972, 1975) emphasized the universal features and innate mechanisms reflected in language. The biological aspects of language and speech were highlighted by the linguist and psychologist Eric Lenneberg (1967). He specifically placed language acquisition in the context of developmental neurology. The split-brain studies, reported by Roger Sperry and his colleagues (1969), when the commissural tracts between the hemispheres were severed, indicated specific functions of the right hemisphere as different from the left.

Major anatomical differences in the right and left language centers were also demonstrated in the human brain. Most significant are larger areas in the left temporal lobe in the fetus, infant, and adult (Wada, Clark, & Hamm, 1975; Witelson & Pallie, 1973; Geschwind & Levitsky, 1968). These differences suggest an anatomical basis for cerebral dominance for language and contradict a theory of progressive lateralization of speech centers.

Throughout the 1960s and 1970s considerable attention was paid to neurologic speech disorders. Neurologists and speech pathologists in the Mayo Clinic Neurology Department (Darley, Aronson, & Brown, 1969a,b, 1975) documented the acoustic-perceptual characteristics of the major dysarthrias in a viable classification scheme. This work has stimulated widespread study of the various adult dysarthrias in the speech science laboratories of the country.

The 1960s and 1970s were also marked by the development of three psychometrically sound and widely used aphasia tests—*The Minnesota Test of Differential Diagnosis of Aphasia* (Schuell, 1965); the *Porch Index of Communicative Ability* (Porch, 1967, 1971); and the *Boston Diagnostic Aphasia Examination* (Goodglass & Kaplan, 1972). Coupled with new neurodiagnostic techniques such as radioisotopic scanning, computerized axial tomography (CAT) scanning, and regional cerebral blood flow and metabolic rate, these tests allowed more accurate study of the correlations between brain and language behavior.

Ingvar (1983) suggested that recent advances in neurodiagnostic imaging techniques may soon lead to precise visualization of neurophysiologic mechanisms of speech and language in the brain of conscious subjects, although present techniques are limited. Regional cerebral metabolic rate, (rCMR) studies, used with positron emission tomography of the whole brain (PETScan), both at cortical sites and in deep structures simultaneously, has spatial resolution and improved temporal resolution. This very promising technique provides more information than does the older regional cerebral flow technique (rCBF).

Thus, in only a century and a quarter there have been dramatic gains in knowledge about brain function as it relates to speech and language. Also in this time, a new discipline, *speech-language pathology*, was born. It has experienced tremendous growth and earned respect as a profession. Today's speech-language pathologist is obligated to continue to advance the profession by being knowledgable in neuroanatomy and neurologic disease as they affect human communication.

How to Study

Most students in speech-language pathology receive a limited introduction in their undergraduate careers to the neurosciences. Often they have not been exposed to course work in the biological sciences. The majority of students are, of course, enrolled in courses designed to acquaint them with the anatomy and physiology of speech, but usually these courses focus on speech musculature. Students often do not receive an adequate introduction to neuroanatomy and neurophysiology of speech and language. It is assumed that students will learn these details in courses in aphasia, adult dysarthria, and rehabilitation of speech in cerebral palsy. Students find a neuroscience course taken as advanced undergraduates or beginning graduate students difficult.

Students often say that neurology courses are difficult because they believe they must learn the technical term for each hill and valley in the complex anatomy of the brain. Second, the technical terms are unfamiliar ones, usually derived from Greek and Roman roots. We will concentrate on crucial terminology for an understanding of speech and language, but we will not burden the student with neuroanatomical terminology that does not affect speech and language directly. A glossary is provided at the end of the book to help readers with terminology.

Part of the strategy in mastering any textbook in the biological sciences is to give the study of drawings, diagrams, and tables in the text as much time as the narrative sections of the textbook. If the reader can come away from a study of this textbook with a set of working mental images of the structures and pathways of the nervous system that are important to communication, and can recall them at critical times, then one of the purposes of this textbook will be realized.

The reader, of course, must also master the verbal material in the text. An integration of verbal material with eidetic imagery means that students must call on all their brain power, bringing into play the special capacities of both the right and left hemispheres of the brain. We now know that the left hemisphere is specialized for its capacities of verbal analysis and reasoning, whereas the right hemisphere is specialized for its imagery functions. Utilization of functions of both hemispheres will facilitate learning in neurology.

With our emphasis on imagery as one of the better ways to learn neurology, it should be no surprise that we urge readers to use as a teaching aid their own drawings of structures and pathways. Even crude sketches, carefully labeled, will teach the necessary anatomic relationship and will fix pathways, structures, and names in the mind.

Anatomical Orientation

In order to aid this visualization process of learning, we have used many drawings throughout the text. When viewing drawings in textbooks or creating your own set of anatomic sketches, one must constantly orient oneself in terms of the standard anatomical position and planes. The human body itself may be defined in terms of an anatomical position—one in which the body is erect, the head, eyes, and toes pointed forward. The limbs are at the side of the body and the palms face forward. From this fundamental position, other positions, planes, and directions may be defined. These positions, planes, and directions apply to the brain as well as other sections of the body. Three planes are traditionally defined:

- The *median* plane, or section, passes longitudinally through the brain and divides the right from the left.
- A *sagittal* plane divides the brain vertically at any point and parallels the medial plane.
- A *coronal*, or frontal, section is any vertical cut through the brain that separates into front and back halves.
- A *horizontal* plane divides the brain into upper and lower halves and is at right angles to the median and coronal planes.
- A *transverse* cut is any section that is at right angles to the longitudinal axis of the structure.

Directions

Several terms are used to designate direction in neuroanatomy. Some of these terms are used synonymously. *Anterior* means toward the front, and *posterior* indicates toward the back. *Superior* refers to upper; *inferior* means lower. The term *cranial* or *cephalic* is used in place of superior. The word *rostral*, meaning near the mouth or front end, may sometimes be substituted for *cranial* or *cephalic*.

Medial means toward the medial plane, and *lateral* means further from the median plane. *Ventral* means toward the belly or front; *dorsal* is toward the back. *Ventral* is sometimes used to indicate structures lying at the base of the brain (Figure 1-1).

FIGURE 1-1 Diagram of the major terms of position and the basic planes of reference in the body

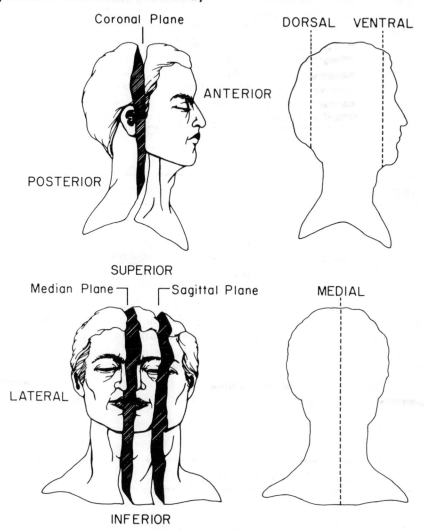

Connective Pathways

A particularly confusing class of terms for the student are those terms used for nerves or nerve fibers or connective pathways. The terms are redundant and follow no particular logic. Students must accept this bothersome fact and should realize that these terms have historical tradition behind them. The words generally derive from Latin and Greek roots. Table 1-1 provides information helpful in understanding the words through their root meanings.

TABLE 1-1
Terms for Connective Pathways in the Nervous System

Bundle: A group of fibers; a fasciculus
Column: A pillar of fibers
Fasciculus: A small bundle
Funiculus: A cord; a cord of nerve fibers in a nerve trunk
Lemniscus: A ribbon; a ribbon of fibers
Tract: A large group of nerve fibers; a pathway

Summary

The brain is the source of all speech and language behavior. Hence, current knowledge concerning its anatomy and functioning must be studied and absorbed by the speech-language pathologist. The study of the relationship between the brain and speech and language function has a rich history in the past century and a quarter, and the disciplines of speech-language pathology and neurology have often been cooperative in the study of neurologically based communication disorders. In the study of neuroanatomy and neurology, clinicians must take advantage of diagrams and drawings and must initially orient themselves to the anatomical directions and terminology used in neuroanatomy texts. Employing both verbal reasoning (left-hemisphere function) and visual imagery (right-hemisphere function) will contribute to a successful experience.

References and Further Readings

Broca, P. (1861). Remarques sur le seige de la faculte du language articule, suivies d'une observation d'aphemie (perte do la parole). *Bull. Anat. Paris,* 2ᵉ serie 6, 332–333, 343–357. Translated in D. A. Rottenberg & F. H. Hockberg (1977), *Neurologic classics in modern translation.* New York: Hafner Press.

Charcot, J. M. (1890). *Oeuvres complete de J. M. Charcot.* Paris: Lecrosnier et Babe.

Chomsky, N. (1972). *Language and mind.* New York: Harcourt and Brace.

Chomsky, N. (1975). *Reflections on language.* New York: Pantheon Books.

Darley, F. L.; Aronson, A. E.; & Brown, J. R. (1969a). Differential diagnostic patterns of dysarthria. *Journal of Speech and Hearing Research,* 12, 246–249.

Darley, F. L.; Aronson, A. E.; & Brown, J. R. (1969b). Clusters of deviant speech dimensions in the dysarthrias. *Journal of Speech and Hearing Research,* 12, 462–469.

Darley, F. L.; Aronson, A. E.; & Brown, J. R. (1975). *Motor speech disorders*. Philadelphia: W. B. Saunders.

Dejerine, J. (1892). Contribution a étude anatomopathologique et clinique des differentes variétés de cectie verbal. *Memoires de la Société de Biologie*, 27, 1–30.

Freud, S. (1953). *On aphasia: A critical study*. Translated by E. Stengel. New York: International Universities Press.

Geschwind, N. (1974). *Selected papers on language and the brain*. Boston: D. Reidel.

Geschwind, N., & Levitsky, W. (1968). Human brain: Right-left asymmetries in temporal speech region. *Science*, 168, 186–187.

Goodglass, H., & Kaplan, E. (1972). *Assessment of aphasia and related disorders*. Philadelphia: Lea and Febiger.

Gowers, W. R. (1888). *A manual of diseases of the nervous system*. Philadelphia: Biakiston.

Head, H. (1926). *Aphasia and kindred disorders* (2 vols.). London: Cambridge University Press.

Ingvar. D, (1983). Serial aspects of language and speech related to prefrontal cortical activity. *Human Neurobiology*, 2, 177–189.

Liepmann, H. (1900). Das Krankheitbild der apraxie ("motorischen asymbolie") *Monatsschr. Psychiatr. Neurol.*, Bd. 8, *Monographie*, Berlin.

Lenneberg, E. (1967). *Biological Foundations of Language*. New York: Wiley.

Meynert, T. (1885). *Psychiatry*. Translated by B. Sachs. New York: Putnam.

Ogle, W. (1867). Aphasia and agraphia. *St. George's Hospital Reports*, 2, 83–122.

Orton, S. T. (1937). *Reading, writing and speech problems in children*. New York: W. W. Norton.

Penfield, W., & Rasmussen, T. (1950). *The cerebral cortex of man*. New York: Macmillan.

Penfield, W., & Roberts, L. (1959). *Speech and brain mechanisms*. Princeton, N.J.: Princeton University Press.

Porch, B. (1967, 1971). *The Porch index of communicative ability*. Palo Alto, Calif.: Consulting Psychologists Press.

Schuell, H. (1965). *The Minnesota test for differential diagnosis of aphasia*. Minneapolis: University of Minnesota Press.

Sperry, R. W.; Gazzaniga, M. S.; & Bogen, J. E. (1969). Interhemispheric relationships: The neocortical commissures; syndromes of hemispheric disconnection. In P. J. Vinken & G. W. Bruyn (Eds.), *Handbook of clinical neurology* (Vol. 4). Amsterdam: North Holland.

Starkweather, C. W. (1983). *Speech and language: Principles and processes of behavior change*. Englewood Cliffs, N.J.: Prentice-Hall.

Travis, L. E. (1931). *Speech pathology*. New York: Appleton-Century-Crofts.

Wada, J. A.; Clark, R.; & Hamm, A. (1975). Cerebral asymmetry in humans. *Archives of Neurology*, 2, 239–246.

Wepman, J. (1951). *Recovery from aphasia*. New York: Ronald Press.

Wernicke, C. (1874) Der aphasische Symptomenkomplex. Breslau: Cohn and Weigert. Translated in G. H. Eggert (1977), *Wernicke's works on aphasia: A sourcebook and review*. The Hague, Netherlands: Mouton.

Whitaker, H. A. (1976). Neurobiology of language. In E. C. Carterette & M. P. Friedman (Eds.), *Handbook of perception* (Vol 7), *Language and speech*. New York: Academic Press.

Witelson, S. F., & Pallie, W. (1973). Left hemisphere specialization for language in the newborn: Neuroanatomical evidence of asymmetry. *Brain*, 96, 641–647.

CHAPTER TWO

The Organization of the Nervous System I

"The brain is the organ of destiny. It holds within its humming mechanism secrets that will determine the future of the human race. Speech might be called the human brain's first miracle. . . . Speech it was that served to make man what he is, instead of one of the animals."

—Wilder Graves Penfield, *The Second Career*, 1963

The Human Communicative Nervous System

The nervous system is the source of all communication in humankind. Only humans can talk. Their special talent for speaking identifies them as unique in the animal kingdom. The special human capacity for speech, or oral language, is the result of an aggregate of intricate nervous mechanisms that have developed in the human brain through a series of dramatic evolutionary changes. Over a period of thousands of years, there has been created in the human brain a novel representation and organization of neural structures and processes that result in what may be called the human communication nervous system. How does this nervous system differ from the communicative nervous system of lower animals? A clear answer to this old question is beginning to emerge from attempts to teach the great apes, particularly the chimpanzee, different types of communication systems. Attempts to teach oral speech to the chimpanzee have been notably unsuccessful; on the other hand, attempts to teach chimpanzees using visual and gestural representations of human language have been undeniably successful. Chimpanzees have been taught to use colored plastic chips to represent morphemes, and in other cases have mastered the American Sign Language of the deaf to a degree that they can communicate adequately and even creatively in rudimentary sign language. How characteristically human these nonoral languages are is open to question, but it is clear that humans and chimpanzees share some characteristics of communication. It is highly likely that the chimpanzee is using cortical structures of the brain to master visual and gestural components of human language. What are the differences between the human brain and that of the chimpanzee? It has been suggested that overall brain size, which reflects the total volume of the cerebral cortex, the total number of nerve cells in the brain, and the degree of dendrite growth or proliferation of the processes of the nerve cell, are crucial to both information processing and communication processing in the brain.

The chimpanzee's ability is reflected by its average brain weight of 450 grams, as compared to an average weight of 1,350 grams for the human brain. Generally, a lack of uniqueness has been found in the parietal, occipital, and temporal lobes of both chimpanzees and humans. In the frontal lobe of the brain, however, humans are distinguished by an area called *Broca's area,* which has been associated with the control of expressive oral speech. With the exception of Broca's area, the primary difference between the human and chimpanzee cortex is quantitative, with the temporal lobe, the inferior parietal lobe, and the frontal lobe anterior to Broca's area being larger in humans. The temporal lobe, the inferior parietal lobe, and the unique Broca's lobe area, as we will learn in later chapters, are those portions of the cerebral cortex that make speech possible. These particular species-specific brain structures, plus the human's special vocal tract and the significant increase in the quantity of information and communicative processing cortex, make the oral speech of humans unique in the animal world.

Divisions of the Nervous System

In order to understand the human communicative nervous system thoroughly, one must first tackle a basic understanding of the organization of the nervous system as a whole. First, think of the nervous system as separated from the other tissues and structures of the body. Imagine the major parts of the nervous system as if they were displayed on a dissection table spread out for your study. You should see in your mind's eye an oval-shaped brain, with a taillike appendage, called the *spinal cord,* hanging from its base. A series of nerves attached to the base of the brain are called the *cranial nerves.* Another set of nerves, called the *spinal nerves,* project from both sides of the spinal cord (Figure 2-1). Of all

FIGURE 2-1 The central nervous system (CNS), including the brain and spinal cord. The CNS is synonymous with the term *neuraxis*.

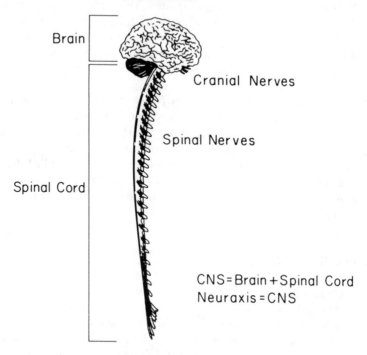

Brain

Cranial Nerves

Spinal Nerves

Spinal Cord

CNS = Brain + Spinal Cord
Neuraxis = CNS

these parts—the brain, cord, and nerves—the brain is by far the most important for communication. It is within the brain that the new evolutionary neural mechanisms of the communicative nervous system are developed.

The nerves that exit from the brain merely transmit sensory or motor information to and from the brain to carry out the control of the speech, language, and hearing mechanisms. The nerves that are attached to the spinal cord innervate muscles of the neck, trunk, and limbs and bring sensation from these parts to the brain.

From this oversimplified first mental image of the structure and function of the communicative nervous system, we hope to acquire a more precise and complex picture of the several aspects of the anatomy, physiology, and diagnosis of neurogenic speech, language, and hearing disorders.

The Central Nervous System

As you inspect the dissected nervous system in display in Figure 2-1, you will see that it can be divided naturally into two gross divisions: *brain* and *spinal cord.* The brain and spinal cord taken together are called the *central nervous system* (CNS) or *neuraxis.*

The brain is gray in color, shaped like an oval melon, and slightly soft to the touch. The average brain weighs about 1,350 grams or approximately 3 pounds. The brain normally is housed in the part of the bony skull called the *cranium.* A synonym for *brain* is *encephalon.* The largest mass of brain tissue is identified as the *cerebrum.* The human cerebrum, through its evolutionary development from the brains of lower animals, includes three parts: the *cerebral hemispheres,* the *basal ganglia,* and the *rhinencephalon.*

The cerebral hemispheres are the two large halves of the brain that are readily discernible, even if you merely glance quickly at the brain on display. The cerebral hemispheres are connected by a mass of white matter called the *corpus callosum.* During development the cerebral hemispheres become enormously enlarged and overhang the structures deep in the brain called the brainstem. The cerebral hemispheres are extremely crucial for speech, since, particularly in the left hemisphere, we find the major neurologic mechanisms of speech and language.

The Cerebral Lobes

The cerebral hemispheres are identical twins in looks, although the functions of the various parts may differ dramatically on the left and right sides of the brain. Each hemisphere has been divided anatomically into four different primary lobes—the *frontal, temporal, parietal,* and *occipital* lobes. These lobes can be located on the brain surface by using certain landmarks, the gyri and sulci. A *gyrus* is an elevation on the surface of the brain caused by the folding in of the cortex. A *sulcus* is a groovelike depression on the brain surface that separates the gyri. Another name for a *sulcus* is *fissure.* You should seek to become very adept at locating the gyri, sulci, and lobes shown in figures 2-2 through 2-4.

The frontal lobe is bounded inferiorly by the *lateral sulcus* or *Sylvian fissure* and posteriorly by the *central sulcus* or *Rolandic fissure.* It comprises about one-third of the surface of the hemisphere. In the frontal lobe there is a long gyrus immediately anterior to the central sulcus. This very prominent gyrus is called the *precentral gyrus.* This makes up the majority of what is known as the *primary motor cortex.* You will also read and use the term *motor strip* for this area. The cells in this area are responsible for voluntary control of skeletal muscles on the opposite, or contralateral, side of the body. This has important clinical significance, which we will discuss later. Motor pathways called the pyramidal tract descend into the brain and spinal cord from starting points in the primary motor area. Immediately anterior to the primary motor area is the *premotor* or *supplemental motor area.* Stimulation studies of this area show that muscular movement is also produced here, but that a stronger stimulus must be used than in the primary motor area.

FIGURE 2-2   Superior view of the cerebral hemispheres

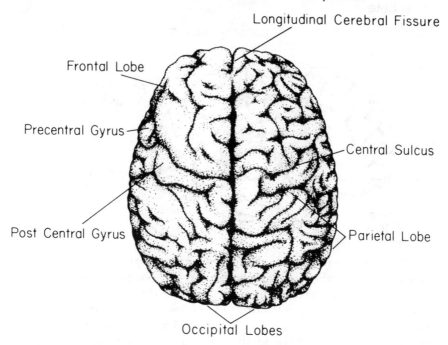

FIGURE 2-3   Lateral view of the left cerebral hemisphere

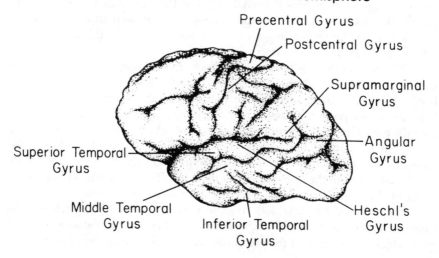

FIGURE 2-4   Medial view of the right cerebral hemisphere

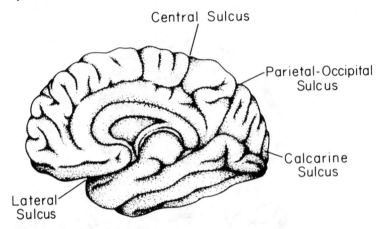

Central Sulcus

Parietal-Occipital Sulcus

Calcarine Sulcus

Lateral Sulcus

The connections between the controlling area on the motor strip and the voluntary muscles served are arranged so that it is possible to draw a map of motor control on the cerebral cortex to show how the muscles are innervated from the cortex. The map is referred to as a *homunculus*, or "little man" (Figure 2-5). You will see that the areas are represented in almost an upside-down or inverted fashion. You will also see that the area of cortical representation given to that particular part does not appear to be strongly related to the size of that part of the body, as the leg and arm are given smaller areas than the hand or mouth. Rather, it is those body parts that require the most precision in motor control that are apportioned the larger cortical areas.

Another important area of the frontal left lobe, known as *Broca's area,* is located in the inferior (third) frontal gyrus of the lobe (Figure 2-6). In most people, Broca's area is vital for the production of fluent, well-articulated speech. Ablation of the corresponding area in the nondominant hemisphere, on the other hand, usually has no effect on speech.

The parietal lobe is bounded anteriorly by the central sulcus, inferiorly by the posterior end of the lateral sulcus, and posteriorly by an imaginary border line. The primary sensory, or somesthetic, area is found in the parietal lobe, the major portion of which is the *postcentral gyrus* (Figure 2-2). This lies directly posterior to the central sulcus, or Rolandic fissure. On this sensory cortex can be mapped the sensory control of various parts of the body. Somesthetic sensations (pain, temperature, touch, and the like) are sent to the sensory cortex from the opposite side of the body. This arrangement is a mirror image of the motor strip and is sometimes called the *sensory strip.*

Located in the parietal lobe are also two other gyri with which speech-language pathologists should become familiar. The first is the *supramarginal gyrus* which curves around the posterior end of the lateral Sylvian fissure. The

FIGURE 2-5 Homunculi. "Maps" of the cortical sensory and motor control of the parts of the body.

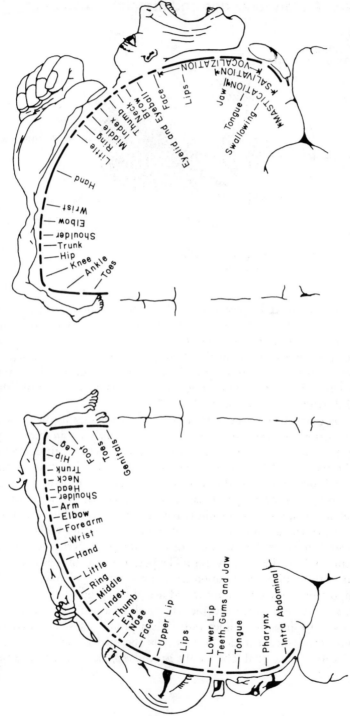

Source: Adapted from W. Penfield and T. Rasmussen, *The Cerebral Cortex of Man: A Clinical Study of Localization of Function* (New York: Macmillan, 1950).

FIGURE 2-6   Primary language and association areas of the cortex

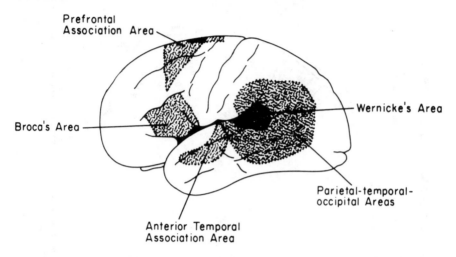

second gyrus lies directly posterior to the supramarginal gyrus and curves around the end of the prominent sulcus in the temporal lobe, the superior temporal sulcus. This gyrus is called the *angular gyrus* (Figure 2-3). Damage in the area of the angular gyrus in the dominant hemisphere may cause word-finding problems (anomia), reading and writing deficit (alexia with agraphia), as well as left-right disorientation, finger agnosia (inability to identify the fingers), and difficulty with arithmetic (acalculia).

The temporal lobe is the seat of auditory processing in the brain. It is bounded superiorly by the lateral fissure and posteriorly by an imaginary line that forms the anterior border of the occipital lobe. There are three prominent gyri on the temporal lobe, the superior, middle, and inferior temporal gyri (Figure 2-3). If one pulls apart the two borders of the lateral fissure, a structure called the *insula* or the *Island of Reil* may be seen. Fiber connections to the insula are not well defined, but it is thought to have connections to the *viscera* (internal organs). The primary auditory cortex is situated in the inferior wall of the lateral fissure. *Heschl's gyrus*, or the anterior transverse temporal gyrus, represents the cortical center for hearing (Figure 2-3). The posterior part of the superior temporal gyrus is the auditory association area, best known as Wernicke's area, and is very important to the development and use of language.

The *occipital lobe*, which occupies the small area behind the parietal lobe and is marked by imaginary lines rather than prominent sulci, is concerned with vision. Two sulci that can be found on the medial surface of the brain that help locate the occipital lobe are the *parietal-occipital sulcus* and the *calcarine sulcus* (Figure 2-4).

The portions of the cortex on the various lobes that are not assigned as primary motor or sensory areas—such as the primary motor or sensory strip, the primary auditory area, and the primary visual area—are categorized as *association cortex*. This type of cortical area comprises most of the hemisphere. Association cortex has a different cellular makeup than the primary sensory and motor areas. There appear to be multiple inputs and outputs in these areas, and many of them are apparently independent of the primary motor and sensory areas. Three main association areas that are widely recognized are the *prefrontal*, *anterior temporal*, and *parietal temporal–occipital areas* (Figure 2-6).

Cerebral Connections

Your knowledge of the cerebral hemispheres should also include the types of fibers found in these areas. *Association fibers* connect areas within the hemisphere. *Commissural fibers* connect an area in one hemisphere with an area in the opposite hemisphere. The aforementioned corpus callosum is the largest set of commissural fibers in the brain. Association fibers form *association tracts* between areas. Short association tracts are within lobes and long ones between lobes. One association tract with which you should be familiar is the *arcuate fasciculus*. *Fasciculus* means "little bundle" and is used to describe a bundle of nerve fibers within the central nervous system. The arcuate fasciculus travels from the posterior temporal lobe forward via another set of fibers, the *superior longitudinal fasciculus*, to the motor association cortex on the frontal lobe (Figure 2-7). Lesions in the area of the arcuate fasciculus are thought to cause a certain major syndrome of aphasia called conduction aphasia.

FIGURE 2-7   Association fiber tracts of the left cerebral hemisphere

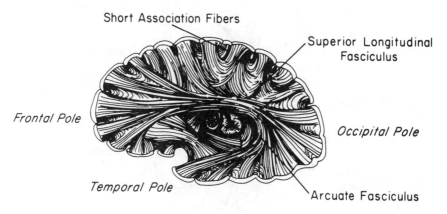

Short Association Fibers

Superior Longitudinal Fasciculus

Frontal Pole

Occipital Pole

Temporal Pole

Arcuate Fasciculus

Subcortical Structures

The basal ganglia are masses of gray matter deep within the cerebrum, below its outer surface or *cerebral cortex*. The division of the structures known as basal ganglia has been very confusing in the literature. Various anatomists categorize the structures differently. For our purposes we will think of the basal ganglia as consisting of three main parts: the *caudate nucleus*, the *globus pallidus*, and the *putamen* (Figure 2-8). Some neuroanatomists also include a structure called the *claustrum*. The *substantia nigra* and *subthalamic nuclei* are functionally related but not a part of the basal ganglia. The three main parts are often grouped together and referred to as the *corpus striatum*. The putamen and globus pallidus are sometimes grouped and called the *lentiform nucleus*. (The subcortical neural cell masses of the basal ganglia are associated with motor functions; these functions will be highlighted in a later chapter.)

The rhinencephalon is part of what is called the "old brain." The prefix *rhino* means "nose," so it is easy to see that the functions of the old animal brain dealt primarily with the sense of *olfaction* or smell. Since smell is a much more crucial sense to animals for their adaptation to the environment than it is to humans, the old brain was relatively large in animals and the cerebral hemispheres less well developed. Right now, however, concentrating too much on the structures of the cerebrum will distract you from your main tasks at the moment—conceptualizing the major subdivisions of the central nervous system or neuraxis.

FIGURE 2-8   Horizontal section of the cerebrum showing the basal ganglia

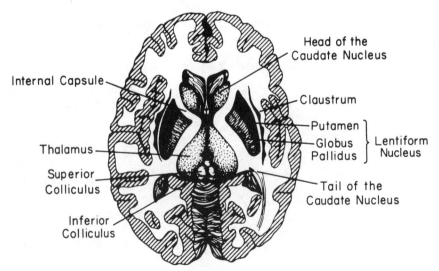

Cerebellum and Brainstem

The brain contains two other major parts in addition to the large cerebrum: the *cerebellum* and the *brainstem*. Both structures are extremely important to an understanding of the neurology of speech, so do not pass over them quickly at this point as you did the basal ganglia and rhinencephalon.

The word *cerebellum* means "little brain," and the cerebellum is indeed a much smaller structure than the cerebrum, weighing only about one-eighth as much. The cerebellum is located at the rear of the brain, below and at the base of the cerebrum (Figure 2-9). It is reminiscent of a small orange wedged into the juncture of the attachment of the spinal cord to the melon-shaped cerebrum. The cerebellum, a recent evolutionary addition to the nervous system, functions to provide fine coordination to the movements of the body. It appears to play a particularly important role in coordinating the extremely rapid and precise movements needed for the normal articulation of speech.

The Brainstem

The third major part of the brain is the *brainstem* (Figure 2-10). The brainstem and its subdivisions cannot be viewed directly unless the cerebral hemispheres are cut away and we are allowed to see the internal structures of the brain. The brainstem appears as a series of structures that seem to be an upward extension of the spinal cord, thrust upward into the brain between the cerebral hemispheres. Often the parts of the brain stem are depicted as extending as vertical segments one above the other, but in fact the parts of the brainstem do not sit in a vertical plane. The upper structures are crowded together to fit within the cranium.

A confusing point for the speech student is the fact that the structures that define the brainstem are not universally agreed on. We have chosen a definition of the brainstem that is reasonably popular and that fits logically into

FIGURE 2-9 Medial view of the right cerebrum and cerebellum

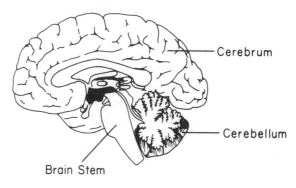

Cerebrum

Cerebellum

Brain Stem

**FIGURE 2-10   Ventral view of the
brainstem**

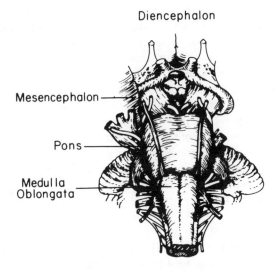

the neuroanatomy and physiology of communication. We will include the following four structures in our definition of the brainstem. From the rostral (head)
end of the neuraxis to the caudal (tail) end of the nervous system, the brainstem
structures are:

1.   Diencephalon
2.   Mesencephalon
3.   Pons
4.   Medulla oblongata

The following variations in the definition of the brainstem will be found in
many neurology textbooks. The basal ganglia, described earlier as part of the
cerebrum, are classified by some experts as part of the brainstem. Other authorities only include the medulla oblongata and the pons as brainstem structures. They consider the mesencephalon and diencephalon as cerebrum. As a
compromise, some neurologists have designated the diencephalon and mesencephalon as *upper brainstem* and the pons and medulla oblongata as *lower brainstem*.

Before describing the brainstem structures, we will review what we have
learned so far so that you may check your mental picture of the nervous system.
The nervous system is made up of the brain and the spinal cord. The major
anatomical units of the central nervous system are the cerebrum, the cerebellum,
the brainstem, and the spinal cord. The brainstem has four major subdivisions,
which we will now describe.

Medulla Oblongata

This is the most caudal brain stem structure. Older terminology identified it as the *bulb*. It appears as a rounded bulge that is an enlargement of the upper spinal cord (Figure 2-10). It contains ascending and descending tracts plus the nuclei of several of the nerves that control phonation, velopharyngeal closure, swallowing, and articulation. It is extremely important for the control of speech production. There is a *median fissure* (furrow) on the anterior surface. On either side of this fissure are landmark swellings called *pyramids*. Other landmarks are oval elevations called *olives*, produced by the *olivary nuclei*, which are important way-stations in the pathways of the auditory nervous system. The olives are posterior to the pyramids. The *inferior cerebellar peduncles* (feet) are also found on the medulla. The peduncles connect the cerebellum to the brainstem at the level of the medulla.

Pons

Just above the medulla in the neuraxis is the pons, a massive rounded structure that serves in part as a connection to the hemispheres of the cerebellum. The connections to the cerebellum are made by a number of transverse fibers on the anterior surface of the pons. The pons is aptly named, since the Latin term for bridge is *pons*, and the pons is a bridge to the cerebellum (Figure 2-10).

Mesencephalon

This area, immediately above the pons, is also called the *midbrain* (Figure 2-10). The midbrain is the narrowest part of the brainstem. The midbrain contains the *tectum* or roof of the brainstem. On the tectum are four swellings, or little hills, called *colliculi*: two *inferior colliculi* and two *superior colliculi*. The tectum and the four colliculi are known collectively as *corpus quadrigemia*. The inferior colliculi serve as way-stations in the central auditory nervous system, and the superior colliculi are way-stations in the visual nervous system.

Diencephalon

Above the midbrain is a double oval structure, the diencephalon (Figure 2-10). It is almost completely hidden from the surface of the brain and is made up of two structures, the *thalamus* and the *hypothalamus*. The thalamus is placed ventrally (toward the belly), and the hypothalamus is placed dorsally (toward the back). The thalamus is a large, rounded structure consisting of gray matter. It is made up of two egglike masses that lie on either side of the third *ventricle*, one of the large openings in the brain through which the cerebrospinal fluid (CSF) flows. The posterior end of the thalamus expands in a large swelling, the *pulvinar*. Wilder Penfield (1891–1976), a famous twentieth-century neurosurgeon, was the first to ascribe special subcortical speech and language functions to this thalamic structure.

The thalamus is a structure that integrates sensation in the nervous system. It brings together and organizes sensation from the classic sensory pathways.

Its nuclei act as thalamic relays, sending sensory information upward to sensory areas on the cerebral cortex. The to and fro sensory pathways between the thalamus and cerebral cortex are so numerous, and the two structures so interdependent, that it is sometimes difficult to assign a sensory deficit to the thalamus or the sensory cortical areas of the cerebrum.

The hypothalamus forms part of the *third ventricle*. The lower part of its lateral wall and the floor of the third ventricle make up the hypothalamus. Two important landmarks on the base of the brain are found on the floor of the third ventricle: the *optic chiasm* and the *mamillary bodies*. The optic chiasm is the point at which optic nerves cross over. The mamillary bodies are two nipple-shaped protuberances that contain nuclei important to hypothalamic function.

The hypothalamus controls several aspects of emotional behavior, such as rage and aggression, as well as escape behavior. In addition, it aids in regulation of body temperature, food and water intake, and sexual and sleep behavior. The hypothalamus exerts neural control over the pituitary gland, which releases *hormones* involved in many bodily functions.

The Spinal Cord

We said earlier that the two natural anatomic divisions of the nervous system are the brain and the spinal cord. Up to now we have described some of the important structures of the brain. Now, moving to the more caudal, or lower, end of the nervous system, we will describe the spinal cord. Recall our mental image of the dissection of the nervous system. Looking at the brain, one sees a long pigtail of flesh hanging from its base. This is the spinal cord. It is normally found in an opening in the center of the bony vertebral column. The spinal cord is strictly defined. It is what is caudal to the large opening at the base of the skull called the *magnum foramen*; the nervous tissue encased in the skull proper is brain.

A cross-section of the spinal cord reveals an H-shaped mass of gray matter in the center of the spinal segment. The ventral or anterior portion of the cord mediates motor output. The anterior horn cell of the ventral gray matter is the point of synapse of the descending motor tracts with the ventral roots of the spinal cord. The dorsal or posterior portion of the cord mediates sensory input from the spinal cord. The dorsal root relays sensory information to the cord. Major anatomic landmarks of a cross-section of the spinal cord are shown in Figure 2-11. Inspecting the cord closely on the dissection table, you can see a series of thin, regularly placed filaments extending from each side of the cord. These are the *spinal nerves*. Branching off the spinal nerves are the *peripheral nerves*, which go to muscles, glands, and skin. The spinal nerves and the extensions, called the peripheral nerves, along with their branches, are one part of what is called the *peripheral nervous system*. If we add the cranial nerves, we have a complete definition of the peripheral nervous system.

FIGURE 2-11   Cross-section of the spinal cord

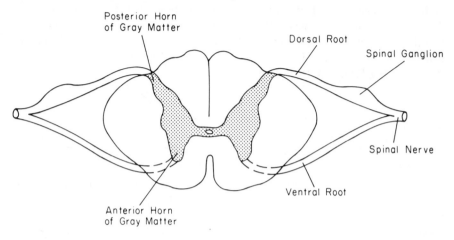

The spinal cord is divided into five regions (Figure 2-12). Each of these regions is named for a section of the thirty-one spinal vertebrae that surround the spinal cord itself. The regions of the cord are (1) cervical, (2) thoracic, (3) lumbar, (4) sacral, and (5) coccygeal. There are eight cervical nerves, twelve

FIGURE 2-12   Divisions of the spinal cord

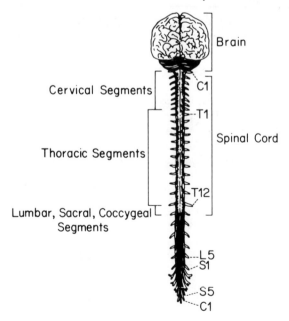

thoracic, five lumbar, five sacral, and one coccygeal nerve. There are, however, eight cervical nerves and only seven cervical vertebrae. There are four coccygeal vertebrae and only one nerve. The spinal cord does not extend the complete length of the vertebral column. In the adult it terminates at the level of the lower border of the first lumbar vertebra. In the child, it is longer, ending at the upper border of the third lumbar vertebra.

Summary

The human communicative nervous system is a novel representation and organization of neural processes and structures that allow humans to communicate at a complex level unique in the animal world. The speech-language pathologist must be knowledgeable in the area of neurology and neurological disease to participate in the treatment of communication disorders. The nervous system is organized into brain, spinal cord, and nerves. This chapter presented an overview of the central nervous system, which includes the brain and spinal cord. At the end of Chapter 3, the structures reviewed herein will be outlined for your continued study.

References and Further Readings

Barr, M. L., & Kiernan, J. A. (1983). *The human nervous system*. Philadelphia: Harper and Row.

Chusid, J. (1985). *Correlative neuroanatomy and functional neurology* (19th ed.). Los Altos, Calif.: Lange Medical Publications.

DeMyer, W. (1980). *Technique of the neurologic examination*. (3rd ed.). New York: McGraw-Hill.

Gardner, E. (1975). *Fundamentals of neurology*. (6th ed.). Philadelphia: W. B. Saunders.

CHAPTER THREE

The Organization of the Nervous System II

"The charm of neurology . . . lies in the way it forces us into daily contact with principles. A knowledge of the structure and function of the nervous system is necessary to explain the simplest phenomena of disease and it can only be attained by thinking scientifically."

—Henry Head

THE CENTRAL NERVOUS SYSTEM is the controlling influence in the human communicative nervous system. However, the CNS would not be functional, nor necessary, without the lower-level structures reviewed in this chapter.

The Peripheral Nervous System

The peripheral nervous system includes (1) the cranial nerves with their roots and rami (branches), (2) the peripheral nerves, and (3) the peripheral parts of the autonomic nervous system. The cranial nerves exit from the neuraxis at various levels of the brainstem and the uppermost part of the spinal cord. Ordinarily the peripheral nerves include the spinal nerves plus their branches.

Spinal peripheral nerves are described as mixed nerves, meaning that they carry both sensory and motor fibers. Each spinal nerve is connected to the spinal cord by two roots: the *anterior root* and the *posterior root*. The anterior root of the spinal nerve consists of bundles of nerve fibers that transmit nerve impulses away from the central nervous system. These nerve fibers are called *efferent* fibers. Those efferent fibers that go to the muscles and make them contract are called *motor fibers*. The motor fibers of the spinal nerves originate from a group of cells or motor nucleus in the spinal cord called the *anterior* (or *ventral*) *horn cell*. The anterior horn cell is the point of *synapse*, or connection, with the spinal nerves as they leave the neuraxis. When nerve impulses have left the neuraxis, they have reached what the great British neurophysiologist Charles Sherrington (1857–1952) called the "final common pathway"—the terminal route of all neural impulses acting on the muscles.

The posterior root of the spinal nerve consists of afferent fibers that carry impulses to the central nervous system. Afferent fibers carry information to the CNS about the sensations of touch, pain, temperature, and vibration. They are called *sensory fibers*. The cell bodies of the sensory fibers are a swelling on the posterior root of the spinal nerve called the *posterior root ganglion*.

The motor and sensory roots leave the spinal cord at the *intervertebral foramina*, where the roots unite to form a spinal nerve. At this point the motor and sensory fibers mix together.

The organization of the spinal roots allow us to understand some clinical principles when there is damage to the spinal cord or spinal nerves. First, recall that we can make the generalization that the anterior or ventral half of the spinal cord is devoted to motor or efferent activity, and the posterior or dorsal half is devoted to sensory or afferent activity. A *lesion*, or damaged area, will impair motor or sensory activities at the cord level depending on the specific site of the lesion. Naturally, large lesions in the spinal cord will impair both sensory and motor functions. If there is a high spinal cord injury or lesion at the level of the cervical cord, speech production may be affected because the respiratory muscles are controlled by spinal nerves exiting from the intervertebral formina of the cervical and thoracic region. If respiration is stopped, death may follow with a lesion above the third, fourth, and fifth cervical nerves. These nerves, called the *phrenic nerves*, innervate some of the breathing muscles, particularly the diaphragm. Spinal cord injuries involving the caudal portion of the cord do not affect speech production and are of only indirect interest to the speech-language pathologist. They are instructive, however, in understanding the effect of lesions at various levels of the nervous system. Injuries in the spinal cord may produce partial or complete loss of function at the level of the lesion. Function is also completely or partially impaired below the level of the lesion. Spinal cord injuries must be considered serious because they impair functions beyond those controlled directly at the lesion point.

The Cranial Nerves

The cranial nerves, in contrast to the spinal nerves, are of more significance to the speech pathologist since all the cranial nerves have some relation to the speech, language, and hearing process, and seven of the twelve nerves are directly related to speech production and hearing. The twelve pairs of cranial nerves look on dissection like thin cords, gray-white in color. They consist of nerve fiber bundles surrounded by connective tissue. Like the spinal nerves, they are relatively unprotected and may be damaged by trauma. The cranial nerves leave the brain and pass through the foramina of the skull to reach the sense organs or muscles of the head and neck with which they are associated. Some are associated with special senses such as vision, olfaction (smell), hearing, and others. Cranial nerves innervate the muscles of the jaw, face, pharynx, larynx, tongue, and neck. Unlike the spinal nerves, which attach to the cord at regular intervals, the cranial nerves are attached to the brain at irregular intervals. They do not all have dorsal (sensory) and ventral (motor) roots. Some are motor, some are sensory, and others are nerves with mixed functions. Their origin, distribution, brain and brainstem connections, functions, and evolution are complicated. Details will be discussed in Chapter 7. It is traditional to designate them with Roman numerals: (I) olfactory, (II) optic, (III) oculomotor, (IV) trochlear, (V) trigeminal, (VI) abducens, (VII) facial, (VIII) acoustic-vestibular, (IX) glossopharyngeal, (X) vagus, (XI) spinal accessory, and (XII) hypoglossal (Figure 3-1).

Autonomic Nervous System

The innervation of involuntary structures such as the heart, the smooth muscles, and the glands is accomplished through the *autonomic nervous system*. Although this system has primarily indirect effects on speech, language, and hearing, you must be familiar with its contribution to total body function in order to understand how involuntary but vital functions such as hormonal secretions, visual reflexes, and blood pressure are controlled within the nervous system.

The autonomic nervous system is distributed throughout both the central

FIGURE 3-1 Cranial nerves exiting from the brainstem

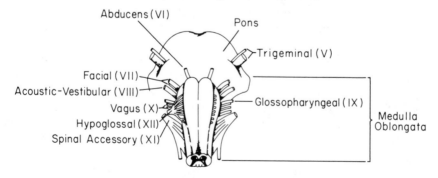

nervous system and the peripheral nervous system. It may be divided into two parts, *sympathetic* and *parasympathetic*, which have almost antagonistic functions. The sympathetic system is the body's alerting system, sometimes referred to as the fight-or-flight system. This part of the autonomic nervous system is responsible for such preparatory measures as accelerating the heart rate, causing constriction of the peripheral blood vessels, raising the blood pressure, and redistributing the blood so that it leaves the skin and intestines to be used in the brain, heart, and skeletal muscles if needed. It serves to raise the eyelids and to dilate the pupils. The sympathetic part will also decrease peristalsis (the propelling wave of contractions of the intestine) and will close the sphincter.

The parasympathetic part of the autonomic nervous system has an almost opposite calming effect on bodily function. It serves to conserve and restore energy by slowing the heart rate, increasing intestinal peristalsis and opening the sphincters. As a result of parasympathetic action, other functions, such as increased salivation and increased secretion of the glands of the gastrointestinal tract, may take place.

Both the sympathetic and the parasympathetic parts work together in the autonomic nervous system along with the *endocrine system* to maintain the stability of the body's internal environment. The endocrine system is a group of glands and other structures that release internal secretions called *hormones* into the circulatory system. These hormones influence metabolism and other body processes. The endocrine system includes such organs as the pancreas, the pineal gland, the pituitary gland, the gonads, the thyroid, and the adrenal glands. These work more slowly than the autonomic nervous system.

The autonomic nervous system is composed of both *efferent* (conducting away from the central nervous system) and *afferent* (conducting toward the central nervous system) nerve fibers. Both kinds of fibers travel routes that include either synapsing on or passing through a ganglion—a group of nerve cell bodies, usually outside the central nervous system. Before reaching the ganglion, the fiber is referred to as *preganglionic*. After synapsing on or passing through the ganglion, it becomes a *postganglionic* fiber. All the fibers of the sympathetic part course through or synapse on a chain of ganglia running adjacent to the cerebral bodies called the *sympathetic trunk*. The parasympathetic part has no comparable structure, and its peripheral ganglia are scattered through the body (Figure 3-2).

The higher nervous system control of the autonomic nervous system is thought to be centered in the *hypothalamus*. This structure in the diencephalon appears to have a controlling influence over the autonomic nervous system, as well as functioning to integrate the autonomic and neuroendocrine systems. As a result of the different connections of its ascending and descending tracts, the reticular formation also exerts influence over autonomic nervous system function.

As stated earlier, the autonomic nervous system is of importance to the

FIGURE 3-2 The efferent part of the autonomic nervous system showing selected ganglion and glands

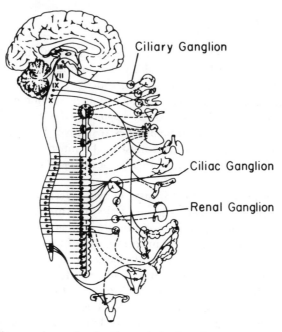

Source: Redrawn and reproduced with permission from R. Snell, *Clinical Neuroanatomy for Medical Students* (Boston: Little, Brown and Company, 1980).

speech-language pathologist because of its indirect effect on communication functioning. If you have ever experienced the sweaty palms, dry mouth, and blushing associated with anxiety before delivering a public speech, you have some idea of the power of the autonomic nervous system. Those indirect effects may make a great deal of difference in how well one communicates!

The Protection and Nourishment of the Brain

Up to this point we have been concerned with the three major controlling mechanisms of the human body: the central nervous system, the peripheral nervous system, and the autonomic nervous system. The brain and the spinal cord, which make up part of these systems and house most of their mechanisms, must be protected in some way and must be nourished to continue to function.

The following is a discussion of the protection and nourishment of these structures.

The Meninges

Since the spinal cord and the brain are the major coordinating and integrating structures for all physical and mental activities of the body, it is fortunate that they are very well protected. The brain and the spinal cord are covered by layers of tissue called the *meninges*. Within certain layers of these meninges there is a cushioning layer of fluid called *cerebrospinal fluid* (CSF).

The meninges are three membranes that cover both the brain and the spinal cord. Moving from the outermost to the innermost covering, they are known as the *dura mater* ("tough mother"), the *arachnoid mater*, and the *pia mater* (Figure 3-3).

The dura mater actually consists of two layers that are closely united except where, in certain spots, they separate to form the venous sinuses. The dura mater of the spinal cord is continuous with that of the brain through the opening in the skull called the foramen magnum. In the brain, the dura mater is marked by complex folds that divide the contents of the cranial cavity into different cerebral subdivisions. These folds are the *falx cerebri* (between the cerebral hemispheres), the *tentorium cerebelli* (projecting between the cerebellar hemispheres), and the *diaphragma sella* (forming the roof of the sella turcica) (Figure 3-4). These folds serve to brace the brain against rotary displacement. They receive blood from the brain through the cerebral veins and receive cerebrospinal fluid from the subarachnoid space. The blood ultimately drains into the internal jugular veins in the neck.

Beneath the dura mater is a space called the *subdural space*, which is filled

FIGURE 3-3 Cerebral meninges

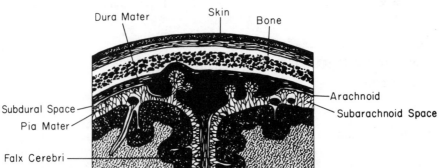

Source: Redrawn and reproduced with permission from R. Snell, *Clinical Neuroanatomy for Medical Students* (Boston: Little, Brown and Company, 1980).

FIGURE 3-4   Folds of the dura mater

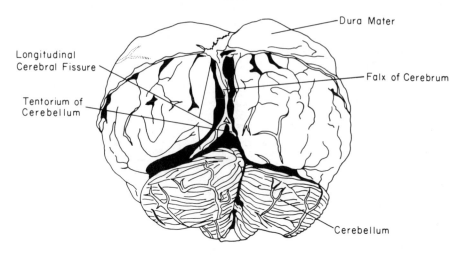

with fluid. Immediately below this fluid is the second membrane covering, the arachnoid mater. This membrane bridges over the sulci or folds of the brain. In some areas it projects into the venous sinuses to form arachnoid villi, which aggregate to form the arachnoid granulations where cerebrospinal fluid diffuses into the bloodstream.

Separating the arachnoid and the third membrane, the pia mater, is the *subarachnoid space*, filled with cerebrospinal fluid. All cerebral arteries and veins as well as the cranial nerves pass through this space. The pia mater adheres closely to the surface of the brain, covering the gyri (ridges) and going down into the sulci. The pia mater also fuses with the ependyma (a cellular membrane lining the ventricles) to form the choroid plexuses of the ventricles.

The Ventricular System

The ventricular system of the brain has three parts: the lateral ventricles, the third ventricle, and the fourth ventricle. These are actually small cavities within the brain and are joined to each other by small ducts and canals (Figure 3-5). Each ventricle contains a tuftlike structure called the *choroid plexus*, which is concerned mainly with the production of cerebrospinal fluid.

The lateral ventricles are paired, one in each hemisphere. Each is a C-shaped cavity and can be divided into a body located in the parietal lobe and anterior, posterior, and inferior horns, extending into the frontal, occipital, and temporal lobes, respectively. The lateral ventricle is connected to the third ventricle by an opening called the *intraventricular foramen* or the foramen of

FIGURE 3-5   The ventricular system

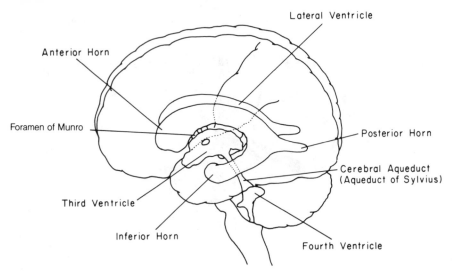

Munro. The choroid plexus of the lateral ventricle projects into the cavity on its medial aspect.

The third ventricle is a small slit between the thalami. It is connected also to the fourth ventricle, through the cerebral aqueduct or the aqueduct of Sylvius. The choroid plexuses are situated above the roof of the ventricle.

The fourth ventricle sits anterior to the cerebellum and posterior to the pons and the superior half of the medulla. It is continuous superiorly with the cerebral aqueduct and the central canal below. The fourth ventricle has a tent-shaped roof, two lateral walls, and a floor. There are three small openings in the fourth ventricle, the two lateral foramina of Luschkea and the median foramen of Magendie. Through these openings the cerebrospinal fluid enters the subarachnoid space. The choroid plexus of the fourth ventricle has a T-shape. The ventricular system serves as a pathway for the circulation of the cerebrospinal fluid (Figure 3-5). The choroid plexuses of the ventricles appear to secrete the cerebrospinal fluid actively, although some of the fluid may originate as tissue fluid formed in the brain substance.

Cerebrospinal Fluid

The brain and the spinal cord are suspended in a clear, colorless fluid called *cerebrospinal fluid*, which serves as a cushion between the central nervous system and the surrounding bones, thereby protecting the brain against direct trauma. This fluid aids in regulation of intracranial pressure, nourishment of the nervous tissue, and removal of waste products.

The path of circulation of the cerebrospinal fluid is illustrated in Figure

3-6. It flows from the lateral ventricles into the third ventricle, to the fourth ventricle, and into the subarachnoid space. It then travels to reach the inferior surface of the cerebrum and moves superiorly over the lateral aspect of each hemisphere. Some of it moves into the subarachnoid space around the spinal cord.

The cerebrospinal fluid is important in medical diagnostic procedures. The pressure of the fluid can be measured; if it is abnormally high, such abnormalities as intracranial tumor or hemorrhage, hydrocephalus, meningitis, or encephalitis may be suspected. Chemical and cell studies may be made on cerebral spinal fluid that is drawn out of the nervous system through a procedure called a *lumbar puncture*. This route also may be used to inject drugs to combat infection or to induce anesthesia.

FIGURE 3-6   Circulation of the cerebrospinal fluid

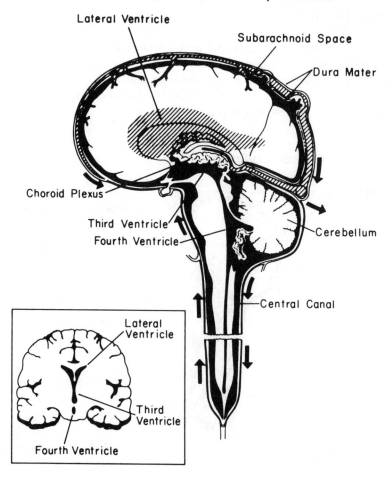

The Blood Supply of the Brain

The blood serves the brain as much as food serves the body: to nourish it by supplying its most important element, oxygen. The brain uses about 20 percent of the blood of the body at any one time and requires approximately 25 percent of the oxygen of the body to function maximally. Initially, blood is delivered to the brain through four main arteries. There are two large *internal carotid arteries*, one on either side of the neck. These are a result of bifurcation, or splitting, of the common carotid artery from the heart. The other two main arteries supplying the brain are the *vertebral arteries* (Figure 3-7).

The Internal Carotid Arteries and Their Branches

The internal carotid arteries ascend in the neck and pass through the base of the skull at the carotid canal of the temporal bone. Each artery then runs horizontally forward and perforates the dura mater. After entering the sub-arachnoid space, it turns posteriorly and, at the medial end of the lateral sulcus, divides into the anterior and middle cerebral arteries. Other cerebral arteries

FIGURE 3-7   Cerebral arteries

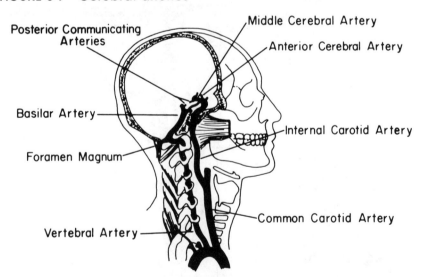

Source: Redrawn and reproduced with permission from R. Snell, *Clinical Neuroanatomy for Medical Students* (Boston: Little, Brown and Company, 1980).

are also given off by the internal carotid artery. The *ophthalmic artery* supplies the eye, the frontal area of the scalp, the dorsum of the nose, and the ethmoid and frontal sinuses. The *posterior communicating artery* runs posteriorly above the occulomotor nerve and joins the *posterior cerebral artery*, forming part of the *circle of Willis*. The anterior communicating artery joins the two anterior cerebral arteries together in the circle of Willis.

Through these cortical branches, the internal carotid artery provides the blood supply to a very large portion of the cerebral hemisphere. The *anterior cerebral artery* supplies all the medial surface of the cortex as far back as the parieto-temporal-occipital sulcus. It also supplies the so-called leg areas of the motor strip. Branches of this artery supply a small portion of the caudate nucleus, lentiform nucleus, and internal capsule.

The middle cerebral artery is the largest branch of the internal carotid. Its branches supply the entire lateral surface of the hemisphere except for the small area of the motor strip supplied by the anterior cerebral artery, the occipital pole, and the inferolateral surface of the hemisphere, which are supplied by the posterior cerebral artery. The middle cerebral artery's central branches also provide the primary blood supply to the lentiform and caudate nuclei and the internal capsule.

The Vertebral Artery and Its Branches

The vertebral artery passes through the foramina in the upper six cervical vertebrae and enters the skull through the foramen magnum. It passes upward and forward along the medulla and at the lower border of the pons and joins the vertebral artery from the opposite side to form the *basilar artery*. Prior to the formulation of the basilar artery, several branches are given off, including:

1. The meningeal branches, which supply the bone and dura of the posterior cranial fossa
2. The posterior spinal artery, which supplies the posterior third of the spinal cord
3. The anterior spinal artery, supplying the anterior two-thirds of the spinal cord
4. The posterior inferior cerebellar artery, which supplies part of the cerebellum, the medulla, and the choroid plexus of the fourth ventricle
5. The medullary arteries, which are distributed to the medulla

After the basilar artery is formed by the union of the opposite vertebral arteries, it ascends and then divides at the upper border of the pons into the two *posterior cerebral arteries*. These arteries supply the inferolateral surface of the temporal lobe, and the lateral and medial surfaces of the occipital lobe (that is, the visual cortex). They also supply parts of the thalamus and other internal structures (Figure 3-8).

Other branches of the basilar artery include:

1. The pontine arteries, which enter the pons
2. The labyrinthine artery, which supplies the internal ear
3. The anterior inferior cerebellar artery, supplying the anterior and inferior parts of the cerebellum
4. The superior cerebellar artery, which supplies the superior portion of the cerebellum

The Circle of Willis

The circle of Willis, or the circulus arteriosus, is formed by the anastomosis of the two internal carotid arteries with the two vertebral arteries. The anterior communicating, anterior cerebral, internal carotid, posterior communicating, posterior cerebral, and basilar arteries are all a part of the circle of Willis (Figure 3-9). This formation of arteries allows distribution of the blood entering from the internal carotid artery or vertebral artery to any part of both hemispheres. Cortical and central branches arise from the circle and further supply the brain.

The bloodstreams from the internal carotid artery and vertebral artery on both sides come together at a certain point in the posterior communicating artery. At that point the pressure is equal and they do not mix. Should, however, the internal carotid artery or the vertebral artery be occluded or blocked, the blood will pass forward or backward across that point to compensate for the reduced flow. The circle of Willis also allows blood to flow across the midline

FIGURE 3-8 Distribution of the cerebral arteries of the lateral and mesial surfaces of the left cerebral hemisphere

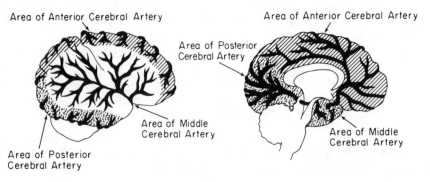

Area of Anterior Cerebral Artery

Area of Anterior Cerebral Artery

Area of Posterior Cerebral Artery

Area of Middle Cerebral Artery

Area of Middle Cerebral Artery

Area of Posterior Cerebral Artery

Lateral View

Medial View

FIGURE 3-9   Circle of Willis

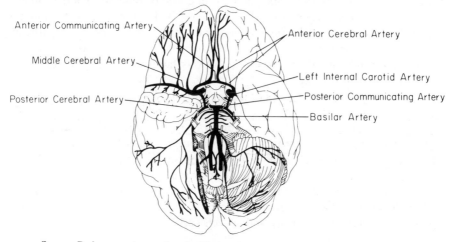

Anterior Communicating Artery

Middle Cerebral Artery

Posterior Cerebral Artery

Anterior Cerebral Artery

Left Internal Carotid Artery

Posterior Communicating Artery

Basilar Artery

Source: Redrawn and reproduced with permission from R. Snell, *Clinical Neuroanatomy for Medical Students* (Boston: Little, Brown and Company, 1980).

of the brain if an artery on one side is occluded. The circle of Willis thereby serves a safety valve function for the brain, allowing collateral circulation (or flow of blood through an alternate route) to take place if the flow is reduced to one area. The state of one's collateral circulation will help determine the outcome after a vascular lesion occurs and affects blood flow to the brain.

General Principles of Neurologic Organization

Now that we have surveyed the general anatomic organization of the nervous system for communication, it is appropriate to extract some fundamental principles of neurologic organization that are particulary crucial to the understanding and diagnosis of communication disorders. We will build on these principles in later chapters.

Contralateral Motor Control

The first principle to remember is that major movement patterns in humans have contralateral neurologic control in the brain. The arms and legs are represented in the motor strip of the cerebral cortex in a contralateral fashion. In other words, the cerebral hemisphere on one side of the body controls movements of the arm and leg on the other side of the body. This contralateral motor control is brought about by the crossing of the major voluntary motor pathway at the level of the lower brainstem. Auditory and visual sensory systems also have some contralateral organization, and this fact will become clinically important as you read Chapter 6.

If a patient sent to the speech-language pathologist has a severe language disorder and some paralysis of the right arm and leg, it suggests that the brain lesion causing this motor deficit is probably in the left cerebral hemisphere. The severe language disturbance accompanying the right limb paralysis serves as a confirming sign of left-sided brain lesion (discussed later). Why the nervous system is organized in such a manner to provide contralateral motor control of the limbs is not completely known, but the fact illustrates that knowledge of principles of neurological organization can be used to locate and lateralize causative lesions seen in neurology and speech pathology.

Ipsilateral Motor Control

If a lesion occurs in the nervous system below the crossing of the major descending motor pathways, the effect of the lesion is observed below the level of lesion on the same side of the body where the lesion occurs. In many spinal cord injuries there is paralysis and sensory loss below the point of injury. Thus second important principle is to determine whether effects of lesions are ipsilateral or contralateral.

Bilateral Speech Motor Control

For the most part, the midline muscles of the body in the head, neck, and trunk tend to be represented bilaterally and the nerve fibers supplying these regions, with certain exceptions, descend from both cerebral hemispheres. This bilateral neural control provides smooth, symmetrical movement for those muscles used in speaking—the lips, tongue, soft palate jaw, abdominal muscles, and diaphragm. The principle of bilateral control of speech muscles suggests that serious involvement of the speech muscles usually results from diseases that affect bilateral neurologic mechanisms. With unilateral damage to the nervous system, effects on speech are generally less serious, and compensatory mechanisms are made available from the other side of the midline speech system.

Representation of the body is found in an inverted fashion on the motor areas of the cerebral cortex. Pathways that are concerned with movements of the lower limbs originate in the upper parts of the motor strip, whereas movements of the head and neck originate at the lower end of the motor strip, just above the Sylvian fissure. The area surrounding the left Sylvian fissure contains major areas for language processing. The anatomic relationship of motor speech areas and language suggests that is not uncommon for speech and language disturbances to coexist because of the close proximity of their control areas on the cortex.

Unilateral Language Mechanisms

An impressive facet of cerebral asymmetry is that language mechanisms, for the most part, are unilaterally controlled in the brain, as compared to the bilateral speech muscle mechanism. Among the adult population, over 95 percent of right-handed people have their language mechanisms in the left cerebral hemisphere. Language dominance the world over is primary in the left brain. Left-handers are more variable. Some are right-brained for speech, others have bilateral representation of language. The obvious clinical principle suggested by these facts is that major language disturbance is a neurologic sign of left cerebral injury and that the left hemisphere has special anatomical properties for language.

Scheme of Cortical Organization

Although later chapters will detail the specifics of cortical localization, it is helpful for the student and clinician to have in mind a general scheme of organization of the cortex, since it is the site of most language functions. Although any such scheme is oversimplified and exaggerated, it nevertheless provides a crude but workable framework for conceptualizing functional localization.

The right and left hemispheres may be designated as nonverbal and verbal, and the anterior and posterior portions may be characterized as motor and sensory areas. The central sulcus divides the cerebral hemispheres into anterior and posterior regions. In humans approximately half the volume of the cerebral cortex is taken up by the frontal cortex. The frontal lobe contains the primary motor cortex and the premotor cortex as well as Broca's area, the primary motor speech association areas. In the anterior portion of the frontal lobes are the prefrontal areas, which are generally concerned with behavioral control of both cognitive and emotional functions. Lesions here produce slowed behavior, lacking in spontaneity. Difficulties in making mental shifts occur, and perseveration and rigidity are observed, as are lack of self-awareness and a tendency toward concreteness. In brief, the frontal lobe appears to excel in the control, integration, and regulation of emotional and cognitive behavior.

In contrast, the posterior cortex appears dominated by the control, integration, and regulation of sensory behavior. The defects arising from the posterior cortex are related to the specific sensory association areas that are implicated by a lesion.

The left parietal lobe is associated with constructional disturbances and visuospatial defects. Disorders of recognition, called *agnosias*, are common. The inferior parietal lobe concerns itself with language association tasks, and lesions there cause defects in reading and writing.

The occiptal lobe, as noted earlier, contains the primary visual cortex and visual association areas. Deficits in the primary cortex result in blind spots in the visual field, and total destruction of the cortex produces complete blindness. Visual imperception and agnosias (see Chapter 10) are associated with the visual association areas.

The temporal lobe on the left is concerned with hearing and related functions. It contains the primary auditory area and association areas. Auditory memory storage and complex auditory perception are among the functions of the temporal lobe. An area known as the *speech zone* surrounds the Sylvian fissure and appears to contain the major components of the language mechanism. Damage in the speech zone produces the aphasias.

With a clinical knowledge of primary sensory and related association areas and behavioral correlates to these areas, the speech-language pathologist will be able to infer the approximate location of a lesion from the patient's behavioral symptoms and will be able to recognize the well-known speech-language syndromes associated with cortical dysfunction. The general clinical principle is that specific cortical deficits can be associated with behavioral syndromes.

Summary

A vast amount of information is provided in Chapters 2 and 3. In order to help you review and organize what you have learned, we have prepared an outline of the most important structures discussed. In using this outline, ask yourself the following questions concerning the outline item:

1. What is it?
2. Where is it?
3. What does it do?

When appropriate, go back and see if you can label drawings of some of the various structures for which illustrations were used. The effort you put into doing this will be rewarded with your feeling knowledgeable about and comfortable with the information in these chapters—information that is basic to your understanding of subsequent chapters.

I. The human nervous system
   A. Central nervous system
      1. Brain
         a. Cerebral hemispheres
            (1) Four lobes
            (2) Fissures
            (3) Sulci
            (4) Gyri
            (5) Association cortex
            (6) Connecting fibers
         b. Basal ganglia
            (1) Corpus striatum
               (a) Caudate nucleus
               (b) Lentiform nucleus: putamen, globus pallidus
            (2) Claustrum
         c. Cerebellum
         d. Brainstem
            (1) Medulla oblongata
               (a) Pyramids
               (b) Olives
               (c) Peduncles
            (2) Pons
            (3) Mesencephalon
               (a) Tectum
               (b) Colliculi
      2. Spinal cord
         a. Spinal nerves
         b. Peripheral nerves
         c. Five regions
      3. Meninges
         a. Dura mater
         b. Arachnoid
         c. Pia mater
      4. Ventricles
         a. Choroid plexuses
         b. Cerebrospinal fluid
      5. Blood supply
         a. Internal carotid artery and its branches
         b. Vertebral artery and its branches
         c. Circle of Willis
   B. Peripheral nervous system
      1. Spinal peripheral nerves
         a. Anterior horn cell
         b. Efferent fibers

References and Further Readings

Angevine, J. B., & Cotman, C. W. (1981). *Principles of neuroanatomy*. New York: Oxford University Press.

Liebman, M. (1983). *Neuroanatomy made easy and understandable*. 2nd ed. Baltimore: University Park Press.

Snell, R. S. (1980). *Clinical neuroanatomy for medical students*. Boston: Little, Brown and Company.

CHAPTER FOUR

Neuronal Function in the Nervous System

> But strange that I was not told
> That the brain can hold
> In a tiny ivory cage
> God's heaven and hell.
>
> —Oscar Wilde

Neuronal Physiology

The Neuron

The *neuron*, or nerve cell, is the basic anatomic and functional unit of the nervous system, underlying all neural behavior including speech, language, and hearing. Each neuron consists of a cell body known as a *soma* or *perikaryon*. Neurons vary greatly in size, but most of the billions of neurons of the central nervous system are small (Figure 4-1). Each neuron contains a cell nucleus and a series of one to a dozen projections of varying length. These projections receive stimuli and conduct neural impulses. Those receiving neural stimuli, called *dendrites*, are the shorter and more numerous projections of the nerve cell. Generally the dendrites of a neuron are no more than a few millimeters in length.

The other process of a neuron is the *axon*, a longer single fiber that conducts nerve impulses away from the neuron to other parts of the nervous system, glands, or muscle. Axons range in length from several micrometers to several

FIGURE 4-1   Schematic drawing of a neuron, myelinated axon, and synapse

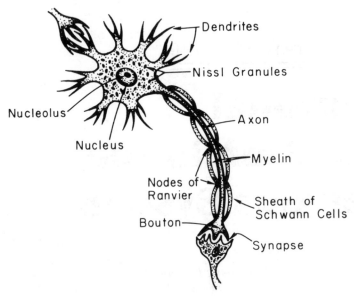

Source: Redrawn and reproduced with permission from M. Liebman, *Neuroanatomy Made Easy and Understandable* (2nd ed.) (Baltimore: University Park Press, 1983).

meters. The diameter of individual axons varies greatly, and their conduction velocity ranges from 2 to 100 meters per second, depending on the fiber size. The larger the diameter, the greater the conduction velocity. In a physiologic sense, the term *axon* refers to a nerve fiber that conducts impulses away from a nerve cell body. Any long nerve fiber, however, may be referred to as an axon, regardless of the direction of the flow of nervous impulses.

In the brain itself, most of the neurons conduct neural impulses to other neurons, which are clustered very close together, providing a high neuronal density in the cerebrum. This high density creates an almost unlimited capacity for complex neuronal activity.

Cellular Electrical Potentials
Like other cells of the body, the neuron is enclosed by membranes made up of protein and lipid layers. The intracellular portion of the neuron contains a high concentration of potassium and a low concentration of sodium and chloride in relation to the extracellular fluids. In the extracellular fluids, the concentrations are reversed. Sodium and chloride are found in high concentrations, about 10 times that of intracellular concentrations. Potassium is found in low concentrations. The difference in chemical concentrations produces ionic differences across the membrane of the cell. These ionic differences create small electrical

potentials across the surface membrane of the neuron and produce a flow of electric current. The electrical charge within the nerve cell is strongly negative compared to the outside of the cell. The term *resting potential* is employed to describe the differences in potential across the cell membranes.

Changes in electrical potential are conducted along the membranes of both the cell body and the nerve fibers. During the transmission of neural impulses, the primary mechanism is a change in the resting potential and a propagation of electrical current across the membrane. The conduction of the nerve impulse is actually brought about by an abrupt change in electrical potential, known as the *action potential*. The flow of current that occurs during the action potential is called the *action current* (Figure 4-2).

Action Potential

The action potential develops as the result of a rapid depolarization of the cell membrane, and there is a decrease in negativity inside the nerve cell relative to the outside of the cell. During the action potential, there is a transient reversal of the polarity of the electrical potential. At the peak of the action potential, the inside of the cell becomes positive with respect to the outside. The action potential is thus brought about by an initial inward current developed by a flow of sodium from the exterior to the interior of the cell.

The action current is propagated along the nerve fiber for long distances without change in the wave form and at a constant velocity. This means that all the neuronal signals of coded information that are transmitted in the nervous

FIGURE 4-2 A typical action potential

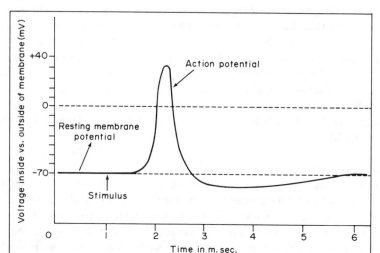

Source: Redrawn and reproduced with permission from S. Rose, *The Conscious Brain* (New York: Knopf, 1973).

system are conveyed by a series of uniformly sized impulses. The information transmitted in the nervous system is therefore signaled by the frequency of the action potentials rather than by their amplitude. The action potential functions in an all-or-nothing manner. A stimulus sets up either a full-sized impulse or nothing.

During the passage of an action potential across a nerve cell membrane, the membrane becomes incapable of responding to another stimulus. This period of unresponsiveness is called an *absolute refractory period*. The absolute refractory period is relatively short, lasting approximately 0.8 millisecond. Following the absolute refractory period, an action potential may be produced by a very intense stimulus initially and then by stimuli of less intensity. The period after the absolute refractory period is called the *relative refractory period*.

The Synapse

Neuromuscular Synapse
As the electrical nerve impulse, in the form of an action potential, moves along an axon, it comes to a point where it must be transmitted to another neuron, a gland, or a muscle. This point is known as a *synapse*. Until it was realized that small junctures occur at the synapse, it was assumed that neurons were connected in one continuous network.

The transmission of a neural impulse across the synaptic juncture or gap is primarily a chemical process, sometimes an electrical process, and very occasionally a combination of both. The transmission of nerve impulses to muscle impulses in the peripheral nervous system was the first well-established example of chemical synaptic transmission. About fifty years ago, many neurophysiologists believed that the impulse transmission of one thousandth of a second was too fast for any type of chemical mediation. It was held that an electrical nerve impulse directly excited the muscle fiber. The large electrical mismatch, however, between the tiny nerve fiber and the large muscle fiber indicated that an electrical explanation would be faulty by at least two orders of magnitude. In the 1930s, it was established that synaptic transmission in nerve-to-muscle synapses was due entirely to chemical mediation by a substance called acetylcholine (ACh).

Chemical Transmission
In peripheral-nerve-to-muscle transmission, or neuromuscular transmission, the nerve is known to be a structure on the muscle surface, making contact with the muscle fiber but not fusing with it. There is a special structural enlargement of the muscle fiber at the synaptic junction called the *motor endplate*. Near the motor endplate is the nerve terminal, or *synaptic knob* (Figure 4-3). With the advent of electron microscopy, a series of vesicles on the nerve terminal were identified. These became known as *synaptic vesicles*, and they release chemical

FIGURE 4-3 Reconstruction of what a synapse may look like in three dimensions

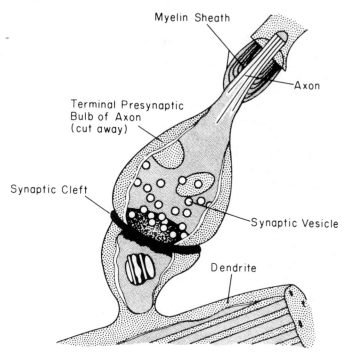

Source: Redrawn and reproduced with permission from S. Rose, *The Conscious Brain* (New York: Knopf, 1973).

transmitters at the synapse. In addition to the synaptic vesicles, a space known as the *synaptic cleft* has been observed. The synaptic cleft is the junction in the synapse across which transmission occurs. In the peripheral nervous system, electrical currents generated by the action of the transmitter substance, acetylcholine, flow across the synapse to the membrane known as the postsynaptic membrane. In nerve-to-muscle impulses, this is the membrane of the motor endplate. From the endplate, the impulse triggers muscle contraction. In brief, the primary mechanism of the synapse occurs when a nerve impulse causes some of the synaptic vesicles to liberate their contents into the synaptic cleft. The vesicles contain acetylcholine, which is prepackaged with about 10,000 molecules in each vesicle. It is released in a quantal, or packetlike, fashion. The acetylcholine transmitters act to change the direction of depolarization. This, in turn, sets up an impulse on the motor endplate. An impulse is then generated along the muscle fiber and sets off a complex series of events for muscle contraction.

The chemical transmitters in either the peripheral nervous system or the central nervous system are removed by either reuptake or destruction by enzymes. Specific enzymes have been found to be involved for different types of transmitters.

Transmission Disorders

Disorders of chemical transmission can cause neurologic disorders. In the neuromuscular disease known as *myasthenia gravis*, the patient shows muscle weakness on sustained effort. Neuromuscular transmission appears to fail after continuous muscle contraction as a result of reduced availability of acetylcholine at the myoneural junction. Antibodies interfere with the transmission of the acetylcholine. These antibodies are an autoimmune disease reaction to postsynaptic receptor protein, with an involvement of the postsynaptic membranes.

The prime symptom of weakness often affects the speech muscles. The nerve innervating the larynx and palate is sometimes the first to be affected by the disease. The weakened vocal folds do not close appropriately, and the voice becomes breathy and weak in intensity. A hypernasal voice quality may develop after sustained speaking because of weakness of the soft palate. As the speech deteriorates, the tongue, lips, and respiratory muscles may be involved. Speech symptoms will be discussed further in Chapter 8.

Certain drugs—prostigmine and Tensilon—will temporarily relieve the symptoms promptly and aid the neurologist in diagnosing the disease. Treatment to reduce the antibodies blocking the acetylcholine transmission is effective in reversing the neuromuscular problem in the muscles of the body as well as the speech muscles.

Synaptic Excitation and Inhibition

Synaptic transmission in the brain, as opposed to neuromuscular transmission, is the result of synaptic action between neuron and neuron rather than nerve fiber and muscle fiber. Neurons connected to each other are called *interneurons*. The basic synaptic mechanism, however, is much the same. Synaptic vesicles release transmitter substances, and action potentials are triggered. The main transmitters are epinephrine, acetylcholine, dopamine, serotonin, γ-aminobutyric acid (GABA), glutamate, and glycine. Excitatory and inhibitory potentials are established before and after the action potential. Before an action potential in the postsynaptic nerve fiber is triggered, there is an intervening potential developed called the *postsynaptic potential*. This potential may be either excitatory (E) or inhibitory (I). The excitatory postsynaptic potential (EPSP) persists for several milliseconds and may be strong enough to trigger an action potential, or it may summate in space and time to achieve the necessary voltage to trigger an action potential. Several individual nerve endings converging on one postsynaptic membrane may summate, or several subthreshold events may summate over time to evoke an action potential in an all-or-none manner.

The inhibitory postsynaptic potential (IPSP) is almost a mirror image of

EPSP. The peak voltage is in the opposite direction, and the duration is almost the same except for minor alterations. The EPSP acts to depolarize the membrane, and the membrane potential may be driven beyond a threshold to trigger the action potential. The IPSP stabilizes the membrane potential so that the action potential is not triggered.

An action potential may be triggered when a series of impulses of the EPSP type arrive at a neuron. If the series of impulses occur in rapid succession, the action potential is more likely than when a single or a few impulses arrive at the neuron. Excitatory states that assist the conduction of action potentials along a chain of neurons are called *facilitation*.

Both the EPSP and the IPSP are graded responses that will summate, resulting in plasticity and variability of function at the synapse. The individual synapse is subject to an almost infinite number of influences that affect the rate of firing in individual neurons. This allows for the notion of a probabilistic aspect in neuronal functioning in the brain.

Principles of Neuronal Operation

The central nervous system is constantly bombarded by volleys of sensory nerve impulses. The excitatory and inhibitory influences of the nervous system provide for a process of selectivity of impulses for transmission at the level of the synapse. This selectivity of transmission of nerve impulse may be the basic function of the synapse. The synapse allows transmission in an all-or-none manner also. In other words, all that can be transmitted is either a full-sized response for the condition of the axon, or else nothing.

Further, the central nervous system is characterized by the principle of divergence. Charles Sherrington observed that within the human nervous system there are numerous branchings of all axons with a great opportunity for wide dispersal of impulses because the impulses discharged by a neuron travel along its branches to activate all its synapses. Thus the central nervous system is made up of an almost numberless series of sources and routes for widespread or accessory neuronal activity. This accessory neuronal activity forms what may be considered neuronal pools of activity.

There is a complementary principle of convergence in the nervous system. This principle, also enumerated by Sherrington, implies that all neurons receive synaptic information from many other neurons, some of an excitatory nature and some of an inhibitory nature. The number of synapses on individual neurons is generally large, measured in hundreds or thousands, with the largest being about 80,000. Therefore, both excitation and inhibition play a large role in the nervous system.

The principles of divergence and convergence also suggest that although individual neurons are neither excitatory or inhibitory, certain neuronal systems act primarily as either excitatory or inhibiting mechanisms for effective overall neuronal functioning. An example is the large excitatory and inhibitory neuronal system in the reticular formation deep within the brain, which both activates and suppresses levels of consciousness expressed during wakefulness and sleep.

The complexity of the neuronal firings and synaptic connections, particularly on the surface of the brain called the cerebral cortex, provides an intricate weaving of impulses into very complex spatial and temporal patterns. Sherrington has compared this neuronal activity to the weaving of an enchanted loom. No doubt these ever-changing neuronal designs are the basis for the integrative activity of the nervous system and are the foundations of emotion, thought, language, and action as well as that most human of behaviors—speaking.

It is sometimes difficult to grasp, and even harder to believe, that the rich range of behavior that we assume is specifically human, including the uniqueness of oral language, can ultimately be reduced to and equated with the mere ebb and flow of minute chemical and electrical changes in tiny, but intricate, synaptic mechanisms. This present-day interpretation of neuronal function, reductionist as it appears, highlights the vast and mysterious frontier between mind and brain that faces the neuroscientist. Despite this great gulf between mind and matter, it is well for the speech-language pathologist to remember that this view of neuronal functioning provides the neurophysiologist a basis for seeing the workings of the brain as a vast abstract complex of neuronal design on the enchanted loom of Sherrington. Despite our sophistication in studying neuronal function, the specifics of the neuronal patterns for understanding and producing language and speech in the brain are unknown.

Servomechanism Theory in Neuronal Function

Feedback

Several fruitful engineering concepts have been applied to neuronal transmission problems in the nervous system. These concepts have been particularly useful in explaining the possible control of neural impulses in the speech mechanism. The basic concept, known as the theory of servomechanism control systems, implies the concept of *feedback*. Feedback describes the functioning principle in self-regulating systems, either mechanical or biological. Feedback assumes that the output of any self-regulating system, such as a thermostat, is fed back into the system at some point so as to control or regulate the output of the system. This concept of self-monitoring is most appropriate for understanding the biologic system known as the speech motor control system. For instance, the questions of how a speaker monitors speech and what neuronal feedback mechanisms are available to control speech movements seem likely ones for explanation by servomechanism theory.

Open and Closed Control Systems

Two types of bioengineering control systems have been described as applicable to neuronal transmission in speech production: closed- and open-loop control systems. A closed-loop system employs a positive feedback wherein output is returned to input to control further output. For example, if you are copying a complex and delicate drawing, the sensory input to your visual system guides the motor output of your hand. Similarly, hearing our own speech as we talk may at times serve to control the motor speech output as we continue to talk more. In these two examples it is assumed that our motor output by hand or tongue is guided by the sensory input of vision or audition. We would further assume that if the sensory feedback were blocked, our drawing or speech would go awry.

In an open-loop system, the output is generally preprogrammed, and the performance of the system is not matched with the system. For instance, if you have learned a short poem by heart and practiced it over and over again, you may well be able to say the phonemes of the words in the poem without error even though your ears are stuffed with cotton. In an open-loop system the notion of *feedforward*, rather than feedback, is important. Once you have uttered a phrase of a well-learned poem, it will cue the next preprogrammed phrase of speech without the need to hear what was said through auditory feedback. An open-loop system thus typically generates another input via its output system. The term *negative feedback* is also used in control systems of the servomechanism type. It implies that when errors are fed back into the system, this error information will act to keep a given output activity within certain limits. Correcting an articulation error on hearing it is an example of utilization of negative feedback in speech activity.

Much speech research has viewed speech motor control as the product of a closed-loop feedback system with sensory monitoring from hearing, touch, and deep muscle sense guiding the movements of the speech muscles. Circumstantial evidence for this position has come from studies of sensory dysfunction in some speech disorders (see Chapter 6). Yet there is evidence that much of speech motor control is preprogrammed by the brain and that feedforward control is also important in speech motor control. It may well be that neurologic control of speech involves combinations of both open and closed loops in a multiple-pathway, hierarchical system that provides the necessary flexibility, speed, and precision to program and execute the everyday movements of speech with such complexity and ease.

Myelin

Nerve fibers, or axons, may be classified as myelinated or unmyelinated. Large peripheral nerves as well as the large axons of the central nervous system acquire a white fatty sheath of wrapping as the brain develops. This is *myelin*. The myelin sheath is composed of *Schwann cells*. The Schwann sheet outside is called the *neurolemma*. Myelin is white, contrasting sharply with the gray unmyelinated nerve. The myelin sheet is thick and can be revealed by a special myelin stain. The thick insulation of myelin is interrupted at intervals by structures called the *nodes of Ranvier*. The design of myelin sheaths enhances rapid propagation of the electrical impulse along the nerve fiber. The impulse moves along the myelinated fiber by hopping from node to node, without any active contribution from the long internodal spaces. Action potentials develop only at the nodes (Figure 4-1). This mode of transmission is extremely efficient compared with the slow gliding along of the nerve impulses on unmyelinated fibers. The type of transmission in myelinated fibers is called *saltatory transmission*. The efficiency of saltatory transmission is achieved because of the insulation that prevents current flow between nodes as well as the fact that there is little leakage of current from the fibers. The conduction velocity of a myelinated fiber is directly proportional to the diameter of the fiber, whereas in an unmyelinated fiber the velocity is approximately proportional to the square root of the diameter. On the average, a transmission along myelinated fiber is roughly 50 times as fast as one along an unmyelinated fiber.

Unmyelinated fibers are more common in the smaller nerve fibers of the peripheral nervous system, though the cranial nerves, which are part of the peripheral nervous system, are relatively large in diameter, and are myelinated. Six of the cranial nerves innervate the speech muscles and provide neuromotor control for talking. The rapidity of transmission in these nerves helps supply neural innervation for the rapid muscular movements underlying speech.

Development of Myelin

Myelin is laid down in the nervous system as the brain develops. At birth, the human brain is relatively low in myelin. Most of the pathways that have been formed in prenatal life are unmyelinated, so the gray matter of the cortex is hard to distinguish from the white matter of the subcortical tissue at birth. The major increase in the laying down of the myelin lipid sheaths is in the first two years of life. The development of myelin parallels the development of *glia* in the brain. Glia are cells other than neurons that are found in the cortex of the brain. The term *glia* is from the Latin and means "glue." The cells appear to stick together and seal up the available spaces in the cerebral cortex; they outnumber the neurons about ten to one. Not all the functions of the glia cells are clear, but one that is well established is that of fabricating the myelin sheaths in which the myelinated axons are wrapped. The cells that make the myelin are called *oligodendroglia*. The other glial cells are known as *astrocytes*.

Since the infant brain shows a distinct lack of myelin at birth, its development has frequently been considered a significant index, among several others, of the maturation of the nervous system. Specific attempts, discussed in Chapter 11, have been made to relate major speech and language milestones, such as the appearance of babbling, first words, and word combinations, to the development of myelin in the nervous system. Although a case can be made for a positive relation between communicative milestones and development of myelin, there is not substantial evidence to suggest that delays in the development of myelin are necessarily related to syndromes of speech and language delay. The area of neurologic developmental delays of myelin awaits further research.

Myelin Disorders

Multiple sclerosis is a disorder of myelin that produces a variety of neurologic symptoms, including a severe motor disturbance. It is caused by an autoimmune inflammatory response that damages the myelin sheath. If this inflammatory reaction is intense, the axons, too, may be damaged, producing irreversible neurologic deficits that show irregular fluctuating periods of exacerbation and remission.

About half the patients with multiple sclerosis have speech defects. A speech disorder, resulting from involvement of the neuromuscular aspect of the nervous system, is called *dysarthria*. Clinical symptoms of dysarthria will be detailed in Chapter 8.

Summary

The neuron is the basic functional unit of the nervous system. Its primary property is excitability. The afferent processes of the neuron are called dendrites, and the efferent process is the axon. Neural transmission is a function basic to the nervous system, and the neuron with its processes serves as a basic conductive unit of the nervous system.

The synapse is a juncture point at which electrical impulses are transmitted from nerve to muscle, gland, or another neuron. Interneuron transmission occurs in the brain from nerve to nerve. Electrical transmission at the synapse is aided by the release of biochemical transmitters. Peripheral neuromuscular synapses release acetylcholine. Other neurotransmitters have been found in the brain. Firing at the synapse occurs as the result of the trigger of an action potential. This potential is influenced by the excitatory presynaptic potential (EPSP) and the inhibitory presynaptic potential (IPSP).

Neuronal function at higher levels is accomplished in neuronal patterns and networks. The principles of network excitation and inhibition, as well as convergence and divergence and probabilistic selectivity of impulses at the synapse, are important in brain function. There remains a significant knowledge gap between understanding the electrical and biochemical properties in neuronal transmission and explaining the neuronal activity necessary for speech and language.

Myelin, an insulating covering on some nerves of the central and peripheral nervous system, allows rapid and efficient transmission of impulses. The six cranial nerves innervating the speech mechanism are myelinated, and this allows for the rapid muscular actions necessary for speech. Acquisition of myelin appears to be one index of nervous system maturation in the first two years of life, but there is no substantial evidence to suggest that speech and language delays in preschool children are associated with lack or delay of myelination. Multiple sclerosis (MS) is a disorder of myelin that sometimes produces a motor speech disorder known as dysarthria. Currently there is no cure for the myelin deterioration in multiple sclerosis. Reduction of acetylcholine at the synapse as part of an autoimmune disease is a cause of another neuromuscular disorder, usually with an associated dysarthria. This disorder is myasthenia gravis, and it is marked by extreme weakness of muscles on sustained effort. Drug therapy may alleviate the speech problems and weakness appreciably.

References and Further Reading

Eccles, J. C. (1973). *The understanding of the brain*. New York: McGraw-Hill.

Grillner, S.; Lindblom, B.; Lubker, J.; & Persson, A. (1982). *Speech motor control*. Oxford: Pergamon Press.

Jewett, D. L., & Rayner, M.D. (1984). *Basic concepts of neuronal function*. Boston: Little, Brown.

CHAPTER FIVE

Neurosensory Organization of Speech and Hearing

"Speech is normally controlled by the ear."
                    —Raymond Carhart, *Hearing and Deafness*, 1947

Bodily Sensation

Classification

During the nineteenth century, neurophysiologists conceived of the execution of skilled motor acts primarily as the result of programming in the motor areas of the cerebral cortex, with some additional influences on the descending motor impulses from cerebellar and extrapyramidal mechanisms. This view of the nervous system has been modified during the twentieth century to include the concept of sensory feedback control in motor acts. Audition, of course, plays a special and primary feedback role in the control of speech. Recently, specific efforts have been directed at determining the nature of other neurosensory controls exercised in speaking. Before we discuss sensory control in speech, it is necessary to understand in general the types of sensation mediated by the nervous system.

Sherrington's Scheme

Charles Sherrington proposed a classification of sensation that is in wide use today and has application for the sensory control of speech. He divided the sensory receptors into three broad classes: (1) exteroceptors, (2) proprioceptors, and (3) interoceptors. *Exteroceptors* mediate sight, sound, smell, and cutaneous sensation. Cutaneous superficial skin sensation includes touch, superficial pain, temperature, itching, and tickling. *Proprioceptors* mediate deep somatic sensation from receptors beneath the skin, in muscles and joints, and in the inner ear. Proprioception includes the following senses: pressure, movement, vibration, position, deep pain, and equilibrium. *Interoceptors* include sensation from the viscera, as well as visceral pain and pressure or distension. Pain receptors, either from cellular or tissue injury, are known as *nociceptive receptors*.

In addition, multisensory functions have been called the higher sensations. The higher sensations include recognition of form, size, and texture, as well as weight and two-point discrimination.

Neurophysiologists have classified the senses as special and general senses. The term *special senses* reflects the traditional layperson's concept that certain of the senses are primary. For the neurophysiologist, hearing, vision, taste, smell, and balance are the special senses. The *general senses*, in this classification scheme, include the remainder of the senses.

Anatomy of Sensation

The neuroanatomy of the senses is complex. The general somatic sensory pathways—those dealing with bodily sensation—utilize the spinal cord and spinal nerves. Sensation to the head and vocal mechanism—larynx, pharynx, soft palate, and tongue—utilize the cranial nerve pathways.

The pathways of somatic sensation are composed in general of a three-neuron pathway from the periphery to the cerebral cortex. There is some variation within this three-neuron organization for the sensations of light touch, pain, temperature, and proprioception. The first-order, or primary, neuron for sensation for any given spinal nerve is found on the dorsal or posterior spinal root in a mass known as a spinal ganglion. For instance, the superficial sensations of light touch and pain and temperature begin in special receptors in the skin and are transmitted by spinal nerves to the spinal cord through the spinal ganglion. From the first-order neuron, an axon is sent centrally to the central nervous system to synapse on the second-order neuron. Fibers of the second-order neuron then cross the midline, and an axon ascends to the third-order neuron in the thalamus. A general name for the tract formed by the axon of the second-order neuron is *lemniscus*.

Lateral Spinothalamic Tract

The crossed ascending sensory pathway in the spinal cord, known as the lateral spinothalamic tract, transmits the sensations of pain and temperature (Figure 5-1). The fibers enter the cord through the spinal root ganglion and end in the dorsal root of the gray matter. At this point the first-order neuron synapses

FIGURE 5-1 The pathways mediating the sensations of pain and temperature

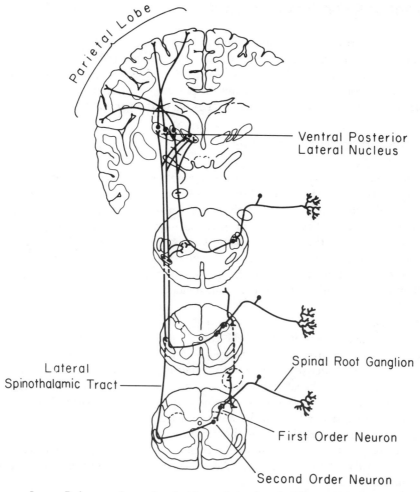

Source: Redrawn and reproduced with permission from S. Gilman and S. Winan, *Manter and Gatz's Essentials of Clinical Neuroanatomy and Neurophysiology* (6th ed.) (Philadelphia: F.A. Davis, 1982).

with the second-order neuron and promptly crosses to the other side of the spinal cord. There the fibers enter the lateral white column or the lateral spinothalamic tract, and ascend to the ventral posterior lateral nucleus in the thalamus. The axons of the lateral spinothalamic tract synapse with a third-order neuron that leaves the thalamus, ascends in the internal capsule, and reaches the postcentral cortical gyri in the parietal lobe (areas 3, 1, 2). This is the primary somatic sensory area of the brain, where pain and temperature sensations as well as pressure and touch are interpreted.

Ventral Spinothalamic Tract

This tract carries sensory information of light touch, including light pressure and touch and tactile location (Figure 5-2). The light touch fibers synapse within the dorsal gray horn cells in the spinal cord, and ascend in the ventral spinothalamic tract to the brainstem and the posterior ventral nucleus of the midbrain. The tract ends in the postcentral gyrus of the parietal lobe.

Proprioception Pathways

Proprioception, two-point discrimination, vibration, and form perception follow different pathways than those of the spinothalamic tracts. Proprioception is the sense that allows us to know exactly where our body parts are in space and in relation to one another. Two-point discrimination allows us to distinguish two adjacent points on the skin. Two-point sensitivity varies over the body surface. The lips and fingertips are the most sensitive and the back the least sensitive. Vibratory sensation allows us to recognize vibrating objects. Form perception allows the recognition of objects by touch alone.

Spinocerebellar Tract
Proprioception is conveyed by fibers from muscle tendons and joints, and takes two major routes after entering the spinal cord. One of these major pathways is the spinocerebellar pathway, and the other is the dorsal column pathway.

The spinocerebellar pathway has two tracts, dorsal and ventral. These tracts arise from the posterior and medial gray matter of the cord. The dorsal tract ascends ipsilaterally, but the ventral tract crosses in the cord. Both tracts terminate in the cerebellum and allow proprioceptive impulses from all parts of the body to be integrated in the cerebellum. It has been proposed that the spinocerebellar pathway functions in unconscious perception of already learned motor patterns.

Dorsal Columns
Conscious proprioception, two-point discrimination, and form perception have been called the sensory modalities of the dorsal, or posterior, columns of the spinal cord. The axons of the dorsal columns enter the cord after entering the

FIGURE 5-2 The pathways mediating the sensation of touch

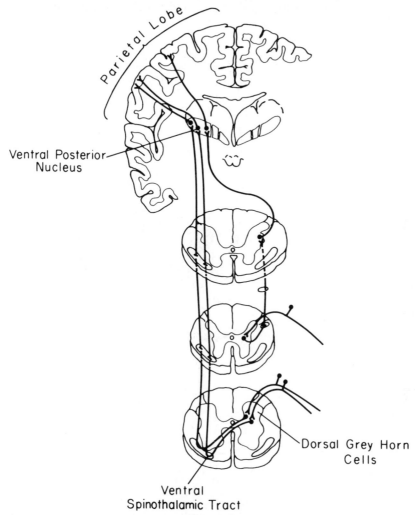

Ventral Posterior
Nucleus

Parietal Lobe

Dorsal Grey Horn
Cells

Ventral
Spinothalamic Tract

Source: Redrawn and reproduced with permission from S. Gilman and S. Winan, *Manter and Gatz's Essentials of Clinical Neuroanatomy and Neurophysiology* (6th ed.) (Philadelphia: F. A. Davis, 1982).

peripheral nerves of the spinal cord with the first-order neuron at the dorsal root ganglion (Figure 5-3). The axons then ascend in the dorsal white columns to the medulla. Axons entering the cord at the sacral and lumbar regions, which mediate proprioception from the leg and lower body, are found in the medial dorsal columns, called the *fasciculus gracilis*. Axons from the more lateral dorsal columns, from the thoracic and cervical regions, are generally related to the arm and upper body. They are found in the *fasciculus cuneatus*. The second-

FIGURE 5-3   The pathways mediating proprioception. These pathways are those that are known as the dorsal column modalities

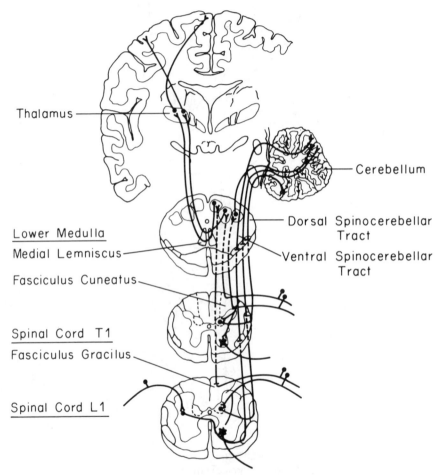

Source: Redrawn and reproduced with permission from S. Gilman and S. Winan, *Manter and Gatz's Essentials of Clinical Neuroanatomy and Neurophysiology* (6th ed.) (Philadelphia: F. A. Davis, 1982).

order neurons leave the nucleus gracilus and nucleus cuneatus and cross over to the other side of the medulla, where they form a bundle called the *medial lemniscus*. The pathway then ascends to the third-order neuron at the thalamus and finally proceeds to the parietal lobe.

Proprioceptive Deficits
Damage to the postcentral gyrus of the parietal lobe, the dorsal columns, or the dorsal root ganglion may produce a loss of proprioception, astereognosis,

loss of vibratory sense, and loss of two-point discrimination in the trunk or extremities. If there is damage to the dorsal column fibers from the upper body and arms below the level of the medulla, the loss in proprioception is on the same side of the injury. Damage above the level of the medulla produces a loss in proprioception on the opposite side of the body. If the fibers of the spino-cerebellar tract are damaged, proprioceptive loss occurs on the same side as the injury.

Damage to the spinothalamic tracts of pain and temperature usually result in loss to the opposite side of the body. The fibers of light touch take two routes, one ipsilaterally and one contralaterally. The ipsilateral fibers ascend with the proprioceptive fibers in the dorsal columns, and the crossed fibers ascend in the spinothalamic tract. The fibers of light touch branch extensively; because of this branching, touch is unlikely to be abolished by injury to a specific pathway in the spinal cord.

Sensory Examination

The neurologist employs several traditional and standard procedures for determining sensory loss. These are incorporated into the standard neurologic examination (see Appendix B).

The senses of light touch, pain, and temperature are mediated by the fibers of the dorsal root of the spinal cord, which come from a circumscribed area of the skin known as a *dermatome*. In peripheral nerve injuries, impairment of touch corresponds to dermatomal zones; but at the boundary of each segmental dermatome is an overlap area that is supplied by the adjacent segmental nerves. For instance, if the fifth thoracic nerve (T5) is severed, T3 and T6 will carry many of the pain and temperature sensations supplied by T5. This segmental overlap also is present in the spinal cord. Thus overlap is greater for pain and temperature than for touch.

Light Touch

The sense of light touch is tested by determining the patient's ability to perceive light stroking of the skin with a wisp of cotton. Disorders of the sensory pathways from skin to cortex will show abnormal sensory reactions. Decreased tactile sensation is called *hypoesthesia*, and complete loss of sensation is called *anesthesia*. If tactile sensation is abnormally increased, it is known as *hyperasthesia*.

Inability to localize touch is called *atopognosis*. Topognosis is tested by touching the patient's body. With the eyes closed, the patient is asked to point to the spot where he or she was touched. The neurologist compares similar areas on both sides of the body. Atopognosia is usually associated with a lesion of the parietal lobe.

Two-Point Discrimination

Two-point discrimination, or the ability to discriminate the shortest distance between two tactile points on the skin, is sometimes tested with points of a caliper. Right and left sides of the body are compared. Loss of discrimination suggests a parietal lobe lesion.

Double stimulation may also be tested to determine a cortical sensory disorder. Two simultaneous tactile stimulations are presented to both sides of the body in similar areas, or to different areas. Lateralized sensory loss can then be determined. Frequently, sensory pathway or cortical sensory losses accompany lesions that produce cerebral language disorders.

Pain and Temperature

Pain and temperature disturbance are more likely to be sensory pathway disorders, and lesions of the ventral and lateral spinothalamic tracts may be present. Pain perception is lost on the side contralateral to the lesion. Pain is tested by the ability to perceive a pinprick or deep pressure. Increased pain, or tenderness, is called *hyperalgesia*. A diminished sense of pain is *hypoalgesia*, and a complete lack of pain sensibility is an *analgesia*.

Temperature disturbances are tested by the ability to distinguish between warm and cold. For this test, the neurologist usually asks the patient to identify a test tube of warm water and one of cold water.

Dorsal Column Lesions

Dorsal column lesions produce disorders of proprioception and astereognosis and related impairments. The following defects may be present with dorsal column lesions.

Inability to Recognize Limb Position
The patient cannot say, without looking, whether a joint is in flexion or extension, nor can the direction of displacement of limbs or digits—fingers and toes—during movement be identified.

Astereognosis
Astereognosis is the inability to recognize common objects, such as coins, keys, and small blocks, by touch with the eyes closed. If this disorder is caused by a cortical sensory lesion rather than a dorsal column proprioceptive lesion, it is called tactile agnosia (see Chapter 9).

Two-Point Discrimination Disorder
Separating two tactile points from a single one is called two-point discrimination. Deficits are associated with a dorsal column lesion.

Vibratory Sensibility Disorder
The sensation evoked when a vibrating tuning fork is applied to the base of a bony prominence is lost in dorsal column problems. The patient cannot differentiate a vibrating tuning fork from a silent one on bony surfaces.

Body Sway Test
This test, called the Romberg test, requires the patient to stand with the feet together. The neurologist notes the amount of sway with the eyes open and compares with the amount of sway with the eyes closed. An abnormal accentuation of swaying or actual loss of balance is called a positive Romberg sign. The visual sense can compensate for this loss of proprioception of muscle and joint position, if it is a dorsal column disorder, so the patient may correct balance problems if he opens his eyes. If the lesion is in the cerebellum rather than the dorsal columns, the cerebellar ataxia of balance will not be corrected by visual compensation as is the case in the sensory ataxia of the dorsal column.

Anatomy of Oral Sensation

The neuroanatomy of oral sensation is different from that of the trunk and extremities in that the cranial and oral sensations are mediated by the cranial nerves, as opposed to mediation by the spinal nerve and cord in bodily sensations. This is summarized in Table 5-1. Of particular importance to oral sensation is the trigeminal nerve (cranial nerve V). This cranial nerve is the primary somatic sensory nerve for the skin of the face, the anterior portion of the scalp, the anterior two-thirds of the tongue, the teeth, and the outer surface of the eardrum. It mediates the sensations of pain, temperature, touch, pressure, and proprioception for the oral and cranial regions.

The glossopharyngeal nerve (cranial nerve IX), which is primarily sensory, also plays a role in mediating general somatic sensation in the cranial and oral regions. It mediates sensation from the posterior third of the tongue, the palatopharyngeal muscles, and the external ear.

Sensory Pathway of Cranial Nerve V

In studying the spinal pathways for sensation, it has been found that it is logical to separate the pathways for pain and temperature and the pathways for touch and pressure. This general model of the pathways for sensation is similar, with

TABLE 5-1
Sensory Innervation of the Speech Mechanism

Structure	Cranial Nerve(s)
Face	V: pain, temperature, touch to face VII: proprioception to face
Tongue	V: touch to anterior two-thirds IX: touch to posterior third
Palate	IX: sensory to soft palate
Pharynx	IX: sensory to lateral and posterior pharyngeal walls
	X: sensory to pharynx; with IX, forms pharyngeal plexus
Larynx	X: sensory to most of the laryngeal muscles

minor variations, for both the oral-cranial regions and the body and extremities. Pain and temperature receptors in the skin and mucous membranes in the face and muscles project to the neural cell bodies of the Gasserian ganglion. This ganglion in the face is analogous to the dorsal root ganglion of the spinal nerves. The Gasserian ganglia are called first-order neurons. Axons from the ganglion enter the pons and become a fiber bundle called the descending tract of cranial nerve V. The descending tract may sometimes reach the upper cervical region of the spinal cord. Fibers enter the adjacent spinal nucleus of cranial nerve V and synapse with second-order neurons. These cross over to the contralateral side upon leaving the nucleus. Those contralateral fibers, called the *secondary trigeminothalamic tract*, then ascend to the level of the thalamus. From the thalamus, third-order neurons pass into the internal capsule and finally terminate in the primary somatosensory cortex in the postcentral gyrus of the parietal lobe.

The pressure and touch pathways of cranial nerve V have the same general organizational plan as the pain and temperature pathways. The first-order neurons are the cell bodies of the Gasserian ganglion. The axons of the cell bodies terminate in the main sensory nucleus of cranial nerve V. The second-order reach the thalamus via the secondary ascending tract of cranial nerve V. Fibers travel both ipsilaterally and contralaterally, unlike the pain and temperature pathways of V. The third-order neurons are the relay fibers from the thalamus to the postcentral gyrus of the cerebrum.

The contralateral pathway's organization of pain and temperature and the bilateral organization of pressure and touch can be observed clinically if a unilateral sensory cortex lesion is present. The patient suffers no major loss of touch or pressure from the face but will lose pain and temperature sensations on the side of the face contralateral to the lesion.

Proprioceptive pathways of V are made up primarily of fibers from the muscles of mastication and the temporomandibular joint. The first-order neurons, the cell bodies of the mesencephalic nucleus, are located in the midbrain. The pathway from this point to the postcentral gyrus of the parietal lobe is not known.

The jaw reflex is mediated by the sensory input from the muscles of mastication and temporomandibular joint, acting on the motor neuron of nerve VII, or the facial nerve. A hyperative jaw reflex (see Chapter 7) suggests a lesion in the corticobulbar fibers above the level of the pons.

Sensory Pathway of Cranial Nerve IX

The glossopharyngeal nerve has its first-order neuron in the ganglion of cranial nerve IX. Fibers pass to the solitary fasciculus from the ganglion. The route of the second-order neuron, the ascending central pathway to the thalamus, is not precisely known, but probably involves the reticular formation, with termination in the thalamus. The path of the third-order neuron to the cortex is likewise unknown.

In summary, the sensory pathway plan in the orofacial region and the body involves a sensory ganglion close to the primary sensory receptors. This is a first-order neuron. A second-order neuron is the pathway to the thalamus, and a third-order neuron projects from the thalamus to the sensory cortex.

Oral Sensory Receptors

Generally, sensory receptors in the oral region and respiratory system are excited by chemical or mechanical stimulation. Taste, of course, is based on chemical stimulation. Mechanicoreceptors respond when stimuli distort them. For instance, the tongue touching the teeth, alveolar ridge, or palate will compress mechanicoreceptors, and the receptors in turn will generate electrical impulses to the fibers.

The tongue mucosa and the tongue surface in particular are served by many different types of mechanicoreceptors. The endings in these receptors have been divided into diffuse, or free, endings and compact, or organized, endings. Some speech experts believe that free endings provide a general sense of touch in sensory control of speech articulation, and that organized endings provide sensitive acuity in speech articulation.

Oral Proprioceptors

In addition to receptors in the mucosa of the oral region, there are receptors in the oral muscles themselves, in the joints of the jaw, and in the membranes of the teeth. The receptors in the temporomandibular muscles, the pterygoids, the masseter, and the temporalis, place stretch on the joint.

The periodontal receptors are fine filaments in the teeth that are responsive to extremely slight touch on the teeth. The pressure sense of these receptors is extremely sensitive and no doubt plays a role in sensory control of articulation.

Studying Oral Sensation

The role of the tactile receptors in the oral region has been widely studied in the speech science laboratory over the past two decades. Two-point discrimination for tactile sensation is assessed by speech scientists with an instrument called an *esthesiometer*. Subjects are asked to discriminate if they feel one or two points on the surface of the tongue. Normals can separate two points on the tongue tip when the points are only one to two millimeters apart. The sensitivity of the tongue tip is extremely delicate, but the back of the tongue and the lateral margins are less sensitive. Differences of less than 1 centimeter cannot be clearly distinguished at these points.

To determine the significance of tactile sensation in the sensory control of speech, the technique of *nerve block* has been used. An anesthetic, usually lidocaine, is injected into the branches of the trigeminal nerve. Tactile sensation of the tongue is mediated by the lingual branch of V (Figure 5-4). Nerve block techniques have resulted in some distortion of the articulation of speech, but for the most part speech remains intelligible. The consonants /s/ and /z/ are frequently distorted with tongue anesthetization.

Oral Stereognosis

Another laboratory procedure used for the study of sensory control in speech is called *oral stereognosis testing*. Stereognosis (*stereo* = "form"; *gnosis* = "knowing") is the ability to recognize three-dimensional forms through the senses. Neurologically, it implies that the sensory receptors of the speech mechanism are functioning normally and that the sensory pathways to the cerebral cortex are also intact. Finally, it assumes that cortical sensory recognition and association areas in the cerebral cortex of the brain itself are unimpaired. Small acrylic forms representing common three-dimensional geometric shapes are placed in the subjects' mouth without their knowing the shape of the form. Subjects identify the shapes through either recognition or discrimination. The results of these experiments have been equivocal. In general, the ability to identify shapes by feeling them with the tongue and palate has little or no relation to speech proficiency in most cases. In fact, in one study, a spastic quadriplegic person with poor oral form recognition, poor two-point discrimination, and an inability to report his tongue position performed with acceptable articulation. Other studies, however, have indicated that subgroups of children with speech dis-

FIGURE 5-4   The sensory control of the tongue

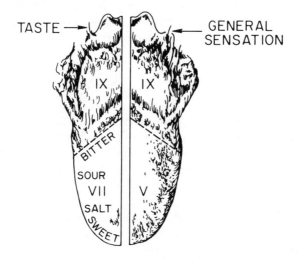

TASTE ———→ GENERAL SENSATION

IX   IX

BITTER

SOUR
VII   V
SALT
SWEET

orders could be differentiated by oral stereognosis scores. There is, however, no clear-cut syndrome of sensory loss present in speech-defective cases. The research to date has only demonstrated that oral stereognosis may have an influence in sensory control of speech, but that specific instances of oral astereognosis, or oral form recognition disorder, may be compensated for by other skills employed in speech production.

Sensory Control Modalities

The apparent importance of stereognosis and two-point discrimination raises the question of the relative significance of the various sensory control mechanisms in speech production. Intuitively, audition would appear to be the most powerful sensory mechanism to control our speech. If we misspeak, as in uttering a "slip of the tongue," we often hear our error and correct it. Additionally, congenitally deaf individuals, who do not hear their speech, show deviations in articulation and voice. Under certain conditions, as those cited, hearing of our own speech provides a strong sensory control. But individuals who have developed normal speech and then become deafened do not immediately show articulation and vocal deviations. Deafened persons rely on sensory mechanisms other than audition to control most of their speech performance. For many speech sounds, the average auditory processes that provide feedback occur too late to be of help in ongoing speech. Where the tactile sensory receptors of the tongue have been interfered with by nerve block of the trigeminal nerve, it has been found that the addition of auditory masking does not increase the articulation error scores significantly. In brief, it seems that although audition, touch and oral stereognosis play a role in speech motor control, their exact significance is unclear. Orosensory testing has not been widely used as an everyday clinical practice by neurologists or speech-language pathologists. We await more refined methodology. Issues surrounding these aspects of speech physiology and their disorders are still relegated to laboratory studies.

Speech Proprioception

According to Sherrington's classification, proprioception refers to sensory receptors within the body itself. As we already mentioned, the muscle spindles serve as primary afferent proprioceptors in striated muscles, including muscles of the speech mechanism. The distribution of muscle spindles varies considerably within the speech musculature. Muscle spindles are found in all the intercostal muscles and all the laryngeal muscles. The jaw muscles are also rich in spindles, but the facial muscles, including the lips, have very few. The tongue, the primary articulator for speech, assumes an intermediate position between the jaw and the face in a number of muscle spindles. A small number of spindle afferents have been found in the intrinsic tongue muscles. These afferents do not project to the lower motor neurons of the tongue muscle.

As a result of this distribution of spindles in the oral musculature, a stretch reflex can usually be elicited from the jaw, but not from the facial muscles. In addition, the neural pathways for spindle information are not clear in the tongue. It has been suggested that the hypoglossal nerve (CN XII), generally considered to be a motor nerve, may carry some spindle afferents that enter the brainstem by the way of the dorsal cervical nerves, labeled C1 through C3. Others have postulated that proprioceptive impulses from the tongue are conducted by the lingual nerve, a branch of the trigeminal nerve. At this point we do not yet have a clear picture of the proprioceptive pathways from the tongue.

In summary, it is apparent that the oromotor mechanism is richly endowed with exteroceptors and proprioceptors for control of the neuromuscular activity for speech, but no single type of sensory input is superior to another in the control of the muscles for speech. Different types of articulation probably demand different types of sensory feedback. Alveolar stops, for instance, may utilize primarily tactile sensation, while articulations with no contact, such as back vowels, may utilize auditory and proprioceptive feedback.

The Visual System

The Retina

The visual pathway begins with photoreceptors in the retina and ends in the visual cortex of the occipital lobe. The photoreceptors are cells of two types:

rods and *cones*. Rods play a special role in peripheral vision and in vision under low light conditions. Cones, on the other hand, function under bright light and are responsible for central discriminative vision and for color detection.

The central area of the retina, a region about 6mm in diameter, is called the *macula* and is specialized for acuity of vision. A depression in the center of the macula, called the *fovea*, is the area of greatest visual acuity in the retina.

Action potentials generated in the photoreceptors are transmitted to ganglion cells within the retina. These ganglion cells are large neurons that form the last retinal link in the visual path. The axons of these cells form a layer of nerve fibers that converge on a structure called the *optic papilla* or optic disk. This is a blind spot in the eye since it contains only nerve fibers. At this point the fibers pass in bundles through foramina in the sclera and become the optic nerve. They then acquire myelin sheaths.

Pathway of the Optic Nerve

After becoming the optic nerve, the fibers from the ganglion cells travel to the lateral geniculate nucleus. The fibers terminate in a small swelling under the pulvinar of the thalamus called the lateral geniculate body. They then pass through the internal capsule and pass around the lateral ventricle, curving posteriorly. Some of the fibers travel far over the temporal horn of the lateral ventricle and form what is called the temporal loop or Meyer's loop of the visual pathway. These fibers terminate in the visual cortex below the calcarine sulcus. A temporal lobe lesion may involve Meyer's loop and cause a defect in the upper visual field on the side opposite the lesion.

The other fibers of the tract continue posteriorly and terminate in the visual cortex above the calcarine sulcus. A lesion in the parietal lobe may involve that tract and result in a defect in the lower visual field on the contralateral side.

Visual Fields

There is a spatial pattern of cortical stimulation that is based on the retinal image of the visual field, or what is seen by each eye. For purpose of describing the retinal projection, each retina is divided into nasal (inner, at the nose) and temporal (outer, at the temples) halves by a vertical line through the fovea. Upper and lower quadrants are formed by drawing a horizontal line (see Figure 5-5). Fibers from the retina are projected to the lateral geniculate body and then to the visual cortex in accordance with certain rules. Visual defects that result from pathway interruption at any point from the retina to the cortex are described in terms of the visual field rather than the retina. It is important to understand that the image of an object in the visual field is inverted and reversed

FIGURE 5-5   Visual pathways with lesion sites and resulting visual-field defects

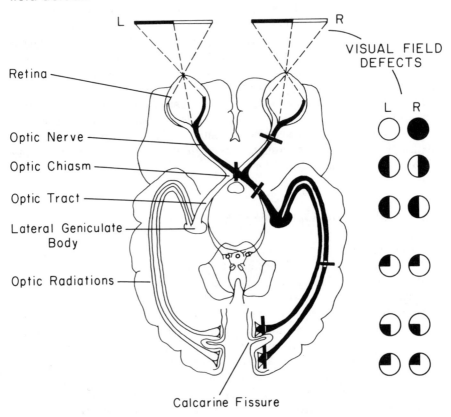

from left to right, much like the image on film from a camera lens. The representation of that visual field on the cortex follows these rules:

1. The left visual field is represented in the right hemisphere visual cortex, and vice versa.
2. The upper half of the visual field is represented below the calcarine sulcus.
3. The lower half of the visual field is represented above the calcarine sulcus.

To understand further what happens with lesions along the optic tract, follow the pathway in Figure 5-5. You will see that fibers from the temporal half of the retina project ipsilaterally. The fibers from the nasal half of each retina, however, decussate at the optic chiasm, or the point where the two tracts meet at midline. The temporal retinal fibers that do not cross are responsible for the nasal half of the visual field, whereas the nasal fibers that do cross midline are responsible for the temporal half of the visual field. Therefore, for example, if a lesion interrupts both the temporal and nasal fiber pathways of the left cerebral hemisphere, a visual field defect called a *right homonymous hemianopsia* will result. This means that the entire right visual field cannot be seen, so that peripheral vision to the right is lost. If you follow the tract, you will see that this is because the temporal fibers of the right eye see the nasal half of the right visual field, and the nasal fibers of the left eye (which have been interrupted because of the decussation at the optic chiasm) see the temporal half of the right visual field. Other types of visual field deficits are shown in Figure 5-5 with the corresponding lesion sites. You should study this chart carefully to understand why visual field defects are often associated with lesions that also produce language deficits.

Visual Integration

The characteristics of neurons in the visual cortex and the responses of individual cells have been studied in a wide variety of experimental animals. Scientists are interested in how patterns are perceived and recognized by the eye. It has been found by such experimenters as Hubel and Wiesel (1968) that there are many different types of receptive fields in the neurons of the visual cortex. These receptive fields are termed simple, complex, hypercomplex, and higher-order hypercomplex. Simple receptive field cells respond to a slit of light of particular width, slant, or orientation and place on the retina. Complex receptive fields respond to slit-shaped stimuli also, but over a large area of the retina rather than a specific place. For hypercomplex fields, the line stimulus must, in addition, be of a certain length. Cells with higher-order hypercomplex fields require more elaborate visual stimuli to respond.

The visual cortex is organized in columns of cells with similar properties. Some respond only to one eye and are monocular. Others respond to both eyes and are binocular columns. Since the eyes are located in different positions on the head, there is a difference of position on the retinas for a stimulus, giving binocular disparity to the columnar cells. This provides information about the depth of objects.

In addition to the primary visual pathways, two other major visual pathways can be distinguished: the *tectal*, or collicular, pathway and the *pretectal* nuclei pathway. Thus fibers from the optic tracts do not all go to the lateral geniculate body. Some of them project to the subcortical pretectal nuclei and ascend to the thalamus and out from there to various regions of the cortex. This system seems to be important in the control of certain visual reflexes as the pupillary reflex and certain eye movements.

The tectal, or collicular, pathway projects to the superior colliculi in the brainstem and to the thalamus and out to many regions of the cortex. The superior colliculi also receive input from somatosensory and auditory systems. The tectal pathway seems to be involved in a major way in our ability to orient toward and follow a visual stimulus.

The visual pathways do not operate independently of each other. They are interconnected at every level from retina to cortex and each receives descending input from the cerebral cortex, providing for the richness of visual perception. The nature of the processes that account for visual perception are only beginning to be understood.

Central Auditory Nervous System

A major aspect of speech and language function is dependent on audition. Audition is classified generally as one of the special senses and as an exteroceptive sense. The neurology of the central auditory pathways is crucial to an understanding of the mechanism of the communicative nervous system. See Figure 5-6 for a schema of these pathways.

Receptor Level

The hair cells in the organ of Corti in the cochlea of the inner ear serve as the primary neural receptors for audition. The cell bodies of the primary neuron of the central auditory pathway are in the *spiral ganglion*. A distinction usually is made between the peripheral auditory system and the central auditory system. For the neurologist, the peripheral system includes the outer ear and eighth cranial nerve, and the central auditory system extends from the cochlear nucleus to the auditory cortex in the cerebrum. The otolaryngologist, on the other hand, considers the peripheral system as extending from the outer ear to the hair cells of the cochlea. The central system is from the auditory nerve to the cerebral cortex.

Cranial Nerve Level

The nerve of hearing, cranial nerve VIII, has two divisions: the *cochlear* branch, associated with hearing, and the *vestibular* branch, associated with balance. The cochlear nerve proceeds from the spiral ganglion through the internal auditory canal. It is accompanied by cranial nerve VII, the facial nerve, in the auditory canal. The two nerves enter the brainstem at the sulcus between the pons and the medulla.

FIGURE 5-6 The central auditory pathways showing the major auditory way-stations

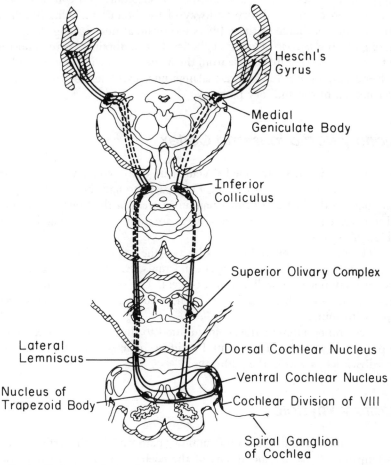

Source: Redrawn and reproduced with permission from S. Gilman and S. Winan, *Manter and Gatz's Essentials of Clinical Neuroanatomy and Neurophysiology* (6th ed.) (Philadelphia: F. A. Davis, 1982).

Brainstem Level

The fibers of the cochlear division of cranial nerve VIII end in the dorsal and ventral cochlear nuclei, which are draped around the inferior cerebellar peduncle. The cochlear nuclei contain the secondary neurons of the auditory pathway. From the cochlear nuclei, some fibers of the auditory pathway proceed to the upper medulla and pons and cross the midline. Other fibers ascend in the brainstem ipsilaterally. Some fibers intermingle at a point called the *trapezoid body*, and many of the fibers terminate at the *superior olivary nucleus*. From the superior olive, fibers course upward, both ipsilaterally and contralaterally, in the ascending central auditory pathway of the brainstem. This is called the lateral lemniscus. Some of these fibers terminate at nuclei along the way, and others go to the *inferior colliculus* at the level of midbrain, where almost all of the fibers terminate. Fibers arise from the nucleus of the inferior colliculus and reach the *medial geniculate body*, a thalamic nucleus. This nucleus is the third-order neuron of the auditory pathways.

Auditory Radiations and Cortex

The fibers arising from the medial geniculate body, coursing to the temporal cortex, are called *auditory radiations*. They pass through the internal capsule in their route to the bilateral primary auditory areas of the brain in the superior and transverse temporal gyrii. These areas are numbered 41–42 and are known as Heschl's gyrus.

The nuclei of the auditory pathway—the trapezoid body, the superior olivary complex, the nucleus of the lateral lemniscus, and the inferior colliculi—serve as relay nuclei as well as reflex centers. The reflex centers make connections with the eyes, head, and trunk, where automatic reflex actions occur in response to sound.

Descending efferent fibers, in addition to the ascending afferent fibers, are present in all parts of the central auditory pathway. They probably serve as feedback loops within the pathways.

Auditory Physiology

Sound is transmitted to the central auditory pathways by a traveling wave that is set up on the basilar membrane of the cochlea. The basilar membrane is narrower at the base of the cochlea than at its apex. The mechanics of the membrane on which the organ of Corti is located varies slightly from base to apex. The traveling pressure wave of a specific frequency causes the basilar membrane to vibrate maximally at a specific point along the length of the membrane. The vibration produces shearing forces in the hair cells that set up electrical charges in the dendrites of the spiral ganglion, in turn causing the nerve cells to fire.

Auditory nerve impulses ascend in the pathways of the central auditory nervous system. The organ of Corti serves as an analyzer of sound frequencies. It is tonotopically organized, meaning that the highest frequencies stimulate hair cells in the most basilar portion of the cochlea, where the basilar membrane is narrowest. The lowest frequencies stimulate the portions of the membrane at the apex. Frequency discrimination, therefore, is dependent on the frequency of the tone and the spatial response of the basilar membrane. Intensity discrimination depends on the length of the basilar membrane set in motion and the amplitude of the vibration. Displacement of a longer area of the membrane will activate more nerve fibers, and a greater amplitude of vibration will increase the frequency of the neural discharge.

Localizing the source of a sound depends on a comparison between the arrival time and the intensity of the sound at the two ears. Localization of sound occurs at higher levels in the auditory pathways. Central auditory structures, generally above the level of the inferior colliculus receiving input from both ears, are capable of making appropriate comparisons for sound localization. Thus in mammals and humans the temporal auditory cortex is not needed for simple sound recognition, but it is essential for sound localization and changes in the temporal sequencing of sounds. Temporal sequencing is a very crucial higher auditory function since it is a significant aspect of speech. Sound localization probably requires the inferior colliculus and auditory cortex, whereas temporal sequencing may require the cochlear nuclei, the medial geniculate nuclei, and the auditory cortex. There is a tonotopic organization in all the central auditory nuclei, but they are used for an analysis of several auditory properties of sound other than the recognition of tones or different frequencies.

Lesions of the Auditory System

Unilateral lesions of the central auditory system that completely destroy the receptors, auditory nerve, or cochlear nuclei will generally cause total deafness in that ear. Unilateral lesions, however, of the auditory cortex, medial geniculate body, or lateral lemniscus will produce impaired hearing, poorer in the contralateral ear, but will not result in total deafness because of the bilateral pathways and an abundance of fibers that cross over in the auditory system. Lesions in Heschl's gyrus bilaterally may cause either cortical deafness, nonverbal agnosia, or auditory agnosia. Unilateral cortical damage does not cause a total deafness.

Summary

Three major pathways carry sensory impulses from the extremities and trunk to higher levels of the nervous system. One of these is the spinothalamic tract, which has two divisions. The lateral spinothalamic tract conveys impulses of pain and temperature. The ventral spinothalamic tract conveys impulses of light touch, light pressure and tactile discrimination.

The second major pathway is known as the dorsal columns. The two tracts of the dorsal columns are the fasciculus gracilus and the fasciculus cuneatus. The fasciculus cuneatus is associated with sensation from the upper extremities and body, and the fasciculus gracilis is associated with the lower extremities and body. Both pathways convey proprioceptive sensations of movement and posture, vibration, stereognosis, and two-point discrimination. Lesions may produce specific sensory losses as well as a sensory ataxia of the dorsal columns.

The third major pathway includes the spinocerebellar tracts. The dorsal pathway ascends contralaterally. Both pathways end in the cerebellum and are thought to mediate unconscious proprioception of movement. Cerebral lesions, marked by language loss, may have accompanying sensory loss involving the parietal lobe or subcortical pathway.

The oral cavity is very rich in sensory receptors. Tactile receptors of the mouth, tongue, pharynx, and teeth play a significant role in the articulation of speech. Tactile sensory receptors have been widely studied in the speech laboratory, but no standard clinical method for assessing the sensory integrity of the oral mechanism is widely accepted. Anesthetization of the tongue surface only distorts vowels and sibilants to a moderate degree. Oral stereognosis, the ability to recognize three-dimensional shapes in the mouth, can be studied clinically with simple materials. Although stereognosis may play a role in the production of speech, no clear-cut syndromes of sensory loss have been found commonly in speech-disordered patients. Stereognostic deficits may be readily compensated for by other sensory functions.

Muscle spindles provide sensory control of muscle contraction through the gamma motor neuron system, jaw muscles, and laryngeal muscles. The tongue has fewer muscle spindles than these muscles, and the facial and lip muscles have even fewer spindles than the tongue. Muscle spindles do not appear to exert a major influence on the highly precise and rapid control of the speech muscles.

Cranial nerve V supplies information to the lips, palate, and anterior two-thirds of the tongue. The lingual branch of V supplies all the muscles of the tongue. Cranial nerve IX, the glossopharyngeal nerve, supplies sensation to the posterior third of the tongue.

The central auditory nervous system is complex. For clinical purposes, the speech-language pathologist need employ only a schematic guide to the major auditory way-stations in the system. The primary auditory receptor is the spiral ganglion in the organ of Corti of the cochlea in the inner ear. The auditory nerve, cranial nerve VIII, enters the brainstem at the pontomedullary junction. Fibers go to the dorsal and ventral cochlear nuclei. From these nuclei, some fibers cross over and reach the trapezoid body and the superior olivary nucleus on the contralateral side. Impulses then travel up the lateral lemniscus end to the inferior colliculus. Some proceed to the medial geniculate bodies at the level of the thalamus. Auditory radiations ascend from the thalamus to

Heschl's gyrus in each of the temporal lobes of the cerebrum. Bilateral cortical damage to Heschl's gyrus produces a spectrum of deficits including cortical deafness, nonverbal agnosia, and auditory agnosia. Unilateral cortical damage to Heschl's gyrus does not produce a total deafness.

References and Further Readings

Bordon, G. J., & Harris, K. S. (1984). *Speech science primer* (2nd ed.). Baltimore: Williams and Wilkins.

DeMyer, W. (1980). *Technique of the neurologic examination* (3rd ed.). New York: McGraw-Hill.

Gilman, S., & Winans, S. S. (1982). *Manter and Gatz's essentials of clinical neuroanatomy and neurophysiology* (6th ed.). Philadelphia: F. A. Davis.

Gregory, R. L. (1970). *The intelligent eye.* New York: McGraw-Hill.

Groves, P. M., & Schlesinger, K. (1979). *Introduction to biological psychology.* Dubuque, Iowa: William C. Brown.

Hubel, D. H., & Wiesel, T. N. (1968). Receptive fields and functional architecture of the monkey striate cortex. *Journal of Physiology,* 206, 419–436.

Mountcastle, V. B. (1980). "Central Neural Mechanisms in Hearing." In V. B. Mountcastle (Ed.), *Medical Physiology.* St. Louis: C. V. Mosby.

CHAPTER SIX

The Neuromotor Control of Speech

"We cannot state exactly the number of muscles that are necessary for speech and that are active during speech. But if we consider that ordinarily the muscles of the thoracic and abdominal walls, the neck and the face, the larynx, and pharynx and the oral cavity are all properly coordinated during the act of speaking, it becomes obvious that over 100 muscles must be controlled centrally."

—Eric H. Lenneberg, *Biological Foundation of Language*, 1967

SPEECH IS ONE of the most complex behaviors performed by human beings. On average, a person will utter approximately fourteen recognizable speech sounds per second when asked to produce nonsense syllables as rapidly as possible. This unusually brisk rate will be maintained even when you speak conversationally or are asked to read aloud. The number of separate neural events supporting this complex coordination of the articulatory muscles is, of course, very large, and the degree of neural integration in the motor system for routine, everyday talk is truly amazing.

Speech also requires the action of major mechanisms at every significant motor integration level of the nervous system. Five major levels may be identified: (1) cerebral cortex, (2) subcortical nuclei of the cerebrum, (3) brain stem, (4) cerebellum, and (5) spinal cord. At each of these five levels of the nervous system, there are components of the motor system that integrate speech. For clinical purposes, the motor integration system of the brain for speech may be divided into three great motor subsystems: (1) the pyramidal system, (2) the extrapyramidal system, and (3) the cerebellar system.

The Pyramidal System

Voluntary movement of the muscles of speech is controlled primarily by the pyramidal system. In fact the pyramidal tract, itself, is the major voluntary pathway for all movement. It is made up of the corticospinal tract, the corticobulbar tract, and the corticopontine tract. The corticospinal tract controls the skilled movements in the distal muscles of the limbs and digits. The corticobulbar tract controls the cranial nerves, many of which directly innervate the muscles of speech. The corticopontine tract goes to the pontine nuclei, which in turn project to the cerebellum. The corticospinal, corticobulbar, and corticopontine tracts are called corticofugal pathways because they all descend from the cortex.

The Corticospinal Tract

The corticospinal tract descends from the cerebral cortex to different levels of the spinal cord. It begins in the motor cortex of the two cerebral hemispheres, primarily in the precentral gyrus of the cerebrum and to a lesser degree in the postcentral gyrus. The bilateral corticospinal fibers, therefore, begin in the frontal and parietal lobes of the brain. The fibers are considered the primary descending motor tracts because they course downward from the cortex to the spinal cord, where they synapse with the spinal nerves of the peripheral nervous system at various levels of the cord. The spinal nerves leave the neuraxis and innervate muscles of the trunk and limbs.

The fibers of the corticospinal tract are some of the longest motor axons in the nervous system. They provide a very direct route for motor commands transmitted from the cortical motor areas and permit extremely rapid voluntary motor response in the nervous system (Figure 6-1).

Descending Motor Pathways

The corticospinal tract descends from the bilateral motor cortices to the subcortical white matter in a fan-shaped distribution of fibers called the *corona radiata*, or radiating crown. The fibers converge to enter into an L-shaped subcortical structure called the *internal capsule*. Since all the corticospinal fibers come together at this point, a small lesion in the internal capsule of one side can be devastating to the motor control of one half of the body. The corticospinal fibers pass through the posterior limb of the internal capsule, and the corticobulbar fibers transverse the genu, or "bend," of the internal capsule. From that point both sets of fibers enter the cerebral peduncle of the mesencephalon,

FIGURE 6-1 The pyramidal tract, including both corticospinal and corticobulbar fibers

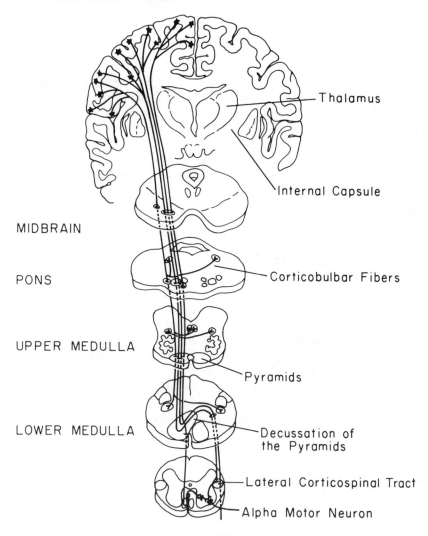

MIDBRAIN

PONS

UPPER MEDULLA

LOWER MEDULLA

Thalamus

Internal Capsule

Corticobulbar Fibers

Pyramids

Decussation of
the Pyramids

Lateral Corticospinal Tract

Alpha Motor Neuron

or midbrain. The fibers enter the pons and are intermingled with pontine fibers and nuclei, providing circuits from the motor cortex that reverberate through the cerebellum and return impulses to the cerebral cortex after cerebellar modulation. After the fibers cross the *basis pontis*, they reach the medulla, situated at the junction of this lower brainstem structure and the spinal cord. This is the medullary-cervical juncture. Here approximately 85 to 90 percent of the corticospinal fibers cross over to the other side of the neuraxis, providing a contralateral motor control of the limbs. The corticospinal fibers in the medulla come together to form the *pyramids*, for which the pyramidal tract is named.

Decussation

The crossing of the right and left corticospinal tract is known as *decussation.* The few fibers, variable in number, that do not cross are known as the uncrossed *anterior corticospinal tract*. The primary corticospinal tract is the *lateral corticospinal tract*. The decussation means that a lesion interrupting the fibers above the crossing will have an effect on the side of the body opposite the site of the lesion. If the corticospinal tract is interrupted in the cerebrum, voluntary movement of the limbs is limited on the *contralateral* side of the body. By contrast, a lesion below the decussation impairs voluntary movement on the same, or ipsilateral, side.

Paralysis, Paresis, and Plegia

A gross limitation of movement is called *paralysis*, and an incomplete paralysis is known as *paresis*. A complete or near complete paralysis of one side of the body is *hemiparalysis*, or more commonly a *hemiplegia*. The presence of a right-sided hemiplegia or hemiparesis is an extremely important sign for the speech-language pathologist. If the lesion is in the cerebrum, above the decussation, it suggests that the left hemisphere is involved. As noted earlier, the left hemisphere is the primary site of brain mechanisms for language, so right hemiplegia is often associated with language disorders. Lesions of the bilateral motor strip or the pyramidal tract alone may produce the motor speech disorder of dysarthria.

The Corticobulbar Tracts

The corticobulbar fibers of the pyramidal tract are the voluntary pathway for the movements of speech muscles, except those of respiration. They are the most important fibers of the pyramidal tract for the speech-language pathologist. Their course is not as direct as that of the corticospinal fibers. The corticobulbar fibers begin with the corticospinal fibers at the cortex and terminate at the motor nuclei of the cranial nerves.[1] Unlike the corticospinal fibers, the corticobulbars have many ipsilateral as well as contralateral fibers. The corticospinal and corticobulbar fibers separate at the upper brainstem level, with the corticobulbars decussating at various levels of the brainstem.

Bilateral Symmetry

The majority of the midline speech muscles work in bilateral symmetry. This is the result of the bilateral innervation that the corticobulbars provide. All the paired muscles of the face, palate, vocal folds, and diaphragm work together in synchrony much of the time in wrinkling the forehead, smiling, chewing, swallowing, and talking. This bilateral innervation of the speech muscles has important implications for the degree of speech muscle involvement in cases of dysarthria.

In corticobulbar lesions, the bilateral innervation provides a safety valve for speech production. Assuming the left corticobulbar fibers to a cranial nerve are damaged, the motor nuclei of that nerve will still receive impulses via the intact right corticobulbar tract, and paralysis of the muscle will not be severe. The innervation of the limbs is primarily contralateral rather than bilateral, so lesions to the corticospinal fibers may produce severe unilateral limb paralysis. Lesions to corticobulbar fibers do not produce as severe weakness, because of the bilateral innervation.

Contralateral and Unilateral Innervation

Each of the cranial nerve nuclei receives varying amounts of unilateral and contralateral innervation, even though they are bilaterally supplied. Those areas with more unilateral supply are more paralyzed. The lower face and trapezius muscles are most affected. An intermediate paralytic effect is found in the tongue with a unilateral lesion. The diaphragm, ocular muscles, upper face, jaw, pharynx, and muscles of the larynx show little paralysis with a unilateral lesion.

The nuclei for the facial nerve are complex. The facial nucleus combines bilateral innervation with contralateral innervation. The muscles of the upper half of the face are far more bilaterally innervated than the muscles of the lower half of the face, which receive more contralateral innervation. Some neuroscientists even hypothesize a cranial nerve nucleus for the upper half of the facial muscles and one for the lower half. In practical terms, this means that among the normal population, most people can wrinkle their forehead or lift both eyebrows together. Only a few people, with more contralateral fibers, are able to lift their eyebrows one at a time. The muscles of the midface receive a more equal combination of bilateral and contralateral innervation. Most, but not all, people can wink one eye at a time because of the increase of contralateral fibers to eyelid muscles compared to forehead muscles.

In the lower face the innervation is primarily contralateral. Most people are able to retract one corner of the mouth alone when asked to do so because of the limited bilateral innervation of the lower face muscles. The principles of bilateral and contralateral innervation are practically applied when a speech cranial nerve examination is performed to determine if there are lesions affecting the corticobulbar fibers, bulbar nuclei, or the cranial nerves themselves. (These principles are summarized for all the cranial nerves in Table 6-1.)

Almost all people can retract one corner of the mouth at a time because of contralateral innervation. The concepts of bilateral symmetry and contralateral independence are of crucial practical clinical utility when analyzing and understanding muscle involvement in dysarthria. We will return to them when discussing the testing of the cranial nerves involved in speech.

Lower and Upper Motor Neurons

A very useful concept in clinical neurology has been the notion of upper motor neuron (UMN) and lower motor neuron (LMN). All the neurons of the anterior and lateral corticospinal tracts, which send axons from the cerebral cortex to the anterior horn cells of the spinal cord, are known as upper motor neurons. These long axons, part of one uninterrupted neuron, are also designated first-order neurons. No upper motor neurons leave the neuraxis. In other words, they are contained within the brain, brainstem, and spinal cord. Lower motor neurons (LMN) are all the neurons that send motor axons into the peripheral nerves—the cranial and spinal nerves. They are designated second-order neurons. Charles Sherrington called the lower motor neuron the "great common pathway." By this he meant that the peripheral nerves—both cranial and spinal—serve as a final route for all the complex motor interactions that occur in the neuraxis above the level of the lower motor neuron. The final muscle contraction is the product of the sum total of all the interaction that has occurred in the central nervous system.

Lesions of the upper motor neuron produce a wholly different set of signs and symptoms from those of the lower motor neuron. This distinction provides

TABLE 6-1
Corticobulbar Innervation in the Cranial Nerves for Speech

Nerve	Innervation
Trigeminal (V)	Bilateral symmetry
Facial (VII)	Mixed bilateral symmetry and contralateral innervation
Glossopharyngeal (IX)	Neither bilateral symmetry or contralateral innervation*
Vagus (X)	Bilateral symmetry
Spinal accessory (XI)	Contralateral innervation
Hypoglossal (XII)	Mixed bilateral symmetry and contralateral innervation

*The motor innervation of IX is to only a single muscle.

the neurologist with a powerful tool in neurologic examination for deciding where a lesion is located in the nervous system. The most striking sign of a lesion in both upper and lower motor neuron disease is paralysis. The type of paralysis, however, is quite different depending on the site of the lesion that produces the paralysis. Understanding the differences is a large step toward establishing a correct diagnosis of a neurologic disease involving motor disturbance.

Lower Motor Neuron Paralysis

If a lesion is in a cranial or peripheral nerve, or in the cell bodies of the anterior horn cell in the spinal cord, or in the cranial nerve axons in the brainstem before they leave the brainstem, neural impulses will not be transmitted to the muscles. This is called *denervation*. The result is that the muscles, innervated by the cranial or spinal nerve, become soft and flabby because of loss of muscle tone. This is a lower motor neuron paralysis. The loss of muscle tone is called *hypotonia*. Hypotonia results in flaccid muscles. Thus, lower motor neuron paralysis is called *flaccid* paralysis. Lower motor neuron paralysis is also sometimes associated with loss of muscle bulk, a condition called *atrophy*. Muscles undergoing atrophy display some degree of degeneration because they become denervated. Signs of this degeneration can be observed clinically. Atrophic muscles will show *fibrillations* and *fasciculations*. These signs are caused by electrical disturbances in muscle fibers resulting from denervation. Fibrillations are fine twitchings of single muscle fibers. Generally these cannot be seen on clinical examination, except perhaps in the tongue, but must be detected by electromyographic (EMG) examination. Fasciculations, on the other hand, are contractions of groups of muscle fibers that can be identified, with training, in skeletal muscles through the skin.

As muscle bulk is lost through atrophy in motor neuron disease, fasciculations may be seen in the muscles of the head and neck, as well as in other muscles of the body. These muscle twitchings may be particularly observed in the relatively large muscle mass of the tongue if the bulbar muscles are involved.[2] Fasciculations have no direct effect on speech itself, but serve only as a sign of lower motor neuron disease.

Interruption of a peripheral nerve by a lower motor neuron lesion also damages the reflex arc that is involved with that nerve. The result is that normal reflex responses mediated through the sensory and motor limbs of the arc become diminished. Reduced reflex response is called *hyporeflexia*. Complete lack of reflex is known as *areflexia*. Hyporeflexia and areflexia, however, are also associated with lower motor neuron disease.

A concept that will help you more fully understand the complexities of lower motor neuron disease is that of the *motor unit* (Figure 6–2a). A motor unit is a structural and functional entity that may be defined as (1) a single anterior horn cell or cranial nerve neuron, (2) its peripheral axon and its branches,

FIGURE 6-2a   The components of the motor unit. It consists of the cell body of the lower motor neuron, the nerve axon, and the muscle fiber. Lesions at any point in the motor unit will produce signs of a lower motor neuron syndrome.

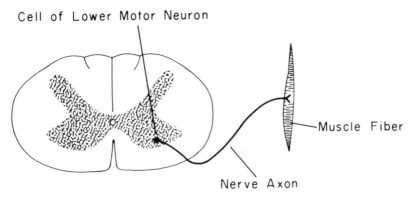

(3) each muscle fiber innervated by these branches, and (4) the myoneural juncture. Lesions may occur at many points within the motor unit and produce lower motor neuron signs (see Figure 6-2b). This figure portrays a motor unit at the spinal cord level. The most obvious example of disorder is a lesion or cut in the spinal nerve (point 2). This damage will paralyze the muscle innervated by the nerve. In addition, the denervated muscle will become hypotonic, areflexic, and atrophic. Finally, fasciculations will appear. If a cranial nerve is denervated, weakness of speech muscles results from hypotonia and loss of muscle bulk.

FIGURE 6-2b   Lesion sites in the motor unit and types of lower motor neuron disorders: (1) cell body (motor neuron disease); (2) lower motor neuron denervation (motor neuropathy); (3) myoneural juncture (neuromyopathy); (4) muscle fiber (myopathy or dystrophy).

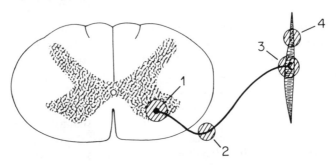

A lesion may also occur in the anterior horn cell in the spinal cord itself and produce paralysis and related lower motor neuron signs (point 1). An example is acute bulbar poliomyelitis, which attacks the high cervical anterior horns as well as the cranial nerve nuclei of the bulbar muscles controlling speech. Speech muscles again may become weak and atrophic.

Lesions of the lower motor neuron type may also occur directly in muscles. An example of this type of lower motor neuron disorder is seen in *muscular dystrophy* (point 4). Speech muscles lose strength and show disturbances of muscle bulk. This type of lower motor neuron disease is called a *myopathy*, as opposed to disease of the peripheral nerves, which is called a *neuropathy*. Lesions may also occur at the neuromuscular junction. An example is seen in myasthenia gravis (point 3). Speech muscles show fatiguable weakness in this *myoneural* disorder.

Upper Motor Neuron Paralysis

Types of Paralysis

Damage to the corticospinal tract, anywhere along this course, will produce a *spastic paralysis*. Spastic muscles display increased tone, or resistance to movement, a condition called *hypertonia*. Spastic hypertonicity can be identified by moving a limb through its full range of motion so that the joint is flexed or bent. The neurological examiner puts an increased stretch on the muscles during the range-of-motion testing. He elicits a muscle stretch reflex (MSR), an increase in tone or tension, which resists the flexion of the joint. The examiner feels this increased resistance to movement. (The MSR controls the degree of contraction in a normal muscle and provides muscles with *tonus* or tone.)

A *clasp knife reaction* occurs in a spastic muscle when the neurologist feels increased tone or resistance to movement in the muscle after the joint has been briskly flexed and then feels the resistance fade. This reaction, which identifies spastic *hypertonicity*, is analogous to the resistance felt when a knife blade is first opened and then followed by a reduction of resistance when the blade is straightened out. Thus we have the term *clasp knife spasticity*. Usually, this occurs more in extension than in flexion of the elbow. There is usually a short span of no tone, then a rapid buildup of tone, then a sudden release as the joint is moved—just as with opening a clasp knife.

Spasticity also is associated with exaggerated muscle stretch reflexes, resulting in *hyperreflexia*. Reflex action is tested at joints by putting stretch on tendons. This elicits the exaggerated MSR. Spastic paralysis, hypertonia, and hyperreflexia have most often been associated with pyramidal tract damage, particularly lesions of the corticospinal tract. However, the corticobulbar tracts are often also involved when a lesion interrupts the corticospinal tract, and signs of spasticity may be found in the midline speech muscles as well as in the distal limb muscles. Therefore, the clinical signs of spasticity, or upper motor neuron lesion, are of equal interest to the speech-language pathologist and the neurologist. Spastic speech muscles may be weak, slow, and limited in range or movement (see Chapter 8). Hypertonia may decrease muscle flexibility of the articulators and limit the ability to achieve a full range of motion of the speech muscles.

Confirmatory Signs
Several signs, in addition to a clinical demonstration of clasp knife spasticity, hypertonia, and hyperreflexia, are used by the neurologist to help verify the diagnosis of spasticity and localize the lesion to the pyramidal tract.

The *Babinski sign*, or extensor plantar sign, in particular, has been identified as an abnormal reflex sign that develops with corticospinal damage. It is the result of the release of cortical inhibition from a lesion. The sign has achieved considerable status in the diagnosis of upper motor neuron lesions because it is a highly reliable abnormal reflex, is new behavior released by the presence of a lesion, and is clearly associated with a relatively specific lesion site—the cortex or the corticospinal tract. The speech pathologist is not directly interested in it because it does not at all involve the midline speech muscles, but its presence as a confirmation of an upper motor neuron lesion of the spastic type is important to all who manage neurologic patients.

The Babinski sign is observed as a reflex toe sign. It is elicited by stimulating the sole of the foot in a strong scratching maneuver. The normal response to stimulation of the sole, or plantar portion of the foot, is a slight withdrawal of the foot and downward turning, or curling under of the toes. With a corticospinal lesion, the great toe extends upward and the other toes fan as the foot withdraws slightly. Physicians will test this response several times to convince themselves that the upturning great toe sign can be repeatedly and automatically elicited. Automatic repetition of a given response such as this defines it as a reflex. The presence of a repeatable abnormal reflex sharply increases the probability of predicting with accuracy the possible site or sites of a neurologic lesion.

The Babinski sign is more reliable in adults than in infants and children. Normal infants are highly variable in display of the sign. The explanation usually given for this variability is that the immature nervous system and the damaged nervous system often show similar symptoms and signs. Damage to the nervous system often releases early reflex behavior that has become inhibited by development of higher centers, so signs of damage at that point in time are signs of immaturity at an earlier time. Clinical neurologists believe that the extensor plantar sign usually reaches stability by the age of two. Other signs such as a persisting *asymmetrical tonic neck reflex (ATNR)* and the *Moro reflex* can be tested to suggest an upper motor neuron lesion in young children (see Chapter 12).

Another confirmatory sign of spasticity is *clonus*. Hyperactive muscle stretch reflexes associated with spasticity may show a sustained series of rhythmic beats or jerks when a neurological examiner maintains one tendon of a muscle in extension. To test for clonus, the Achilles tendon at the ankle is often put under extension. If there is an upper motor neuron lesion, the ankle and the calf will show sustained jerks. A few clonic jerks, called *abortive clonus*, are not clinically significant, but if the clonus is sustained over time, it is considered pathologic and an indicator of hyperreflexia. It is part of the clinical syndrome resulting from an upper motor neuron lesion.

Another set of reflex responses considered as confirmatory signs are the *superficial abdominal* and *cremasteric reflexes*. These reflexes, like the Babinski response, are called superficial reflexes because they are elicited by the cutaneous skin receptors, as opposed to the muscle stretch reflex, which is considered a deep reflex because it is elicited by receptor end organs deep within the tendons. The abdominal and cremasteric reflexes are elicited by stroking the abdominal quadrants or the inner surface of the thigh, respectively. The normal abdominal response is a twitching of the navel toward the quadrant stimulated. A normal cremasteric response is the elevation of the ipsilateral testicle in a male in response to thigh stimulation. No comparable reflex is found in the female. Absence of the reflexes indicates an upper motor neuron lesion. Sometimes, however, it is hard to find abdominal reflexes in normal persons, especially if they have had abdominal surgery (see Table 6-2 for a summary).

Alpha and Gamma Motor Neurons

In the final analysis, motor control of speech muscles, or any other musculature, is brought about by muscle contraction. At one time it was believed that the only route for control of voluntary muscle contraction was via the several de-

TABLE 6-2
Signs of Upper and Lower Motor Neuron Disorder

UMN	*LMN*
Spastic paralysis	Flaccid paralysis
Hypertonia	Hypotonia
Hyperreflexia	Hyporeflexia
Clonus	No clonus
Babinski sign	No Babinski sign
Little or no atrophy	Marked atrophy
No fasciculations	Fasciculations
Diminished abdominal and cremasteric reflexes	Normal abdominal and cremasteric reflexes

scending motor pathways in the nervous system that end in nerve cells called *alpha motor neurons*. These motor neurons are in the anterior horns of the spinal cord. They are anterior horn cells. Homologous motor neurons are the cranial nerve neurons of the brainstem. The alpha motor neurons of the cord are the largest neurons of the anterior horn cells and discharge neuron impulses through the spinal nerves to contract the muscles of the trunk and limbs.

Anatomy of Muscle Spindles

More recently, another level of neuromuscular control has been identified. This is at the level of the muscle spindle. Muscle spindles serve as sensory, or afferent, receptors within striated muscle. They provide sensory information on the status of the normal stretch mechanisms in muscle. The spindles are also innervated by efferent neurons, making them more complex sensory receptors than those found in the tendons and joints. The muscle spindle is encapsulated, containing a limited number of short fibers that are parallel to other muscle fibers (Figure 6-3). Fibers of the muscle spindle are called *intrafusal* fibers. The main muscle fibers, outside the spindle, are *extrafusal* fibers. There are two types of intrafusal fibers: *nuclear bag fibers* and *nuclear chain fibers*. An aggregate of closely packed nuclei are in the nuclear bag fibers, whereas the nuclei in the nuclear chain fibers are in single file. The nuclear bag and nuclear chain fibers are attached in parallel.

FIGURE 6-3   The muscle spindle

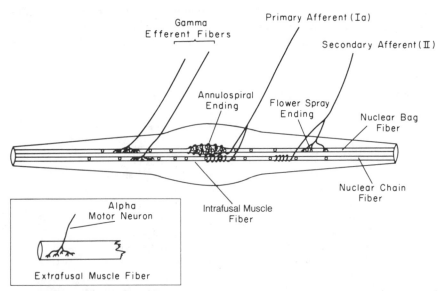

Source: Redrawn and reproduced with permission from W. Hardcastle, *The Physiology of Speech Production* (New York: Academic Press, 1978).

Two types of sensory nerve fibers, called primary and secondary afferents, are associated with the spindle. The primary afferents are rapidly conducting sensory endings wrapped around the center of the intrafusal fibers. They are sometimes called *annulospiral* endings. The secondary afferents lie, for the most part, on the nuclear chain fibers. These are called *flower spray endings* and are more slowly conducting afferents.

Both primary and secondary afferents are stimulated by the lengthening of the intrafusal fibers and by the rate of change of their length. As the muscle fibers are stretched in response to the muscle contraction, the spindle afferents convey information to the alpha motor neurons, which control the neural discharge to extrafusal fibers. The primary afferents are large neurons with a rapid rate of conduction, up to 120 meters per second. The speed with which the spindles convey sensory feedback information to the central nervous system marks them as likely candidates for the neural mechanisms controlling the fine and rapid movements of speech muscles as well as other rapid motor activities.

Gamma Motor Neurons

In addition to afferent neurons, the spindle is also supplied with motor neurons called *gamma efferents* or gamma motor neurons. They control contraction at the muscle level. They are relatively small in size compared to the alpha efferents, but they make up approximately 30 percent of the motor neurons leaving the spinal cord. The gamma motor neurons innervate the muscle spindle at each end. They allow contraction of the intrafusal fibers and increase their sensitivity to stretch. In this way the gamma motor neurons form an important muscle stretch reflex mechanism that acts in conjunction with the alpha motor neurons. As the extrafusal fibers contract, the intrafusal fibers also contract to maintain a consistent length ratio in the muscle. This increases sensitivity to stretch and provides for fine compensations of muscle length and velocity.

Speech muscles, which contain an abundance of spindles, have the potential for making compensations of movement if the specifications of a motor command are met. Evidence from the speech science laboratory indicates that rapid compensatory motor behavior is necessary for intelligible speech. Motor speech acts are rarely performed exactly the same way twice, but in most cases motor speech production meets the broad specification of the motor commands in such a way that the listener can recognize an individual speech sound, or *phon*, as a member of a phoneme class.

Alpha Motor Neurons

One can assume that most motor commands for a given articulatory act are transmitted by the alpha motor neuron system. The alpha motor neuron provides appropriate contraction of the extrafusal fibers innervated by the cranial nerves and the spinal nerves for articulatory acts, but local conditions produce variations on the way the actual articulatory movements are accomplished. The muscle spindle system, or gamma motor neuron system, with its sensory and motor servomechanism capabilities, makes necessary muscle stretch reflex adjustments in the speech muscles for intelligible speech. This theory of muscle spindles provides an explanation of fine coordinated control at the level of the speech muscles. Thus the muscle spindle mechanism has offered a reasonable theoretical explanation for what is known as the problem of *motor equivalence* of speech movements.[3]

Golgi Tendon Organs

Beyond the muscle spindle system, there are joint receptors and special tendon receptors called Golgi tendon organs that are involved in sensorimotor control of the speech muscles as well as other musculature of the body. The Golgi tendon organs are attached directly to the tendons of muscles. They respond when either stretching or contraction places tension on the tendon. The tendon organs serve to temper motor activity and inhibit activity in muscles when high levels of tension are placed on the tendon.

The Extrapyramidal System

We have identified the pyramidal system as the primary pathway for voluntary movement. We also have indicated that a subdivision of that system, the corticobulbar tracts, are the primary pathways for the voluntary control of most of the speech muscles. Still another motor system, the extrapyramidal system, plays a significant role in speech and its disorders. It is made up of a complex set of pathways that connect clusters of subcortical motor nuclei. It also interacts with other motor systems of the nervous system. The neurophysiology of the extrapyramidal system is obscure, but the results of lesions to the system are anything but obscure. The motor disorders that result from damage to the extrapyramidal system are, for the most part, dramatic and blatantly obvious conditions. A neurologist can usually diagnose these conditions by visual inspection alone, because of the obvious abnormality of the movement patterns.

Dyskinesias

The motor disturbances of the extrapyramidal system are usually classified as *involuntary movement disorders*. The most commonly used technical term for them is *dyskinesias* (*dys* = "disorder"; *kinesia* = "movement"). These disorders encompass a full range of bizarre postures and unusual movement patterns. The dyskinesias have long been described with such terms as tremor, writhing, fidgeting, flailing, restlessness, jerking, and flinging. Often the unusual movements that dominate the trunk and limbs of the dyskinetic patient are also reflected in the face and speech mechanism. The result is a serious and typical dysarthria. In general, the dysarthria reflects the specific symptoms of each specific type of dyskinesia.

The term *dyskinesia* is usually used to indicate movement disorders associated with extrapyramidal lesions, but the term may be used in a broader sense to include any excess of movement or reduction in movement. *Hyperkinesia* has been used to indicate those dyskinesias that present too much movement. *Hypokinesia*, on the other hand, refers to too little movement, or reduced movement. In actual clinical usage the terms may not always be applied strictly to a person with extrapyramidal lesions. For instance, neurologists may apply hyperkinesia to the well-known extrapyramidal based twitching or fidgeting of chorea in Huntington's disease as well as to the abnormal hyperactivity of some children, in whom there may not be documented evidence of an organic lesion in the nervous system, let alone knowledge of a lesion localized to the extrapyramidal system.

Hypokinesia may be used to describe the reduced activity level of a depressive patient with no suspected neurologic lesion. By tradition, neurologists do not apply hypokinesia to limitations in movement resulting from lesions of the pyramidal tract or peripheral nerves. In other words, lesions that paralyze voluntary movement are not labeled hypokinetic. Thus hemiplegia, quadriplegia, and paraplegia are not considered hypokinetic disorders.

Anatomy of the Extrapyramidal System

The neuronal activity circuitry of this motor system, like that of the pyramidal system, begins in the cerebral cortex and ultimately exerts an influence on the lower motor neuron. The pathways are indirect, in contrast to the direct pathway of the pyramidal tract. The long axons of the corticospinal tract make only one synapse with the spinal nerves, at the anterior horn cell in the spinal cord. Thus the pyramidal tract is called *monosynaptic*. The extrapyramidal tract is *polysynaptic*, making many synaptic connections before impulses reach the lower motor neuron. It is an indirect motor pathway compared to the direct pyramidal motor pathway. In fact, however, it is difficult to make many significant distinctions between the two systems. They are so closely interconnected that some neurophysiologists have found any sharp distinction between them to be meaningless.

Basal Ganglia

The term *extrapyramidal system* does have some clinical utility in that it is widely used to refer to a group of subcortical nuclei and related structures known as the *basal ganglia* (see Figure 2-8 in Chapter 2). Although the terminology used to describe the basal ganglia is not always agreed on and is generally confusing, there are three structures or major parts of the basal ganglia: (1) the *caudate nucleus*, (2) the *putamen*, and (3) the *globus pallidus* (Figure 6-4).

The caudate nucleus lies just medial to the anterior limb of the interior capsule. The putamen and globus pallidus lie anterior to the genu of the internal capsule. Some authorities would include as part of the basal ganglia another nucleus called the *claustrum*. Two other subcortical structures, the *subthalamic nuclei* and the *substantia nigra* are functionally related to the basal ganglia but are not part of it. The caudate nucleus lies adjacent to the wall of the lateral ventricle, close to the thalamus, which is part of the diencephalon. The structure is divided into a head, body, and tail by some neurologists, but others divide the caudate into only a head and tail.

The *putamen* and *globus pallidus* together make up the *lenticular nucleus*, a thumb-sized structure wedged against the internal capsule. It is separated from the caudate nucleus except at the head of the caudate, where the two nuclear masses border on the anterior limb of the internal capsule. The putamen is the lateral portion of the lenticular nucleus, and the globus pallidus is in the medial region of the lenticular nucleus. The globus pallidus is crossed by myelinated fibers, which give it a pale cast in its fresh state. The lenticular nucleus (that is, the putamen and the globus pallidus) combined with the caudate nucleus make up what is known as the *corpus striatum* (see Table 6-3).

Other structures related in function to the basal ganglia are found near the *reticular formation of the mesencephalon*. These include the *subthalamus*, *substantia nigra*, and *red nucleus*. The *reticular formation* itself is also thought of as part of the subcortical extrapyramidal system. The extrapyramidal system is concerned with coarse stereotyped movements. It has more influence over proximal (midline) than over distal (peripheral) muscles. It maintains proper tone and posture.

FIGURE 6-4　Extrapyramidal nuclei: the basal ganglia

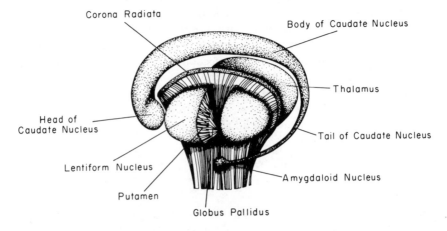

TABLE 6-3
Major Extrapyramidal Nuclei

Basal Ganglia

Globus pallidus	}	Lenticular	}	Corpus
Putamen		nucleus		striatum
Caudate nucleus				

Even with destruction of the pyramidal tract, it can allow a person to eat and walk. It probably is crucial in changing facial expression as we talk, whereas speech itself is probably primarily the result of pyramidal tract action. Most of the efferent fibers from the basal ganglia leave the globus pallidus. In addition to the basal ganglia, the cerebellum and the cerebral cortex interact in a series of feedback loops suggesting complex interaction of motor subsystems to coordinate everyday speech motor performance (see figures 6-5 and 6-6 for a diagram of the major circuitry of the basal ganglia).

Dyskinetic Types

The responsibility of speech-language pathologists does not extend to the identification of lesion sites in the complex circuitry of the extrapyramidal motor system, but they should attempt to recognize the standard dyskinesias of ex-

FIGURE 6-5   Major circuits of the extrapyramidal system: the globus pallidal circuit. The circuit proceeds from the (a) cerebral cortex to (b) corpus striatum to (c) globus pallidus and (d) thalamus. The pathways then return to the cerebral cortex from the thalamus.

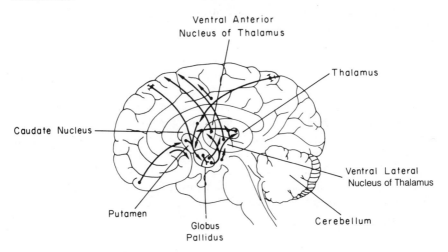

FIGURE 6-6 Major circuits of the extrapyramidal system: the cerebellar circuit. This circuit proceeds from (a) cerebral cortex to (b) ipsilateral pontine nuclei to (c) contralateral cerebellar cortex to (d) dentate nucleus to (e) red nucleus to (f) thalamus. The pathway then returns to the cerebral cortex from the thalamus.

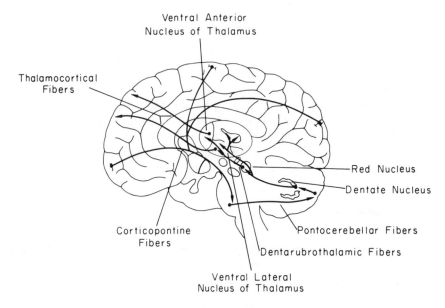

trapyramidal origin and to determine the effect of the symptoms of specific dyskinesias on the dysarthria accompanying it. Undiagnosed cases of dyskinesia demand a referral to a neurologist.

There are several distinct patterns of dyskinesia, but not all of them are related to the dysarthrias. We will describe only those motor signs that produce motor speech symptoms.

Tremors

Tremors are defined as purposeless movements that are rhythmic, oscillatory, involuntary actions. Normal, or physiologic, and abnormal, or pathologic, tremors are usually distinguished. Tremors are pathologic if they occur in a disease and are characteristic of that disease. Normal tremor is called physiologic tremor. There are several classifications of tremor in use today. Table 6-4 provides terminology and definitions of different types of tremor. The types, the amplitude, and the frequency of oscillations in cycles per second are important to the neurologist.

TABLE 6-4
Types of Tremor and Their Definition

Tremor	Definition
Normal or physiologic	
1. Rest tremor	Tremor occurs when body parts are relaxed 8–12 cps. Barely visible amplitude.
2. Postural (static) tremor	Occurs when body parts are in a sustained position against gravity. 8–12 cps and is irregular. No visible amplitude.
3. Intention (kinetic) tremor	Occurs during the movement of a body part toward a goal. 8–12 cps and is irregular. No visible amplitude.
Abnormal or Pathologic	
1. Rest tremor	Tremor occurs in disease state. Cause unknown, probably extrapyramidal lesion. About 5 cps. Amplitude varies. Seen in parkinsonism.
2. Postural (static) tremor	Frequency is 8–12 cps. Increased amplitude. May appear as vocal tremor. May also affect head and neck. Unknown lesion site; associated with cerebral disorder, cerebellar degeneration, toxic states.
3. Intention (kinetic) tremor	Occurs during the movement of a body part toward a goal and is intensified toward end of movement. Is seen in cerebellar and cerebellar pathway lesions.

The speech-language pathologist should be familiar with three types of tremor that are associated with vocal performance in normal and pathologic conditions.

Rest Tremor

Rest tremor designates a tremor that occurs in Parkinson's disease. A tremor of 3 to 7 movements per second occurs in the patient's limbs and hands at rest. It is temporarily suppressed when the limb is moved, and it sometimes can be inhibited by conscious effort. The voice may be affected by the tremor. Tremulous voice has been described in approximately 14 percent of a large sample of parkinsonian patients. It is a salient vocal deviation that is easily recognized among the other vocal deviations of the hypokinetic dysarthria of parkinsonism.

Physiologic or Action Tremor

Normal people demonstrate a fine tremor of the hands on maintaining posture. The rate may vary with age but usually falls within the range of 4 to 12 cycles per second. An action tremor may affect the laryngeal muscles and produce an organic or essential vocal tremor, the mechanism for which is unknown. This normal tremor is distinguished from pathologic tremors associated with known neurologic diseases such as parkinsonism and cerebellar disorders.

Intention Tremor
This term refers to a tremor that occurs during movement and is intensified at the termination of the movement. Intention tremor has been associated with the ataxic dysarthria seen in cerebellar disease. It is a type of tremor often seen in cerebellar disorder but is not exclusive to cerebellar dysfunction.

Chorea

These are quick, random, hyperkinetic movements simulating fragments of normal movements. Speech, facial, and respiratory movements, as well as the extremities, are affected by choreic symptoms in this dyskinesia. The movement is close to what is popularly described as "fidgets." It is one symptom of a hereditary disorder known as Huntington's disease and is seen in other extrapyramidal disorders as well.

Athetosis

The hyperkinesia of athetosis is a slow, irregular, coarse, writhing, or squirming movement. It usually involves the extremities as well as the face, neck, and trunk. The movements directly interfere with the fine and controlled actions of the larynx, tongue, palate, pharynx, and respiratory mechanism. Like most other involuntary movements, the involuntary movements of athetosis disappear in sleep. In congenital athetosis, the most common type of spastic paralysis may also be observed, indicating involvement of both pyramidal and extrapyramidal systems. Lesion sites in pure athetosis are often in the putamen and the caudate nucleus. Hypoxia, or lack of oxygen at birth, is a common cause, producing death of brain cells before or during birth. *Choreoathetotic movements* have also been described; they appear to be a dyskinesia that lies somewhere between choreic and athetoid movements in terms of rate and rhythm of movement, or that comprises both types of movement. In fact, many of the involuntary movement disorders appear to be blends of one or more of the different clinical dyskinesias, as the term *choreoathetosis* implies.

Dystonia

In this disorder the limbs assume distorted static postures resulting from excess tone in selected parts of the body. The dyskinetic postures are slow, bizarre, and often grotesque, involving writhing, twisting, and turning. Dysarthria and obvious motor involvement of the speech mechanism are common. Often, differential motor involvement occurs in the speech muscles, and some dysarthrias have been observed that primarily affect the larynx. Others affect the face, tongue, lips, palate, and jaw. A rare dystonic disorder of childhood is called *dystonia musculorum deformans*. It may be accompanied by dysarthria in its later stages.

Fragmentary dystonias have been described, and some neurologists assert that they contribute to *spastic dysphonia*, a bizarre voice disorder that is a mixture of aphonia (lack of voice) and a strained, labored whisper. The etiology of spastic dysphonia is unclear.

Myoclonus

This term has been used to describe differing motor abnormalities, but basically a myoclonic movement is an abrupt, brief, almost lightning-like contraction of muscle. An example of a normal or physiologic myoclonic reaction occurs when you are drifting off to sleep and are suddenly awakened by a rapid muscle jerk. This muscle jerk is myoclonus.

Pathologic myoclonus is most common in the limbs and trunk, but also may involve the facial muscles, jaws, tongue, and pharynx. Repetitive myoclonus in these muscles, of course, may affect speech. Myoclonic movements in the muscles of speech have been described as having a rate of 10–50 per minute, but can be more rapid. The pathology underlying these movements has been debated, but since they have been associated with degenerative brain disease, the cerebral cortex, brainstem, cerebellum, and extrapyramidal system all have been considered as possible lesion sites.

A special myoclonic syndrome involving speech muscles called *palatal myoclonus* has been described. It involves rapid movements of the soft palate and pharynx, and sometimes includes the larynx, the diaphragm, and other muscles. The symptoms most often come on in later life and are characteristic of several diseases. This myoclonus has a specific pathology in the central tegmental tract of the brainstem, but the etiology can be varied. The most common cause is a stroke, or cerebrovascular accident, in the brainstem.

Orofacial Dyskinesia or Tardive Dyskinesia

In this syndrome, bizarre movements are limited to the mouth, face, jaw, and tongue. There is grimacing, pursing of the mouth and lips, and writhing of the tongue. These dyskinetic movements very often alter articulation of speech. The motor speech signs of orofacial dyskinesia usually develop after the prolonged use of powerful tranquilizing drugs, the most common class of which are the *phenothiazines*. Drug-induced dyskinesias associated with the phenothiazines and related medications may even produce athetoid movements or dystonic movements of the body. Parkinsonian signs and other symptoms associated with extrapyramidal disorders are also caused by these drugs. Orofacial dyskinesia also occurs in elderly patients without drug use. A rare disorder that includes dyskinesia of the eyelids, face, tongue, and refractory muscles is called *Meige syndrome*.

Other dyskinesias are included in the spectrum of extrapyramidal disorders but generally do not include motor involvement of the speech mechanism. These are defined in Table 6-5.

The Cerebellar System

The third major subcomponent of the motor system that affects speech is the cerebellum. Interacting with the pyramidal and extrapyramidal systems, in addition to the reticular brainstem formation, the cerebellum is known to provide significant coordination for motor speech. As noted, the cerebellum is located dorsal to the medulla and pons. The occipital lobes of the cerebral hemispheres overlap the top of the cerebellum. The anatomy of the cerebellum is complex, and the speech-language pathologist need only understand it in a gross sense in order to see the relations of the cerebellum to speech performance.

Anatomy of the Cerebellum

The cerebellum can be divided into three parts. The thin middle portion is called the *vermis* because of its serpentine or wormlike shape. The vermis lies between two large lateral masses of the cerebellum, the cerebellar hemispheres (see Figure 6-7). The vermis connects these two hemispheres. The vermis and hemispheres are divided by fissures and sulci into *lobes* and also into smaller divisions, called *lobules*. The division into lobes and lobules is helpful in clari-

TABLE 6-5
Nonspeech Dyskinesias

Dyskinesias	*Definition*
Myoclonic movement	Spontaneous transient or persistent movements of a few muscle bundles within a muscle.
Hemiballismus	Forceful, flinging movements that are continuous, wild, and unilateral, and may involve one-half of the body.
Akathisia	Motor restlessness or inability to sit still.

FIGURE 6-7 Schematic diagram of the three lobes, the lobules, and fissures of the cerebellum. Roman numerals refer to portions of the cerebellar vermis only.

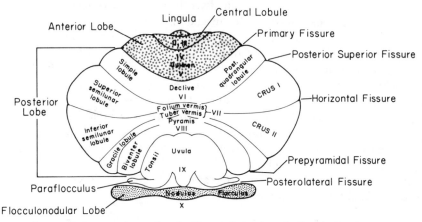

Source: Redrawn and reproduced with permission from J. Chusid, *Correlative Neuroanatomy and Functional Neurology* (17th ed.) (Los Altos, CA: Lange Medical Publications, 1979).

fying the physiologic function of the cerebellum. Although the lobes and lobules have been classified differently by several investigators, we will employ a classification system that divides the cerebellum into three lobes.

Three Cerebellar Lobes

These include (1) the anterior lobe, (2) the posterior lobe, and (3) the flocculonodular lobe. The *anterior lobe* is modest in size and is that part of the cerebellum that is superior to the primary fissure. This part of the cerebellum corresponds roughly to what is known as the *paleocerebellum*, the second-oldest part of the cerebellum in a phylogenetic sense. The anterior lobe receives most of the proprioceptive impulses from the spinal cord and regulates posture.

The *posterior lobe* is the largest part of the cerebellum and is located between the other two lobes. It makes up the major portion of the cerebellar hemispheres. It is the newest part of the cerebellum and is also known as the *neocerebellum*. It receives the cerebellar connections from the cerebrum and regulates coordination of muscle movement.

The *flocculonodular lobe* consists of two small wisplike appendages which are known as *flocculi*, in the posterior and inferior region of the cerebellum. The flocculi are separated by the *nodulus*, the inferior part of the vermis. The flocculonodular lobe, the oldest portion of the cerebellum, contains the fastigial nucleus, fibers that travel from the nucleus to the four vestibular nuclei in the upper medulla. Via these fibers, the cerebellum mediates equilibrium.

Synergy and Asynergy

The connections that the cerebellum has with other parts of the central nervous system are important to its function. It is through these connections that the cerebellum sends and receives afferent and efferent impulses and executes its primary function—a synergistic coordination of muscles and muscle groups. *Synergy* is defined as the cooperative action of muscles. Assuring the smooth coordination of muscles is the prime task of the cerebellum. Specifically, the cerebellum, with other structures of the nervous system, maintains proper posture and balance in walking, and in the sequential movements of eating, dressing, and writing. It also guides the production of rapid, alternating, repetitive movements such as those present in speaking, and in smooth pursuit movements. Voluntary movement, without assistance from the cerebellum, is clumsy, uncoordinated, and disorganized. The motor defect of the cerebellar system has been called *asynergia* or *dysynergia*. Asynergia is a lack of coordination in agonistic and antagonistic muscles.

Cerebellar Peduncles and Pathways

The cerebellum is connected to the rest of the nervous system by three pairs of peduncles or feet. The cerebellar peduncles anchor the cerebellum to the brainstem. All afferent and efferent fibers of the cerebellum pass through the three peduncles and the pons to the other levels of the nervous sytem. The *pons*, which means "bridge," is aptly named: it is literally a bridge from the cerebellum to the rest of the nervous system (see Figure 6-8).

The *inferior cerebellar peduncle*, or *restiform body*, carries primary afferent fibers from the structures close to it; these are the medulla, spinal cord, and eighth cranial nerve. Thus spinocerebellar, medullocerebellar, and vestibular fibers pass through the inferior peduncle.

The *middle cerebellar peduncle*, or *brachium pontis*, connects the cerebellum with the cerebral cortex by pathways that transverse it. The middle peduncle is easily recognized: it is the largest of the three peduncles and also conveys the largest number of fibers to the cerebral cortex and pons. It carries pontocerebellar fibers as well as the majority of the *corticopontocerebellar fibers*. These fibers convey afferent information from the temporal and frontal lobes of the cerebrum to the posterior lobe of the contralateral cerebellum.

The superior cerebellar peduncle, or brachium conjunctivum, conveys the bulk of efferent fibers that leave the cerebellum. The primary efferent fibers arise from an important nucleus deep in the cerebellum called the *dentate nucleus*. The *rubrospinal* and *dentatothalamic pathways*, along with several other tracts, leave via the superior peduncle and terminate in the *contralateral red nucleus* and *ventrolateral nucleus* of the thalamus. From here impulses are relayed to the cerebral cortex. The anatomy of the cerebellum is summarized in Table 6-6.

FIGURE 6-8   Major pathways of the cerebellum

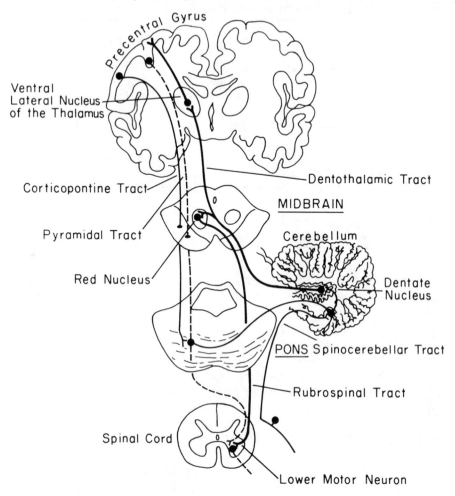

Cerebellar Role in Speech

We have outlined the major pathways and structures of the cerebellum to suggest a rough schematic of the feedback nature of the afferent and efferent connections of the structure. Sketchy as our presentation is, it will highlight the fact that the cerebellar motor subsystem significantly influences the function of the other motor systems in the production of motor speech. The fact that the cerebellum plays an important part in the synergy of rapid alternating movements and the fine coordination of muscles suggests that it interacts in a crucial way with the corticobulbar fibers to provide the specialized rapid and precise motor control needed for ongoing connected speech.

TABLE 6-6
The Cerebellum and Its Pathways

Hemispheres	*Lobes*	*Peduncles*
Right	Superior	Superior
Left	Posterior	Medial
	Floccunodular	Inferior

Major Afferent Pathways and Their Lobes

Vestibulocerebellar tracts	Floccunodular lobe
Spinocerebellar tracts	Superior lobe
Corticopontocerebellar tracts	Posterior lobe

Major Efferent Pathway and Hemispheres

Cerebrocerebellocerebral tracts	Right and left hemispheres

Auditory, tactile, and visual areas exist in the cerebellum. These motor, tactile, and auditory centers in the cerebellum, both cortical and subcortical, project to similar areas in the cerebrum, which in turn project back to corresponding cerebellar areas. The cerebellum, therefore, is neither completely vestibular, proprioceptive, nor motor in function, but serves to reinforce or diminish sensory and motor impulses, acting as a critical modulator of neuronal function. Through its afferent and efferent feedback circuits, it ensures a desired level of neural activity in the motor parts of the nervous system.

Clinical Signs of Cerebellar Dysfunction

Cerebellar lesions or cerebellar pathway lesions manifest themselves in incoordination of volitional movement and, often, in volitionally maintained postures. Clinical signs usually appear on the same side of the body as the cerebellar lesion. Upper motor neuron lesions of pyramidal pathways yield contralateral effects, whereas the cerebellum and its pathways manifest unilateral effects. Several classic signs of cerebellar disorder are as follows.

Ataxia
Ataxia is the prime sign of a cerebellar lesion (*taxis* means "ordering in rank and file"). The term *ataxia* is often used in several senses. It may refer to the general incoordination of motor acts seen with cerebellar system lesions. In this sense it often describes a staggering or reeling gait and abnormal posture seen with cerebellar lesions. The patient compensates for the ataxic gait by standing and walking with feet wide apart in what is called a *broad-based gait*.

Decomposition of Movement

Decomposition of movement is also related to the ataxia. The patient will break a complex motor act into its components and execute the act movement by movement, as if it were being performed by a robot. Decomposition of movement is considered an ataxic movement.

Dysmetria

Dysmetria is the inability to gauge the distance, speed, and power of movement. A patient may stop before the movement is performed or may overshoot the motor goal.

Adiadochokinesia or Dysdiadochokinesia

Adiadochokinesia or dysdiadochokinesia is the inability to perform rapid alternating movement of muscles. Often the rate of alternating movement may be recorded in a neurologic examination. This measure is called an *alternate motion rate* (AMR). Diadochokinetic rate measures of the muscles of the oral mechanism during speech and nonspeech activities have long been used as an assessment task by the clinical speech and language pathologist. These rates, however, are used as measures of the integrity of the oral muscles in speech pathology and have not specifically been related to cerebellar function.

The neurologist may test alternating movements in many muscle groups in persons suspected of cerebellar disorders. Successive pronation or supination of the hands, rapid tapping of the fingers, or rapid opening and closing of the fists are all diadochokinetic diagnostic tests. During the testing of diadochokinesis or alternate motion rates, one may see awkwardness or clumsiness of alternate movements.

Rebound

The rebound phenomenon is the ability to check the contraction of the flexors and rapidly contract the extensor. It may account for lack of smooth diadochokinetic movements.

Hypotonia

Hypotonia, or muscle flaccidity, with a decrease in resistance to passive movement, is seen in cerebellar dysfunction. The muscles of the body are flabby and lack normal tone.

Tremor

Tremor is seen as part of the cerebellar disease. It is usually an intention or kinetic tremor not present at rest.

Nystagmus

Nystagmus is oscillatory abnormalities of the pupil of the eye, often seen in cerebellar disorders. The rhythmic oscillations may be vertical, horizontal, or rotary.

Muscle Stretch Reflexes

Muscle stretch reflexes are normal or diminished. Often, *pendular reflexes* may be seen in cerebellar disease. When the knee jerk reflex is elicited, there are often a series of smooth to and fro movements of the limb before it comes to rest, as would be seen in a pendulum. This is unlike a normal knee jerk response and is designated as a pendular reflex.

Ataxic Dysarthria

Ataxic dysarthria is present with some cerebellar lesions. The typical speech pattern in ataxic dysarthria results from asynergetic movement of the speech muscles. There are disturbances in the force, the speed, the timing, and the direction of the muscles used in speech performance. Articulation is generally imprecise, with distorted vowels and inaccurate consonant production. Articulatory control shows irregularity, and the prosody of speech is disturbed. Rate is slowed and timing of phonemes is abnormal. Stress on syllables is inappropriate, and loudness and pitch are deviant. Prosodic disturbances are obvious in the speech. Cerebellar signs and tests are summarized in Table 6-7.

Cerebellar Syndrome and Dysarthria

Some of the aforementioned signs of cerebellar disorder have been singled out as prominent in a *syndrome of cerebellar disorder*. This syndrome usually includes *ataxia*, *dysarthria*, *nystagmus*, and *hypotonia*. However, not all patients with cerebellar disease show all clinical signs of this syndrome. Dysarthria is not always seen in cerebellar disease. It may appear if the lesion is localized in the speech mechanisms in the cerebellum. The speech mechanisms of the cerebellum are localized to the left cerebellar hemisphere (Lechtenberg & Gilman, 1978).

TABLE 6-7
Cerebellar Dysfunction Signs and Tests

Abnormality	*Signs and Test*
Gait ataxia	Broad-based gait; tandem walking test
Arm ataxia	Finger-to-nose test, hand pronation-to-supination test
Overshooting	Arm-pulling test, rebound noted
Hypotonia	Pendular reflexes; rag doll postures and gait; passive movement test
Nystagmus	Obvious on inspection; follow finger through field of gaze
Dysarthria	Articulation disorder with dysprosody; loudness, pitch, stress disturbance. Often associated with left cerebellar hemisphere lesion

Summary

Traditionally, the neuromuscular control for speaking has been related to three classic motor systems—the pyramidal, extrapyramidal, and cerebellar systems. When the corticospinal tract of the pyramidal tract is damaged by an upper motor neuron lesion, a contralateral hemiplegia (one-sided paralysis) may result. The corticobulbar tracts are the voluntary motor pathways for speech; they are part of the pyramidal system. Corticobulbar fibers innervate the cranial nuclei in the pons and medulla for the cranial nerves that control speech. The crossed and uncrossed fibers of the corticobulbar tracts are arranged so that the midline speech muscles function in bilateral synchrony for many functions. Some speech muscles show mixed bilateral synchrony and contralateral independence.

Clinical lesions in the nervous system have been classically divided into upper and lower motor neuron lesions (UMN and LMN). Each type of lesion presents a different type of paralysis, with its own associated signs. The hallmark of an UMN lesion is clasp knife spasticity (hypertonia), whereas the hallmark of a LMN lesion is a flaccid paralysis (hypotonia). Movement patterns are initiated by the motor cortex and transmitted to lower levels of the nervous system via descending pathways that end on the alpha motor neurons, the anterior horn cells, the spinal cord, or similar neurons of the cranial nuclei. Muscle spindles, which include sensory receptors (proprioceptors) deep within the muscle, aid in controlling movement patterns. An afferent-efferent feedback loop, involving the gamma motor neuron and the muscle spindle, influences the alpha motor neuron in the spinal cord and the cranial nerve nuclei. Although it is apparently important for speech, its exact role is unknown.

The extrapyramidal system is an indirect motor pathway from the cortex involving subcortical nuclei called the basal ganglia. Connections to and from the basal ganglia are made with the cerebral cortex, cerebellum, brainstem, and spinal cord. Involuntary movement disorders, or dyskinesias, associated with special patterns of speech disturbance are tremor, tardive dyskinesia, chorea, athetosis, choreoathetosis, myoclonus, and orofacial dyskinesia. The speech disorders of the extrapyramidal system are dyskinetic dysarthrias. These may be hypokinetic or hyperkinetic dyskinetic dysarthrias. Disturbances of tone—as seen in the rigidity of Parkinson's disease and in dystonia—are also related to basal ganglia disorders.

The cerebellum is responsible for synergistic motor coordination and plays an important part in guiding the rapid, alternating, repetitive movements of speech. It provides afferent and efferent information to the corticobulbar fibers. The primary signs of cerebellar disorder are *ataxia* (incoordination) and *asynergia* (poor cooperative muscle actions). Dysdiadochokinesia is seen in the alternating movement rates (AMR) of the oral musculature. Dysarthria, ataxia, hypotonia, and nystagmus (oscillating pupil) are often described as the classic cerebellar syndrome, but all four signs are not always present with cerebellar pathway lesions. Ataxic dysarthria is not seen in all cases of cerebellar disorder.

Notes

1. The corticobulbar fibers derive their name from their direction. At the longest point they extend from cortex to medulla. In older terminology the medulla was called the *bulb* because it appeared as a bulbous extension of the spinal cord. *Corticomedullar* would be a more consistent modern term, but *corticobulbar* is a term in common usage.

2. The term *bulbar muscles* refers to the muscles whose cranial motor nuclei are found in the medulla oblongata. These are cranial nerves IX (glossopharyngeal), X (vagus), XI (spinal-accessory), and XII (hypoglossal).

3. *Motor equivalence* refers to the fact that the oral structures may be adjusted from several positions to achieve a target position for articulation.

References and Further Readings

Pyramidal System

Feldman, R. G., Young, R. R., Koella, W. P. (Eds.) (1980). *Spasticity: Disordered motor control.* Chicago: Year Book Publishers.

Kuypers, H. G. J. M. (1958). Corticobulbar connections to the pons and lower brainstem in man: An anatomical study. *Brain,* 81, 364–388.

Alpha and Gamma Neurons

Grillner, S., Lindbloom, B., Lubker, J., & Persson, A. (Eds.) (1982). *Speech motor control.* New York: Pergamon Press.

Hardcastle, W. J. (1976). *Physiology of speech production.* New York: Academic Press.

The Extrapyramidal System

Cooper, I. (1969). *Involuntary movement disorders.* New York: Hoeber Medical Division, Harper & Row.

Marsden, C. D. (1982). The mysterious function of the basal ganglia. *Neurology,* 32, 514–539.

The Cerebellar System

Eccles, J. C. (1973). *The understanding of the brain*. New York: McGraw-Hill.

Lechtenberg, R., & Gilman, S. (1978). Speech disorders in cerebellar disease. *Annals of Neurology*, 3, 285–289.

CHAPTER SEVEN

The Cranial Nerves

"To those I address, it is unnecessary to go further than to indicate that the nerves treated in these papers are the instruments of expression from the smile of the infant's cheek to the last agony of life . . ."

—Charles Bell, 1824

Introduction

This chapter is intended to help the speech-language pathologist understand one of the most important parts of the nervous system with respect to the act of speaking. The cranial nerves make up a part of the peripheral nervous system that provides crucial sensory and motor information to the oral musculature. The speech-language pathologist should be very familiar with the names, structure, innervation, testing procedure, and signs of abnormal function of the cranial nerves. This information will be vital in working with the dysarthric adult and child.

Names and Number

Twelve pairs of cranial nerves leave the brain and pass through the foramina of the skull. They are known both by their numbers, written in Roman numerals, and by their names. The names sometimes give a clue to the function of the nerve, but it is best to learn the number, the name, and a concise description of the various functions. Such a description is found in Table 7-1. Many students use a mnemonic device to help them remember the cranial nerves—for example, *On Old Olympus' Towering Top A Finn And German*

TABLE 7-1
The Cranial Nerves

Number	Name	Summary of Function
I	Olfactory	Smell
II	Optic	Vision
III	Oculomotor	Innervation of muscles to move the eyeball, the pupil, & the upper lid
IV	Trochlear	Innervation of superior oblique muscle of eye
V	Trigeminal	Chewing and sensation to face
VI	Abducens	Abducts eye
VII	Facial	Movement of facial muscles, taste, salivary glands
VIII	Vestibular Acoustic	Equilibrium and hearing
IX	Glossopharyngeal	Taste, elevation of palate and larynx, salivary glands
X	Vagus	Taste, swallowing, elevation of palate, phonation, parasympathetic outflow to visceral organs
XI	Accessory	Turning of head and shrugging shoulders
XII	Hypoglossal	Movement of tongue

Vend At Hops. Of course, you can create your own device—an even more memorable one!

Embryological Origin

The nuclei of the cranial nerves are of three different types. The motor nuclei are distinguished by the embryological origin of the muscles they innervate. The development of the body wall in the embryo is from blocks of mesoderm called *somites*. Cranial nerves III, IV, VI, and XII are derived from this somatic segmentation and thus are called the *somatomotor* or *somitic set*.

In the development of the embryo, the branchial (gill) arches are responsible for the structure, muscles, and nerves of the face and neck. Cranial nerves V, VII, IX, X, and XI are thus known as the *branchial set*.

The somites and branchial arches are transverse segments of the embryo. In contrast, the viscera, including the neuraxis, are developed from longitudinal tubes. The elaboration or diverticulation of the hollow tubes gives rise to three cranial nerves (I, II, and VIII) known as the *solely special sensory set*. There are branchial and somatic cranial nerves that do have a visceral component—numbers III, VII, IX, and X.

The Corticobulbar Tract and the Cranial Nerves

The cranial nerves consist of efferent motor fibers that arise from nuclei in the brainstem and afferent sensory fibers that originate in the peripheral ganglia. The motor or efferent parts are axons of the nerve cells within the brain. These nerve cells with their processes are part of the *lower motor neurons*. Groups of these nerve cells form the *nuclei of origin* for the cranial nerves.

The nuclei of origin of the cranial nerves receive impulses from the cerebral cortex through the *corticobulbar tracts*. The tracts begin in the pyramidal cells in the inferior part of the precentral gyrus and also in the adjacent part of the postcentral gyrus. The tracts then follow the path illustrated in Figure 6-1: they descend through the corona radiata and the genu of the internal capsule; they pass through the midbrain in the cerebral peduncles and then synapse either with the lower motor neuron directly or indirectly through internuncial neurons, a chain of neurons situated between the primary afferent neuron and the final motor neuron.

The majority of the corticobulbar fibers to the motor cranial nerve nuclei cross the midline, or decussate, before reaching the nuclei. There is *bilateral innervation* for all the cranial nerve motor nuclei except for portions of the trigeminal, facial, and hypoglossal fibers. These will be discussed later.

Whereas the motor parts of the cranial nerves are formed by axons of nerve cells within the brain, the sensory or afferent parts of the cranial nerves are formed by axons of nerve cells outside the brain. They are situated on the nerve trunks or actually in the sensory organ itself—for example, in the nose, ear, or eye. The central processes of these cells enter the brain and terminate by synapsing with cells that are grouped together to form the *nuclei of termination*. These cells have axons that cross the midline and ascend and synapse on other sensory nuclei, such as the thalamus. The axons of the resulting cells then terminate in the cerebral cortex.

The Cranial Nerves for Smell and Vision

Cranial nerve I, the *olfactory nerve*, is actually a plexus of thin fibers that unite in about twenty small bundles called *fila olfactoria*. The olfactory receptors are situated in the mucous membrane of the nasal cavity. The nerve fibers synapse with other cells in the olfactory bulb and finally end in the olfactory areas of the cerebral cortex, the periamygdaloid and prepiriform areas. These are known as the primary olfactory cortex and they also send fibers to many other centers within the brain to establish connections for automatic and emotional responses to olfactory stimulation.

Cranial nerves II, III, IV, and VI are concerned with vision. The *optic nerve* (II) is the primary nerve of sight. Its nerve fibers are axons that come from the retina, converge on the optic disc, and exit from the eye on both sides. The right nerve joins the left to form the optic chiasma. In the optic chiasma, fibers from the nasal half of the eye cross the midline, and fibers from the temporal half continue to run ipsilaterally. Most of the fibers then synapse with nerve cells in the lateral geniculate body (of the thalamus) and leave it, forming the optic radiation. The optic radiations formed by these fibers then terminate in the visual cortex and the visual association cortex.

Cranial nerve III is the *oculomotor nerve*, the nucleus of which is located at the level of the superior colliculus. It has a somatomotor component that innervates the extraocular muscles to move the eyeball and a visceral component responsible for pupil constriction. Dysfunction of the third cranial nerve causes *ptosis* (drooping) of the eyelid. The eye may also be in abduction and turned down. If the visceral component is impaired, there is loss of the pupillary reflex, and dilation of the pupil

Cranial nerve IV is the *trochlear nerve*, the nucleus of which is at the level of the inferior colliculus. This innervates the superior oblique muscle. Confirmed lesions cause *diplopia* (double vision).

Cranial nerve VI, the *abducens*, has its nucleus located in the floor of the fourth ventricle. Dysfunction prevents lateral movements of the eyeball.

The remaining seven cranial nerves are vital for the production of normal speech and thus will be given more attention than those for smell and vision. The next part of this chapter is intended to lead you through the pathway, structures innervated, functional purpose, signs of dysfunction, and testing procedure for each of these cranial nerves. Digest them one by one. Test them on yourself and then on others until you are firmly acquainted with each cranial nerve. Refer to Figure 2-10 for attachment sites of the cranial nerves to the brainstem.

The Cranial Nerves for Speech and Hearing

Cranial Nerve V—Trigeminal

Anatomy
Both the motor and sensory root of the trigeminal nerve are attached to the lateral edges of the pons. The motor nuclei are restricted to the pons, but the sensory nuclei extend from the mesencephalon to the spinal cord.

Innervation

The motor part of the trigeminal innervates the following muscles: masseter, temporalis, lateral and medial pterygoids, tensor tympani, tensor veli palatini, mylohyoid, and the anterior belly of the digastric muscle.

The sensory fibers have three main branches:

1. The *ophthalmic nerve*, which is sensory to the forehead, eyes, and nose
2. The *maxillary nerve*, which is sensory to the upper lip mucosa, the maxilla and upper teeth, cheeks, palate, and maxillary sinus
3. The *mandibular nerve*, sensory to the tongue, mandible and lower teeth, lower lip, part of the cheek, and part of the external ear

Function

Cranial nerve V is primarily responsible for mastication and for sensation to the face. Innervating the tensor velar palatini, it is partially responsible for flattening and tensing of the soft palate and for opening of the eustachian tube.

Testing

You will be interested in testing the muscles of mastication or chewing and usually will not be testing sensation to the face.

The jaw closing and grinding lateral movement of chewing are the result of the function of the masseter, temporal, medial pterygoid, and lateral pterygoid muscles. The first three contribute to closure of the jaw, but only the masseter can be tested directly. In order to evaluate the *masseter*, palpate the area of the muscle (2 cm above and in front of the angle of the mandible) as the patient bites down as hard as possible and then relaxes. As he bites you should feel the bulk of the muscle rise. Try this on yourself and many others to get the feel of it. The muscle body should feel very firm and bulky. The temporal muscle cannot be well palpated; but if it is atrophied (shrunken) from a lower motor neuron lesion, the temple of the face will be sunken.

You must also evaluate the strength of jaw closure. To do so, place your hand on the tip of the patient's mandible as the jaw is held open. Place the other hand on her forehead to prevent neck extension. Ask her to bite down hard against the resistance of your hand. She should be able to close the jaw against a moderate resistance.

The *lateral pterygoids* enable the jaw to lateralize in chewing. To evaluate, ask the patient to open the jaw against resistance of your hand and note how the tip of the mandible lines up with the space between the upper medial incisors. Ask him to move the jaw from side to side and observe the facility of movement. Finally, ask that he lateralize the jaw against resistance. Have him move the jaw to one side and hold it while you try to push it toward the center. Place your other hand against the opposite cheekbone so that he cannot use the neck to help.

The patient with a unilateral paralysis of cranial nerve V will show a deviation of the jaw to the side of the lesion and an inability to force the jaw to the side opposite the lesion. Atrophy will also be noted after a period of time. These problems result from lower motor neuron lesions. Upper motor neuron lesions that are unilateral do not affect cranial nerves as much, because the nuclei receive so many axons from the other hemisphere. Therefore, the paresis is usually transitory or mild unless there are bilateral UMN lesions.

In bilateral upper motor neuron lesions, there will be an observable limitation of jaw movements. Opening and closing movements of the jaw, though possible, are restricted. Gross chewing movements are seen, but chewing and biting may lack vigor and are performed slowly.

Neurologists frequently test the *jaw* or *masseter reflex* as they are assessing cranial nerve V, since the reflex is mediated by the trigeminal nerve at the level of the pons. To elicit the reflex, the patient is asked to relax the jaw and allow it to remain about half open. The examiner rests his or her forefinger across the chin, pressing firmly downward on the chin. The examiner then strikes the forefinger a gentle blow with a percussion hammer. The examiner's striking of his or her own forefinger cushions the blow, but still elicits a response (Figure 7-1).

FIGURE 7-1   Elicitation of the jaw reflex (jaw jerk). An abnormally exaggerated reflex suggests a possible upper motor neuron lesion at the level of the pons or above.

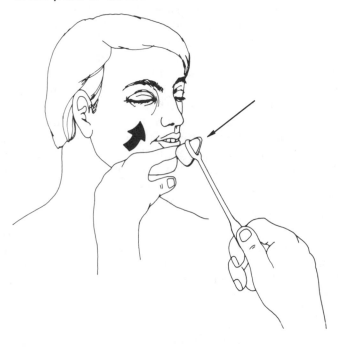

The normal response is a bilateral contraction of the temporal and masseter muscles and a sudden mandibular elevation. Experience is needed to determine whether the jaw reflex is exaggerated or depressed. Often it is difficult to elicit in an adult. In this case, if it is observed without reinforcement, it is often exaggerated beyond the normal level of activity. The reflex can be enhanced by having the subject set the muscles of the jaw to some degree. Often the jaw reflex is exaggerated enough to elicit a *clonus* of the jaw in adults with corticobulbar or supranuclear (above the level of the cranial nerve nuclei) lesions. Frequently, a clonic reaction is also seen in normal newborns and infants. In newborns the reflex may be elicited without the blow of a percussion hammer. The examiner need only strike the forefinger placed across the chin with his or her other forefinger in the small infant to see the response.

Presence of an abnormal reflex response in a child or an adult is usually strong evidence of a supranuclear lesion of the brain. With spastic hemiplegia or quadriplegia, an abnormal reflex may be important in placing the lesion above the level of the magnum foramen and eliminating a spinal cord lesion. Usually, very rapidly closing jaws indicate an exaggerated reflex, but sluggish jaw movement may also point to supranuclear involvement. The speech-language pathologist must be careful in using information derived from the testing of this reflex, since elicitation and interpretation of this reflex are difficult. In experienced hands, however, the reflex yields pertinent information about the corticobulbar fibers innervating the jaw muscles.

Cranial Nerve VII—Facial

Anatomy

The facial nerve is a complex nerve made up of three nuclei: the main motor nucleus, the parasympathetic nuclei, and the nucleus of the tractus solitarius. All lie within the pons near the reticular formation.

The taste fibers of the facial nerve have their primary sensory neurons in the geniculate ganglion. These fibers enter the brainstem in the sensory root of the facial nerve, called the *nervus intermedius*. They run in a bundle, or fasciculus, called the *tractus solitarius*, and are joined in that bundle by the taste fibers from cranial nerves IX and X. These taste fibers then terminate in the nucleus of the tractus solitarius.

The taste fibers will split off from the facial nerve in the middle ear as the *chorda tympani*. This joins the lingual branch of cranial nerve V. The fibers are distributed to the taste buds of the anterior two-thirds of the tongue. Some fibers also terminate in the taste buds in the hard and soft palate. Ascending fibers from the nucleus solitarius run to the ventroposterior thalamus and then project to the cortical area for taste located at the lower end of the sensory strip in the parietal lobe.

The fibers of the motor nucleus of the facial nerve extend to the floor of the ventricle and curve around the nucleus of the abducens (cranial nerve VI) and exit the brainstem near the inferior margin of the pons. These fibers then join those from the nucleus of the tractus solitarius and the parasympathetic nuclei and enter the internal auditory meatus as they extend through the facial canal of the petrosal bone. They will leave the skull through the stylomastoid foramen. While coursing through the facial canal, the facial nerve travels through the tympanic cavity, innervating the stapedius muscle. Therefore, the facial nerve can be involved in pathologies related to the ear. Surgeons removing acoustic tumors must be mindful of the location of the facial nerve.

The part of the nucleus that innervates the lower part of the face receives most of the corticobulbar fibers from the opposite hemisphere; thus innervation to these structures is primarily contralateral. The part that supplies the upper part of the face receives fibers from both cerebral hemispheres (receives crossed and uncrossed fibers), and innervation is *bilateral*.

Innervation

The parasympathetic nuclei are also known as the *superior salivatory* and the *lacrimal* nuclei. The superior salivatory nucleus receives afferent information from the hypothalamus and olfactory system, as well as taste information from the mouth cavity. It supplies the submandibular sublingual salivary glands and the nasal and palatine glands.

The lacrimal nucleus solitarius receives information from afferent fibers from the trigeminal sensory nuclei for reflex response to corneal irritation. The sensory nucleus receives information concerning taste from fibers from the anterior two-thirds of the tongue, the floor of the mouth, and the soft and hard palates.

The motor nucleus gives the face expression by innervation of the various facial muscles: the orbicularis oculi, zygomatic, buccinator, orbicularis oris, and labial muscles. Other muscles innervated are the platysma, stylohyoid, stapedius, and a portion of the digastric.

Function

The facial nerve is responsible for all movements of facial expression. All facial apertures are "guarded" by muscles innervated by the facial nerve: the eyes, the nose, the mouth, and the external auditory canal. This nerve enables you to (1) wrinkle your forehead, (2) close your eyes tightly, (3) close your mouth tightly, (4) pull back the corners of your mouth and tense your cheeks, and (5) pull down the corner of your mouth and tense your anterior neck muscles. It guards the middle ear as well by innervating the stapedius muscle, which acts to dampen excessive movement of the ossicles in the presence of a loud noise. Finally, the facial nerve partly is responsible for taste.

Testing

Tests of facial expression are the primary tests for cranial nerve VII. Before you begin any motor testing, however, *look closely* at your patient's face at rest and note the symmetry. Then begin testing at the upper part of the face.

1. Ask the patient to wrinkle the forehead and look up at the ceiling. Note the symmetry of the wrinkling on both sides. Keep in mind that this ability or inability is very diagnostic for localization. Since the upper part of the face is innervated bilaterally, only a lower motor neuron lesion would cause complete paralysis of this function. An upper motor neuron lesion causes some weakness on the opposite side, but it will not be nearly as perceptible as a result of the ipsilateral fiber innervation.

2. Next, ask the patient to close the eyes as tight as possible. Note the contraction of the orbicularis oculi and the consequent wrinkling around the eyes. The bilateral innervation also is present in this part of the face, though not to the degree that the forehead displays. The lower motor neuron–upper motor neuron difference still holds true for dysfunction of this part of the face.

3. Finally, take a close look at mouth movements. First ask the patient to smile or pull back the corners of the lips. It helps to tell him or her to show the teeth when doing this, as this exaggerates the smile somewhat. Again, observe the symmetry of the two sides. Then ask the patient to pucker the lips and observe the symmetry of constriction. Last, ask him or her to pull down the corners of the lips, (as in pouting) or to try to wrinkle the skin of the neck. Inspect for symmetry.

The patient with a lower motor neuron lesion of cranial nerve VII will have involvement of the entire side of the face on the side of the lesion (ipsilateral). See Figure 7-2 for an example of a unilateral facial paralysis. Though speech may be distorted, it is usually not significantly hindered by peripheral involvement of cranial nerve VII. The patient with an upper motor neuron lesion will show complete involvement of the lips and neck muscles, some degree of involvement of the area around the eyes, and little difficulty with the forehead or frontalis muscle. It should be noted that the paralysis is on voluntary movement. The patient may be seen to have almost normal movement for emotionally initiated movements such as a true smile, but will be unable to lateralize the lips when asked to do so voluntarily.

Since the facial nerve innervates the stapedius muscle, it may be paralyzed by a lesion. If this occurs, the patient may report that ordinary sounds seem uncomfortably loud.

Cranial Nerve VIII—Vestibular Acoustic or Vestibulocochlear

The following explanation assumes that you have completed a study of the anatomy of the ear and are well versed in the structure and function of the cochlea and semicircular canals. It is imperative that you have a good working knowledge of the anatomy of the ear.

Anatomy

As you may ascertain from its name, the vestibulocochlear nerve consists of two distinct parts: the *vestibular nerve* and the *cochlear* or *acoustic nerve*. Both take

FIGURE 7-2   An illustration of a patient with a right lower motor neuron facial paralysis implicating involvement of the right VII nerve. Note lack of contraction of orbicularis oculi indicated by lack of wrinkles around the eye. She lacks forehead wrinkles and has a flattened nasolabial fold on the right. The mouth droops on the right.

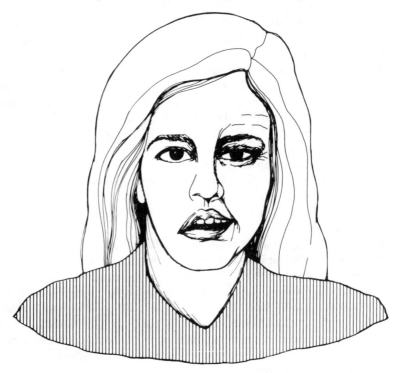

afferent information from the internal ear to the nervous system; but, as their names imply, they carry different types of information.

The vestibular nerve consists of nerve cells and their fibers that are in the vestibular ganglion located in the internal acoustic meatus. The fibers enter the brainstem in a groove between the lower border of the pons and the upper medulla oblongata. They then enter the vestibular nuclear complex, which consists of a group of nuclei located under the fourth ventricle. The four primary nuclei of this group are: (1) the lateral vestibular, (2) the superior vestibular, (3) the medial vestibular, and (4) the inferior vestibular nuclei.

The cochlear nerve consists of nerve cells and fibers located in the *spiral ganglion* of the cochlea. These fibers enter the brainstem at the lower border of the pons on the lateral side of the facial nerve. They are separated from the facial nerve fibers by the vestibular nerve. When the cochlear fibers enter the pons, they divide into two branches. One branch enters the *posterior cochlear nucleus,* and the other enters the *anterior cochlear nucleus.* Both nuclei are situated adjacent to the inferior cerebral peduncle. These nuclei send axons to the *trapezoid body* and are relayed to the posterior nucleus of the trapezoid body on the same or the opposite side. Some fibers also synapse in the *inferior colliculus* and the reticular formation. The axons then form a tract called the *lateral lemniscus* as they ascend through the posterior portion of the pons and midbrain. In the midbrain they will either terminate in the nucleus of the *inferior colliculus* or, by relays through the *medial geniculate body,* terminate in the auditory cortex of the cerebrum through the acoustic radiation of the internal capsule.

Innervation

Both portions of the vestibulocochlear nerve are primarily sensory in nature. The vestibular nerve receives afferent information from the utricle, saccule, and semicircular canal of the inner ear. It also receives afferent fibers from the cerebellum. The vestibular nerve also sends out efferent fibers that pass to the cerebellum through the inferior cerebral peduncles and also to the spinal cord, forming the vestibulospinal tract. In addition to these, efferent fibers are sent to the nuclei of cranial nerves III (oculomotor), IV (trochlear), and VI (abducens) through the medial longitudinal fasciculus. As outlined earlier, the cochlear nerve carries afferent fibers from the cochlea to the inferior colliculus and the auditory cortex. All acoustic nuclei also have efferent fibers that arise within the nucleus and synapse on the next underlying nucleus.

Function

Cranial nerve VIII takes afferent information from the internal ear to the nervous system. It is responsible for sound sensitivity. It also innervates the utricle and the saccule of the inner ear, which are the structures that are sensitive to static changes in equilibrium. In addition, innervation of the semicircular canals takes place through this nerve and controls sensitivity to dynamic changes in equilibrium.

Testing

Although the speech-language pathologist may do hearing threshold screening or testing that may give information about the cochlear nerve, it is the audiologist who is usually responsible for thorough assessment of hearing and cochlear function. Neurologists often perform simple tuning fork tests for acuity and sound lateralization, or they may prefer to use whispered words.

The vestibular function also is not in the parameter of testing of the speech-language pathologist. It is usually investigated with *caloric* tests that involve raising or lowering of the temperature of the internal auditory meatus, thereby inducing current in the semicircular canals and stimulating the vestibular nerve for testing. Neurologists also use maneuvers of changing head position.

The patient complaining of reduced hearing acuity, *tinnitus* (ringing in the ears), or dizziness should always be seen by an otologist and receive an audiological evaluation as well. The dizzy patient may be referred to a neurologist, who will usually also refer for audiological testing.

Cranial Nerve IX—Glossopharyngeal

Anatomy
The three nuclei of the glossopharyngeal nerve are located in the medulla. They are: (1) the nucleus ambiguus, (2) the inferior salivary nucleus, (3) the nucleus of the tractus solitarius.

Innervation
The *nucleus ambiguus* receives corticobulbar fibers from both hemispheres and is the efferent innervation to the stylopharyngeus muscle, which contributes toward the elevation of the palate and larynx. The *inferior salivary nucleus* receives afferent information from the hypothalamus, from the olfactory system, and from the mouth cavity concerning taste. Efferent fibers supply the otic ganglion of the ear and the parotid salivary gland. The *nucleus of the tractus solitarius* receives taste information. The efferent fibers decussate and travel upward to the opposite thalamic and some hypothalamic nuclei. From here the axons pass through the internal capsule and end in the lower postcentral gyrus.

Function
Cranial nerve IX is exclusive to one muscle only—the *stylopharyngeus*. Motor fibers also contribute to the function of the middle pharyngeal constrictor. Secretomotor fibers are also provided for the parotid gland. Sensory fibers carry taste information to the posterior one-third of the tongue. Thus the glossopharyngeal nerve is important to the act of swallowing because of its participation in elevating the palate and larynx and constricting the pharynx. It does not innervate an isolated function and must be tested with cranial nerve X.

Cranial Nerve X—Vagus

Anatomy
Like the glossopharyngeal nerve, the vagus also has three nuclei: (1) the *nucleus ambiguus*, (2) the *dorsal nucleus*, and (3) the *nucleus of the tractus solitarius*. These are also located in the medulla. The nucleus ambiguus has a pharyngeal and a laryngeal branch. The laryngeal branch gives rise to the recurrent laryngeal nerve, which arises considerably below the larynx and ascends to terminate at the larynx. The right recurrent nerve runs in a loop behind the common carotid and subclavian arteries. The left recurrent nerve leaves the vagus at a lower level and loops under and behind the aortic arch. It ascends to the larynx in a groove between the trachea and esophagus and enters through the cricothyroid membrane.

Innervation

The nucleus ambiguus receives an approximately equal number of corticobulbar fibers from both hemispheres that are efferent to the constrictor muscles of the pharynx and the intrinsic muscles of the larynx. The efferent fibers of the dorsal or parasympathetic nucleus innervate the involuntary muscles of the bronchi, esophagus, heart, stomach, small intestine, and a portion of the large intestine. The efferent fibers of the nucleus of the tractus solitarius follow much the same path as those of the glossopharyngeal nerve and terminate in the postcentral gyrus.

Function

Vagus means "wanderer," and one can understand this name when considering the many functions of the nerve. It is motor to the viscera (the heart, the respiratory system, and most of the digestive system). Along with the trigeminal nerve and with some aid from the glossopharyngeal nerve, it innervates the palatal muscles. With the glossopharyngeal nerve it supplies the pharyngeal constrictors. On its own, it innervates the intrinsic muscles of the larynx primarily through the recurrent laryngeal branch. The cricothyroid, however, is innervated by the superior laryngeal branch.

Testing

Remember that you are testing cranial nerves IX and X if you are evaluating palatal and swallowing function. Laryngeal function is covered solely by cranial nerve X.

Palatal function is tested by first observing the palate at rest as the patient opens the mouth to allow your view. Look at the palatal arches and observe their symmetry. Note if one arch hangs lower than the other. Next ask the patient to phonate an "ah" while you observe. The soft palate should elevate and move posteriorly and should do so symmetrically. If the palate does not elevate, the gag reflex, innervated primarily by cranial nerve IX, should be tested by touching the tongue blade against the palatal arches. The gag is a reflex activity, and it is preserved in an upper motor neuron lesion since the reflex arc is still intact. As in all reflexes, it may be lost acutely after an upper motor neuron lesion; then it may become hyperactive. If both volitional and reflex activity of the palate are involved, a lower motor neuron lesion is evidenced. Please bear in mind that palatal elevation is also reduced by a cleft palate, congenital oral malformations, and soft tissue palatal lesions. Do not overlook these vital facts in searching vigorously for an upper or lower motor neuron lesion.

Laryngeal function evaluation is adequately completed only by a direct or indirect laryngoscopy in which the vocal cords can be seen. Damage to the vagus nerve may cause paralysis of the vocal cord. There is bilateral innervation to the larynx, with the crossed and uncrossed fibers being approximately equal.

Therefore, a complete paralysis of a vocal cord from an upper motor neuron lesion is rare.

Preliminary assessment of laryngeal function is done through voice evaluation procedures. The patient is asked to phonate and prolong a vowel such as /a/. Maximum phonation time for normal adults is about 15 seconds, indicating relatively normal laryngeal and respiratory control. Perceptual analysis of the voice is done by the clinician during this phonation and during conversation. The patient may be asked to demonstrate laryngeal function and control by raising and lowering the pitch of a prolonged vowel or singing up and down the scale. Stress testing of the mechanism is done by asking the patient to count to 300 or to keep talking for a prescribed length of time. More sophisticated analyses of the voice may be done employing equipment for acoustical analysis.

In spastic dysarthria cases from UMN lesion, one will hear a harshness upon phonation, sounding somewhat like so-called "glottal fry". In bilateral upper motor neuron lesions (pseudobulbar palsy) there is a characteristic voice quality characterized by what Darley, Aronson, and Brown (1975) describe as "strain-strangle." This voice is harsh, with a very strained, tense quality as if the person is fighting to push the air flow through the larynx and supralaryngeal areas.

A lower motor neuron lesion will cause complete paralysis of the ipsilateral vocal cord. This will result in a hoarse, breathy voice. In some lower motor neuron diseases, the voice will initially be strong; but after the patient talks awhile, it becomes progressively weaker in intensity and more breathy. Transient hoarseness results sometimes from direct damage to the recurrent laryngeal nerve during carotid artery or thyroid surgery.

Cranial Nerve XI—Spinal Accessory

Anatomy
The accessory nerve consists of a cranial and a spinal root. The nucleus of the cranial root is found in the nucleus ambiguus of the medulla. It receives corticobulbar fibers from both cerebral hemispheres. These fibers then join the glossopharyngeal nerve, the vagus nerve, and the spinal accessory nerve.

The spinal root's nucleus is located in the spinal nucleus of the anterior gray column of the spinal cord. The fibers pass through the lateral white column and eventually form a nerve trunk passing through the foramen magnum. It then joins the cranial root as they pass through the foramen. The spinal root separates from the cranial root, however, to find its way to the sternocleidomastoid and trapezius muscles.

Innervation
The cranial root joins the vagus to innervate the uvula and the levator palatini. As mentioned earlier, the spinal root innervates the sternocleidomastoid and trapezius muscles.

Function

The accessory nerve's primary function is as motor to the muscles that help turn, tilt, and thrust forward the head or raise the sternum and clavicle if the head is in a fixed position (sternocleidomastoid) and to the muscle responsible for shrugging the shoulder (trapezius).

Testing

When testing cranial nerve XI, we test the *spinal* part. The *accessory* part is accessory to the vagus and cannot be tested alone.

Initially, look at the size and symmetry of the sternocleidomastoids and palpate them. Do this on yourself and others to get an idea of normal muscle size and firmness. Ask the patient to turn her head to one side and hold it there while you try to push it back to the middle. Put one hand on her cheek and the other on her shoulder to brace her. Gently push against her cheek and observe and palpate the sternocleidomastoid on the opposite side of the neck.

Next have the patient try to thrust her head forward while you are resisting the movement with your hand against her forehead. Again, observe and palpate the sternocleidomastoid.

Finally, ask the patient to shrug her shoulders while you are pressing down on the shoulders. You should feel the shoulders elevate against your gentle resistance.

Cranial Nerve XII—Hypoglossal

Anatomy

The *hypoglossal* nerve runs under the tongue and controls all tongue movements. The nucleus is located in the medulla beneath the lower part of the fourth ventricle. It receives fibers from both cerebral hemispheres, with one exception. The cells serving the genioglossus muscle receive only contralateral fibers. The nerve fibers pass through the medulla and emerge in the groove between the pyramid and the olive.

Innervation

The hypoglossal nerve innervates all the intrinsic muscles of the tongue. It also innervates three extrinsic muscles: genioglossus, hypoglossus, and styloglossus.

Function

The hypoglossal nerve innervates the muscles that are responsible for all tongue movement. The four intrinsic muscles of the tongue control the shortening, concaving (turning the tip and lateral margins upward), narrowing, elongating, and flattening of the tongue. The extrinsic muscles innervated account for tongue protrusion (genioglossus), drawing the tongue upward and backward (styloglossus), and retraction and depression of the tongue (hypoglossus). The hypoglossus also acts with the chondroglossus to elevate the hyoid bone, thus participating in phonation also.

Testing

Initially, ask the patient to open the mouth and let you look at the tongue at rest. Inspect it for signs of atrophy. With a unilateral LMN lesion, one side of the tongue will begin to look shrunken or atrophied. This would occur on the same side as the LMN lesion. With a LMN lesion there may also be fasciculations or fibrillations, seen as tiny ripplings under the surface of the tongue. Actually, authorities often disagree whether these movements in the denervated tongue are fasciculations or fibrillations.

Normal tongues may also show some rippling when they are not completely relaxed. Therefore, if you think you see the fasciculations, ask the patient to move the tongue around and then relax it and again observe the surface for fasciculation. Even in a normal tongue, however, you may continue to see the rippling. Therefore, as DeMyer (1980) points out, the clinician does better to rely on atrophy and weakness for signs of LMN damage. You should also observe the tongue for tremor or random movements at rest.

Next, ask the patient to protrude the tongue, and evaluate the symmetry of this posture. The tongue tip should be at midline. If the patient has weak lip musculature on one side, that side may be lower and cause the tongue to look as if it deviates to that side. Therefore, visually try to align the tip of the tongue with the midline of the jaw. You may also pull that side of the lip back so that it is symmetrical with the other side of the lip and then ask the patient to protrude the tongue. If the cranial nerve is dysfunctional, the genioglossus will not be able to push its side out; the stronger side will overcome the weaker and the tongue will deviate to the weaker side (Figure 7-3). In LMN damage this is the same side as the lesion. In UMN damage, because of the contralateral control, the tongue deviates to the side opposite to the side of the lesion. For example, in many of the cerebrovascular accident (CVA) patients seen for evaluation who have left hemisphere damage to the area of motor strip, the tongue will show a characteristic deviation to the right upon protrusion. This is usually less marked than in LMN tongue weakness.

The patient who has bilateral twelfth nerve damage will have weakness on both sides and will be unable to protrude the tongue beyond the lips. The clinician should try to assess the muscle tone of the tongue by moving the passive tongue with a tongue blade through the range of lateralization and elevation. LMN lesions will result in decreased tone or flaccidity. UMN lesions result in increased tone or spasticity. Again, you must practice on many normals to be familiar with appropriate tonicity of the tongue musculature.

Strength of tongue protrusion may be tested by asking the patient to push against a tongue blade held immediately in front of the lips. You must try all these tests for strength and rate of movement on yourself and your friends in order to familiarize yourself with the normal range of strength.

FIGURE 7-3   Unilateral paresis of the tongue. In the illustration on the left, the resting tongue shows a smaller weak side (atrophy) with a corrugated surface suggesting fasciculations and the effects of atrophy. These tongue signs suggest denervation. In the illustration on the right, the protruded tongue deviates to the weak side. In a lower motor neuron lesion, the deviated tongue points to the side of the lesion.

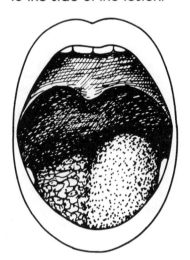 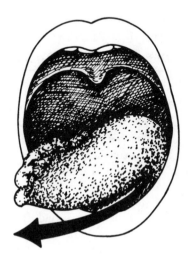

Other movements of the tongue must be evaluated for precisely documenting range, rate, and strength of the tongue for follow-up in treatment and for diagnostic purposes. Next, ask the patient to lateralize the tongue—that is, move it from one corner of the mouth to the other. The tongue should move the full range from one corner to another. Evaluate the strength of lateral movement by asking the client to push the tongue against the inside of the cheek against your fingers placed for resistance on the outside of the cheek ("Make a ball in your cheek with your tongue"). You may also put a tongue blade along the side of the tongue and have the person push against a light resistance. Ability to elevate the tongue can be evaluated by having the person open the mouth to a moderate degree and then hold the mandible down with your finger on it. Ask the client to try to touch the top lip and also the alveolar ridge with the tongue. This should be done with full range of movement and little effort.

Strength of elevation of the tip, blade, or back of tongue is difficult to assess with tongue blade resistance. Your ear is the better assessor of strength of elevation. The tip of the tongue should be able to make firm contact to produce the /t/, /d/, /tʃ/, (as in *ch*um), and /dʒ/ (as in *j*udge) and to elevate fully

for the /l/ and /n/. The blade of the tongue should elevate well to produce a
distinct /i/ (*e* as in *eat*) and /j/ (y as in *young*). Elevation of the back of the tongue
is necessary for production of the velar consonants /k/ and /g/. Careful examination of the production of these consonants and vowels as well as others, in
isolation and in context, will provide the most information regarding tongue
elevation and strength.

Cranial Nerve Cooperation:
The Act of Swallowing

The act of swallowing is highly complex and needs to be studied independently
with respect to its cranial nerve innervation (Figure 7-4). Logemann (1984)
describes normal deglutition as consisting of three phases: (1) the oral phase,
(2) the pharyngeal phase, and (3) the esophageal phase. The oral stage begins
when the lips seal and the back of the tongue begins moving the bolus posteriorly. The tongue forms a central groove that acts as a ramp or chute for the
food. The oral stage is considered the voluntary part of swallowing and typically
takes less than one second. The pharyngeal phase, which also takes one second
or less, begins with the triggering of the swallow response or pharyngeal response at the anterior faucial pillars. The triggering of the swallow causes several
physiological activities to occur in the pharynx simultaneously: velopharyngeal
closure; laryngeal elevation; closure of all sphincters (the epiglottis, false vocal
folds, and true vocal folds); initiation of pharyngeal peristalsis (squeezing); and
relaxation of the cricopharyngeal sphincter to allow material to pass from pharynx to esophagus. If the swallow is not triggered, this response does not occur
and none of these activities take place. The bolus then may be pushed into the
pharynx and come to rest in the valleculae or pyriform sinuses and spill over
into the open airway. Finally, in normal swallowing, the esophageal phase occurs
as the bolus enters the esophagus through the cricopharyngeus and is passed
through into the stomach. Normal transit time is 8–20 seconds.

The trigeminal nerve (V) plays an important part in swallowing because
of the efferent control of the muscles of mastication and the afferent control for
general sensation to the anterior two-thirds of the tongue. Cranial nerve VII,
the facial nerve, controls taste for the anterior two-thirds of the tongue and
controls the lip sphincter for eating. The hypoglossal nerve (XII) controls tongue
movement and may make some contribution to the afferent portion of the
swallow response. The primary efferent and afferent controls for swallowing rest
in cranial nerves IX and X. The glossopharyngeal nerve (IX) is afferent to the
posterior one-third of the tongue, the mucosa of the vallecula, the pharynx, and
the soft palate. It is motor to the pharyngeal constrictors and the stylopharyngeus. The swallow response is thought to be a function of subcortical pattern

FIGURE 7-4 The neurology of swallowing

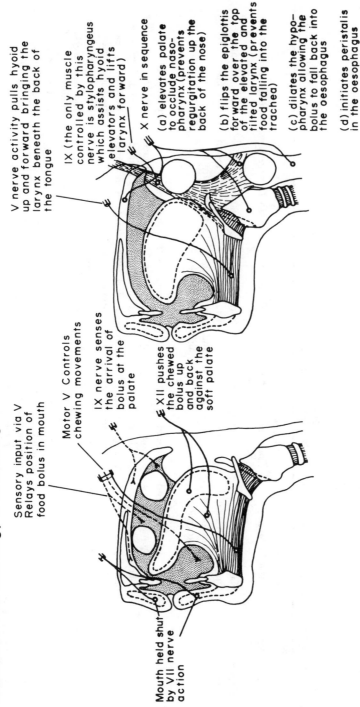

Sensory input via V
Relays position of
food bolus in mouth

Motor V Controls
chewing movements

IX nerve senses
the arrival of
bolus at the
palate

Mouth held shut
by VII nerve
action

XII pushes
the chewed
bolus up
and back
against the
soft palate

V nerve activity pulls hyoid
up and forward bringing the
larynx beneath the back of
the tongue

IX (the only muscle
controlled by this
nerve is stylopharyngeus
which assists hyoid
elevators and lifts
larynx forward)

X nerve in sequence

(a) elevates palate
to occlude naso-
pharynx (prevents
regurgitation up the
back of the nose)

(b) flips the epiglottis
forward over the top
of the elevated and
tilted larynx (prevents
food falling into the
trachea)

(c) dilates the hypo-
pharynx allowing the
bolus to fall back into
the oesophagus

(d) initiates peristalsis
in the oesophagus

Source: Redrawn and reproduced with permission from J. Patten, *Neurologic Differential Diagnosis* (London: H. Starke, Ltd., 1977).

TABLE 7-2
Summary of Cranial Nerve Function for the Oral Musculature

Cranial Nerve	Muscles Innervated	Movements and Sensation Innervated	Test Procedure	LMN Damage Signs	UMN Damage Signs
V: Trigeminal	Masseter, tensor tympani, tensor veli palatini, mylohyoid, digastric (anterior belly)	Jaw closing, lateral jaw movement	Palpation of masseter, closing and lateralization against resistance	Weakness, jaw deviation to lesion side, atrophy	Mild, transitory weakness
VII: Facial	Orbicularis oculi and oris, zygomatic, buccinator, platysma, stylohyoid, stapedius, portion of digastric, stapedius	Forehead wrinkling, closing eyes, closing mouth, smiling, tensing cheeks, pulling down corner of mouth, tensing anterior neck muscles, moving stapedius to dampen ossicles. Taste from anterior two-thirds of tongue and hard and soft palate.	Observation of facial symmetry at rest. Have patient wrinkle forehead, close eyes tightly, smile, pucker, pull down lip corners.	Involvement of entire side of face, weakness, limited range of movement	Complete involvement of lips and neck muscles, less of eye area muscles, little difficulty with forehead, weakness, limited range of movement of affected muscles

IX: Glossopharyngeal	Stylopharyngeus, otic ganglion, parotid salivary gland. Partial to middle pharyngeal constrictor	Elevation of pharynx and larynx. Contributes to pharyngeal constriction, saliva. Taste from posterior one-third of tongue.	Must be tested with X.		
X: Vagus	Inferior, middle, and superior pharyngeal constrictors, stylopharyngeus, salpingopharyngeal glossopalatine, pharyngopalatine, levator veli palatine, uvular, cricothyroid, thyroarytenoid, posterior and lateral cricoarytenoid, interarytenoid, transverse and oblique interarytenoids; and various muscles of the viscera, esophagus, and trachea	Palatal elevation and depression, laryngeal movement, pharyngeal constriction, cricopharyngeal function	Observation of palatal movement, gag reflex, laryngoscopy, evaluation of voice quality, ability to change pitch and phonation time, assessment of swallowing	Absence of gag reflex, poor volitional movement of palate, absent or delayed swallow reflex, aspiration, breathy hoarse voice (may be improved by pushing effort)	Poor palatal movement, harshness or strained-strangled voice quality, delayed or absent swallow reflex, aspiration

TABLE 7-2 (continued)

Cranial Nerve	Muscles Innervated	Movements and Sensation Innervated	Test Procedure	LMN Damage Signs	UMN Damage Signs
XII: Hypoglossal	Superior longitudinal, inferior longitudinal, transverse, vertical, genioglossus, hypoglossus, and styloglossus	All tongue movements as well as some participation in the elevation of the hyoid bone	Observation for atrophy or fasciculations, as well as symmetry on protrusion. Lateralization, protrusion, elevation, retraction to observe range of movement. Movement against resistance for strength testing on lateral, protrusion, and elevation movement, articulation testing	Atrophy, fasciculations, weakness, reduced range of movement, deviation of tongue to side of lesion, decreased tone, consonant imprecision	Weakness, reduced range of movement, deviation of tongue to contralateral side, increased tone, consonant imprecision

generators with the primary afferent being cranial nerve IX. The vagus nerve (X) is sensory to the pharynx, larynx, and viscera and is considered the secondary afferent of the swallow response. The vagus provides motor innervation for the palate, pharynx, and larynx as well as the esophagus.

Summary

The cranial nerves are vital for intact speech production, and the speech-language pathologist must be knowledgeable about their functions. There are twelve pairs of cranial nerves and six of them are directly related to speech production: cranial nerves V (trigeminal), VII (facial), VIII (acoustic-vestibular), IX (glossopharyngeal), X (vagus), and XII (hypoglossal) (see Table 7-2). This chapter refers to the embryologic origin of the cranial nerves, explaining which are somitic or branchial in origin and which are the solely special sensory nerves. The anatomy, innervation, function, and testing of each of the nerves associated with speech is then discussed. The cooperation of several cranial nerves in the act of swallowing is also detailed.

References and Further Readings

Barr, M. L., & Kiernan, J. A. (1983). *The human nervous system.* Philadelphia: Harper & Row.

Darley, F., Aronson, A., & Brown, J. (1975). *Motor speech disorders.* Philadelphia: Saunders.

DeMyer, W. (1980). *Technique of the neurologic examination: A programmed text.* 3rd ed. New York: McGraw-Hill.

Logemann, J. (1984). *Evaluation and treatment of swallowing disorders.* San Diego: College-Hill Press.

Snell, R. S. (1980) *Clinical neuroanatomy for medical students.* Boston: Little, Brown.

CHAPTER EIGHT

Clinical Speech Syndromes of the Motor Systems

"Speech is deranged in a variety of ways by disease of the brain. The process of articulation is immediately effected by a mechanism of nerve nuclei situated in the pons and medulla, but these are excited to action by centers in the cerebral cortex. Thus there are higher and lower mechanisms; the former is cerebral, the latter is bulbar."

—William R. Gowers, *A Manual of Disease of the Nervous System*, 1888

The Dysarthrias

As a speech-language pathologist you will need an understanding of the function of the cranial nerves and the rest of the motor and sensory system for the treatment of the motor speech disorder known as *dysarthria*. Darley, Aronson, and Brown (1969a) define dysarthria as the speech disorder resulting from paralysis, weakness, or incoordination of the speech musculature that is of neurologic origin. Their definition encompasses any symptoms of motor disturbance of respiration, phonation, resonance, articulation, and prosody.

Damage to the motor system responsible for speech production may occur at any point along the pathway from the cerebrum to the muscle itself. In their classic study of types of dysarthria resulting from certain sites of damage in the neural system, Darley, Aronson, and Brown (1969a, b) identified six different dysarthrias from neuroanatomical and acoustic-perceptual judgments of speech.

139

In this chapter we will describe the classic dysarthrias according to neuroanatomical site of dysfunction, associated disease processes, and the effects of these diseases on articulation, resonance, phonation, and prosody. The following is not an exhaustive discussion of the diseases or of the types of dysarthrias resulting from neurological disease. Keep in mind that any disease or trauma that affects the movement, coordination, and timing of the oral musculature may produce a dysarthria and it must be carefully described by the speech pathologist.

Upper Motor Neuron Lesions: Spastic Dysarthria

Recall that upper motor neuron damage results in a spastic paralysis and hyperactive reflexes. The dysarthria associated with upper motor neuron lesions is called *spastic dysarthria*.

Etiology

Upper motor neuron damage may result from cerebrovascular accident, head trauma, tumor, or infection. In this case the damage is to a portion of the corticobulbar or corticospinal tract. Unilateral corticospinal and corticobulbar tract damage may cause a condition known as spastic hemiplegia. Its effects on speech are either transient or mild. A more devastating effect is present with bilateral corticobulbar tract damage, known as *pseudobulbar palsy*. Usually there is involvement of speech, chewing, and swallowing.

Associated Neurologic Characteristics

As mentioned previously, the patient with upper motor neuron damage will show hypertonicity (spasticity) and hyperreflexia upon neurologic examination. Though there is increased tone, the muscles are weak, range of movement is limited, and rate of movement is slow.

The Oral Musculature

With unilateral damage, the face may show an asymmetry, with the nasolabial fold flattened and the side of the mouth opposite the side of lesion showing a droop or decreased range of movement on lateralization and protrusion of the lips. The tongue will deviate to the weak side—that is, the side opposite the site of lesion—and that side of the palatal arches may droop. Palatal movement usually is not greatly affected, and laryngeal function is often preserved. Articulation may vary in degree of impairment, but prognosis is usually good for intelligible speech within a brief period of time post onset.

In pseudobulbar palsy the oral musculature usually shows severe impairment of range and rate of movement. The tongue may extend only to the lips on protrusion. The lips are slow moving and excursion is limited. Palatal movement is severely reduced and very sluggish on phonation. The gag reflex may be absent in the acute stages, but later returns and may be hyperactive. Chewing and swallowing are both frequently affected, and there is drooling in most cases.

Speech Characteristics

The patient with *pseudobulbar palsy* demonstrates a classical spastic dysarthria. Speech characteristics are as follows.

Phonation
The voice of the patient with spastic dysarthria is described as harsh, and many have a characteristic *strained-strangled quality*. An effortful grunt is often heard at the end of vocalizations. Excessively low pitch is frequently found, with pitch breaks in some cases. Very little variation in loudness (monoloudness) and reduced stress are also noted. Occasionally heard in spastic dysarthrias is excess and equal stress (inappropriate stress on monosyllabic words and the usually unstressed syllables of polysyllabic words).

Resonance
Hypernasality is a frequent component of spastic dysarthria. Nasal emission is uncommon, however.

Articulation
As in most dysarthrias, imprecision of consonant production is a noticeable part of the speech disorder in spastic dysarthria. In some cases the musculature is so severely affected that vowels are also distorted. Slow rate of articulation is also frequently observed.

Lower Motor Neuron Lesions: Flaccid Dysarthria

Damage to the lower motor neuron system impairs the final common pathway for muscle contraction. The muscles become hypotonic or flaccid. Thus every type of movement is affected following this damage; that is, voluntary, automatic, and reflexive movement are all impaired, and a flaccid dysarthria may be seen.

Etiology

Any disease that affects a part of the motor unit—the cell body, its axon, the myoneural junction, or the muscle fibers themselves—may yield lower motor neuron symptoms. Thus viral infections, tumors, trauma to the nerve itself, or a brainstem stroke with involvement of the nerve fibers may be the etiology of the dysarthria. A disease known as *myasthenia gravis* (discussed in Chapter 4) results from impairment of transmission across the myoneural junction, or the synapse between the nerve and muscle. Bulbar palsy results from damage to the motor units of the cranial nerves. Mobius syndrome (congenital facial diplegia) involves bilateral sixth (abducens) and seventh (facial) nerve palsies of congenital origin. Mobius syndrome most commonly involves bilateral facial (VII) palsies and bilateral abducens (VI) palsies, not generalized bulbar palsy. Most such patients talk acceptably except for slurring. Direct muscle involvement is found in such diseases as muscular dystrophy, myotonia, and myositis.

Associated Neurologic Characteristics

Damage to the lower motor neuron system causes a flaccid paralysis. Reflexes are reduced; that is, there is hyporeflexia. The affected muscle usually becomes shrunken or *atrophied* over time. Many times the involved muscle, especially the tongue muscles, will be found to show fasciculations—tiny spontaneous muscle contractions of the motor unit or muscle fibers innervated by an axon. The fasciculations appear as spontaneous dimplings of the tongue. The tongue may look as if there are tiny moving worms just beneath its surface.

The Oral Musculature

Since the cranial nerve nuclei are dispersed throughout the brainstem rather than being clustered together, the oral structures may be selectively impaired and should be evaluated carefully.

Muscle tone in lower motor neuron damage is flaccid or hypotonic. Muscles are weak. The affected side of the lips will sag, and in some cases drooling may be present. In bilateral weakness the whole mouth may sag, and the lower lip may be so weak that there is habitual open mouth posture. The patient may have difficulty puckering the lips or pulling up the angles of the lips to smile.

Weakness of the mandibular muscles may not be readily evident in unilateral involvement. Careful observation will reveal that the jaw deviates to the side of weakness. With bilateral damage the jaw obviously sags. With damage to any component of the motor unit supplying the tongue, the muscles become atrophied and shrunken over time and the tongue is flabby. This tends to affect protrusion, lateralization, and elevation, particularly of the posterior portion of the tongue. Fasciculations are often observed after a period of time.

Palatal weakness or immobility may also be present, and there will be reduced or absent gag reflex. There may be pharyngeal involvement, causing swallowing difficulty and possibly nasal regurgitation of fluids.

Speech Characteristics

As a speech pathologist, you are most likely to be consulted concerning patients with a bulbar palsy as the etiology from vascular disease, head trauma, or diseases such as amyotrophic lateral sclerosis. These patients may exhibit a flaccid dysarthria and show some of the following characteristics upon speech testing.

Phonation
Unilateral vocal fold paralysis is relatively unusual with those disease processes affecting the brainstem nuclei. If there is unilateral damage, the quality of phonation will depend on the position of the vocal fold. If it is paralyzed in an adducted position, the voice will be harsh and loudness will be reduced. If it is in the abducted position, more breathiness is heard with reduced loudness.

More likely is bilateral vocal cord involvement. The characteristics of this are a breathy voice, inspiratory stridor (or audible inhalation), and abnormally short phrases. Monotony of pitch and also loudness are distinctive in many patients as well.

Resonance
Hypernasality is noted as an outstanding characteristic of the patients with flaccid dysarthria. Nasal emission of air is also found in a high percentage of patients.

Articulation
Imprecise consonant production may be present from mild to severe (unintelligible speech) degrees. The consonants requiring firm contact from tongue tip elevation are particularly vulnerable. *Plosives* such as /p/, /t/, and /k/, and *fricatives* such as /f/ and /s/ are frequently affected because of the lack of intraoral pressure from palatal dysfunction.

Speech Characteristics in Myasthenia Gravis

Myasthenia gravis is a neuromuscular disease resulting from a reduction of available acetylcholine (ACh) receptors at the neuromuscular junction. Usually changes in the eyes such as ptosis (drooping of the eyelid) or double vision occur. The muscles may be weak, with the jaw sagging accompanied by weak chewing. Swallowing difficulty, or *dysphagia*, is not uncommon, and myasthenia should be considered especially with a history of difficulty with swallowing that worsens in use and improves with rest (Logemann, 1983). There may also be respiratory as well as extremity weakness. The voice symptoms can exist without other signs of dysarthria. The flaccid dysphonia of myasthenia should be suspected when, despite normal laryngoscopic findings, the voice nevertheless becomes progressively more breathy and reduced in intensity as the client speaks.

Mixed Upper and Lower Motor Neuron Lesions

Amyotrophic Lateral Sclerosis

In clinical practice one is very likely to find that the lesion or disease process has not confined itself to one motor system but, rather, has affected both upper and lower motor neuron systems. The most frequently encountered example of this damage is the disease *amyotrophic lateral sclerosis* (also known commonly as Lou Gehrig's disease). Amyotrophic lateral sclerosis, or ALS, causes progressive degeneration of the neurons of the upper and lower motor neuron system and is of unknown etiology. Onset is typically in the fifth decade, although it may be earlier or later and initial symptoms are variable depending on which motor neurons are affected initially. If brainstem nuclei are the first to be affected, the initial signs may be a slurring of speech or a difficulty with swallowing. Often there is only a slight change in voice quality as the first sign. The bulbar or brainstem symptoms are particularly devastating, and verbal communication and oral feedings usually eventually become impossible. This type of ALS patient has a variable life expectancy but typically may survive only one to three years after onset. Pneumonia is frequently the cause of death. There is no known effective treatment or cure for ALS, although there are many pallitive treatments, including drugs for reduction of muscle pain, physical therapy, and speech therapy in some cases.

Associated Neurologic Characteristics

Signs may be present from damage to both upper and lower motor neuron systems. Muscles are weak but reflexes are hyperactive. Spasticity is usually present unless the lower motor neuron damage is well advanced.

The Oral Musculature

The oral peripheral examination will yield indications of a pervasive weakness in lips, tongue, and palate. Range of movement will be reduced and sometimes one side is slightly more affected than the other. The tongue may show fasciculations and, in more advanced cases, atrophy. The patient may report and demonstrate difficulty swallowing, especially liquids, and, with progression, difficulty with handling oral secretions.

Speech Characteristics

Again, we face the signs of involvement of both upper and lower motor neuron systems. It is unpredictable as to which signs will predominate in a given case and what changes may occur through the course of the disease.

The Mayo Clinic study (Darley, Aronson, & Brown, 1975) involved thirty patients with ALS. The characteristics of the speech of this group were as follows.

Phonation

Some patients showed symptoms similar to the pseudobulbar palsy patients with much harshness and strain-strangle quality associated with low pitch. Other patients were more like a predominantly bulbar group, with poor vocal fold adduction resulting in breathiness and short phrases. Audible inspiration was also noted. Monotony of pitch and loudness as well as reduction of stress were present in most patients.

Resonance

Hypernasality was frequent in these cases. Nasal emission, though noted, was not prominent.

Articulation

Imprecise consonant production was a principal characteristic. Vowels were often distorted along with consonant distortion. The slow rate and reduced range of movement of the articulators affected sound production greatly. Hypernasality also contributed to the phoneme distortion, and precision of articulation was often so poor as to render speech unintelligible.

Extrapyramidal Lesions: Dyskinetic Dysarthrias

The extrapyramidal system, as we have discussed, includes the basal ganglia and extrapyramidal pathways. The extrapyramidal system regulates the tone

ıd for changing position. It contributes to complex movements by
nd controlling the component parts of the movements and also
bit unplanned movement. Lesions produce dyskinetic movements
and may yıeld two types of dysarthria, *hypokinetic* dysarthria and *hyperkinetic*
dysarthria.

Hypokinetic Dysarthria: Parkinsonism

The most common disease associated with hypokinetic dysarthria is Parkinson's
disease. In this disorder there are degenerative changes in the substantia nigra
causing a deficiency in a chemical neural transmitter known as *dopamine* in the
caudate nucleus and putamen. Parkinson's disease is usually idiopathic (that is,
spontaneous, not caused by another disease), but parkinsonism (or parkinsonlike
symptoms) is caused by carbon monoxide poisoning, arteriosclerosis, man-
ganese poisoning, and some tranquilizing drugs (for example, Compazine, Ste-
lazine, and Haldol).

Associated Neurologic Characteristics

The major features of parkinsonism include one or more of the following characteristics (Capildeo, Haberman, & Rose, 1981). A tremor may be present at
rest that is absent during sleep and tends to subside during movement. It is
often called a *pill rolling tremor* because of the pattern of movement of the fingers,
as if rolling a small pill between the thumb and the fingers. Rigidity is a common
characteristic and is elicited by passive movement of the limb inducing involuntary contraction in the muscle being stretched. The rigidity may be smooth
or intermittent (referred to as *cogwheel rigidity*). *Bradykinesia*, also common in
parkinsonism, is defined as reduced speed of movement of a muscle through
its range. *Hypokinesia*, or reduced amplitude of movement, is a prime characteristic as well. Dementia is a correlate of Parkinson's disease, with an incidence
between 30 percent and 39 percent (Bayles, 1984). Language characteristics of
this dementia include impaired receptive vocabulary, difficulty in comprehending the meanings of ambiguous sentences, impaired ability to describe
objects verbally, and impaired ability to identify a speaker's intention.

Other features of parkinsonism are referred to as minor, but at least one
of these features should be present for the diagnosis to be made. These include
micrographia, or the tendency for handwriting to be very small in the height of
the letters and to get smaller as the person writes. Excessive salivation and a
dysphonia, described later, may be present. The parkinsonian facies is described
as a *masked facies*, with very little movement used in facial expression. The
parkinsonian posture is stooped and leaning slightly forward. There also may
be a characteristic gait, called a *festinating gait*. This involves short, slow, shuf-
fling steps.

Treatment for parkinsonism usually involves prescription of a drug that contains a chemical called L-dopa, such as Sinemet or Parlodel. Physical therapy and speech therapy are also often prescribed.

Oral Musculature
Frequently the standard oral exam will yield only slow rate of movement of the lips and tongue as the major finding, with some reduced range of movement. Palatal movement may be sluggish. Diadochokinetic rate testing may yield the most interesting information. When the patient is asked to execute the syllable repetition for the diadochokinetic testing, reduction of rate of movement becomes more evident. As repetition continues, constriction for consonant production may become less and less and syllables may seem to run together. Some patients may be using so little movement that there is no differentiation between syllables and more of a humming or whirring sound is heard.

Speech Characteristics
The speech of patients with Parkinson's disease varies tremendously depending on the stage of the disease and the effectiveness of medication. A study of the vocal tract characteristics of 200 Parkinson's patients helped to quantify and describe certain features in this disorder (Logemann, Fisher, Boshes, & Blonsky, 1978). Only 11 percent, or 22 of the patients, were found to have no vocal tract problems.

PHONATION   Laryngeal disorders were found to be present in 89 percent of the patients in the study. Hoarseness was the major perceived characteristic, occurring in 45 percent of the patients. Roughness, breathiness, and tremulousness also occurred. All the patients except one who had articulation problems also showed laryngeal dysfunction.

ARTICULATION   A detailed analysis of the articulatory errors of these 200 Parkinson's patients showed that changes in manner of articulation predominated over changes in place of articulation (Logemann & Fisher, 1981). Stop-plosives, affricates, and fricatives were most affected, as were the features of continuancy and stridency. Inadequate narrowing or constricting of the vocal tract as a result of inadequate tongue elevation appeared to be the reason for these changes. Netsell, Daniel, and Celesia (1975) have termed the result of this phenomena "articulatory undershoot."

RESONANCE   Ten percent of the patients in Logemann's study showed hypernasality. There was no regular pattern of co-occurrence of hypernasality with articulation or laryngeal disorders.

PROSODY   Twenty percent of the patients showed what the authors called a rate disorder. Compulsive repetition of syllables, known as *pallilalia*, occurred in 15 percent. Ten percent of the patients were judged as using syllables that were too short, whereas 6 percent used syllables that were too long. Abnormally long pauses occurred in 2 percent of those tested.

Weismer (1984) found that Parkinson patients had segmental and phrase-level durations that were slightly shorter than corresponding durations in age-matched controls. This may contribute to the often-cited perception that rate is much increased in the speech of Parkinson's patients.

In summary, these studies have revealed that the typical Parkinson's patient will be expected to have a voice-quality disorder and may likely have an articulation disorder as well. Hypernasality and speech rate are less likely to be symptoms of the dysarthria, according to these studies.

Hyperkinetic Dysarthrias

Whereas hypokinetic dysarthria and hypokinesia are related to reduction of movement from extrapyramidal system damage, hyperkinetic dysarthria is related to increase in movement. The involuntary movement disorders of tremor, chorea, athetosis, and dystonia are also a result of extrapyramidal damage. The specific localization of the damage in these disorders is not well understood.

Hyperkinetic Dysarthria: Pathologic Tremor and Voice Disorders

Tremor can be classified as either normal or abnormal—that is, pathologic—depending on whether or not it is associated with a disease state. Both normal and pathologic tremor may occur at rest, in static postures, or with movement.

In speech pathology, we most often encounter essential tremor (also called action, senile, or heredofamilial tremor). Essential tremor of the voice is known in speech pathology as *organic voice tremor*. In this condition the extrinsic and intrinsic muscles of the larynx may show tremor either independently or along with tremor of other parts of the body, such as the hands, jaw, or head.

Speech Characteristics
In a pure organic voice tremor, articulatory and resonance characteristics are normal, and only phonation is affected. On prolongation of a vowel the mildly affected patient's voice will evidence a regular tremor of altering pitch and loudness. With the more severe patient there may be complete voice stoppage, resembling the disorder known as spastic dysphonia. However, significant differences have been found between the two disorders in terms of regularity of voice arrest and accompanying characteristics. Organic voice tremor patients also demonstrate excessively low pitch and monopitch, intermittent or constant strained-strangled harshness, and pitch breaks.

Hyperkinetic Dysarthria: Chorea

The two major diseases in this disorder group are Sydenham's chorea and Huntington's chorea. Huntington's chorea is autosomal dominantly inherited, and a child of a patient has a 50 percent chance of developing the disease. Onset is typically in the fifth decade, although there is a so-called juvenile variant as well as a senile variant. There is no known cause. The disease is progressive and fatal. Pathological changes documented usually include loss of neurons from the caudate nucleus, pallidum, and cerebral cortex, with less constant changes in other areas.

Sydenham's chorea ("St. Vitus Dance" in ancient terminology) is a noninherited disease that may follow strep throat, rheumatic fever, or scarlet fever. The symptoms usually clear up within six months.

Associated Neurologic Characteristics

Huntington's chorea is characterized by dementia and involuntary movements. Choreic movements are rapid, coordinated, but purposeless movements. They occur unpredictably and may involve any group of muscles. Voluntary and automatic movements may be interrupted so that coordinated breathing and speech may be quite difficult. The limbs are hypotonic. Postures cannot be maintained.

The Oral Musculature

The presence of hypotonia and involuntary movement of the oral musculature is variable in chorea. It is very characteristic in Huntington's disease that the patient cannot keep the tongue protruded for more than a few seconds. Sydenham's chorea often involves involuntary movements of the mouth and larynx. Even if there is little involuntary movement of oral musculature, the speech will probably be affected by the movements of other parts of the body.

Speech Characteristics

In the Mayo Clinic study of thirty adults with chorea (Darley, Aronson, & Brown, 1975), the following problems were noted.

PHONATION   A harsh voice quality and/or a strained-strangled sound were found in many patients. Excess loudness variations were prominent as a result of the poor control or ancillary movement. Lower than average pitch levels, voice stoppages, and pitch breaks were other characteristics noted in various patients.

RESONANCE   Forty-three percent of the patients demonstrated hypernasality. The interference with resonance also contributed to the articulatory problems of imprecise consonants and short phrases.

ARTICULATION   The difficulty of muscular adjustment yielded imprecise consonant production and, in twenty-three patients, distorted vowels. Misdirection of movement resulted in a feature called irregular articulatory breakdown. Reduced stress and short phrases were also displayed by many of the chorea patients. Prolonged intervals and variable rate were very prominent and contributed to the perception of prosodic deviations.

Hyperkinetic Dysarthria: Dystonia and Athetosis

Dystonia and athetosis are movement disorders classified as the slow hyperkinesias. Movements are characteristically unstable and sustained, suggesting possible conflicts between flexion and extension of the muscles.

Etiology
Most of these disorders do not have well-established etiologies or focal lesion sites. Encephalitis, vascular lesions, birth trauma, and degenerative neuronal disease are often precipitating diseases. Most show localized damage to the confines of the basal ganglia. Involuntary movement disorders are sometimes due to the effect of drugs such as phenothiazine and related compounds, especially the more powerful tranquilizers.

Athetosis is a rare disorder that is seen as a form of congenital cerebral palsy. It is also seen as a rare progressive disease of adolescence, the cause of which is unknown, and as an accompanying residual deficit with hemiplegia after cerebral infarction. Localization of lesion is difficult, but the putamen seems to be almost always involved.

Associated Neurologic Characteristics
Dystonia implies excess tone in selected parts of the body. Dystonia affects mainly the trunk, neck, and proximal parts of the limbs. These slow movements are usually sustained for more of a prolonged period. The movements usually build up to a peak, are sustained, and then recede, although they occasionally begin with a jerk. Athetotic movements are slow and writhing and are predominantly of the arms, face, and tongue. The movements tend to be exaggerated by attempts at voluntary activity, which make voluntary movements clumsy and inaccurate.

Speech Characteristics
PHONATION   The dystonic patient usually has a harsh or strained-strangled voice quality. Other patients, though fewer in number, may demonstrate intermittent breathiness and also audible inspiration. Monopitch and monoloudness are also a problem with these patients. Because of the involuntary movements, the dystonic patients often experience voice stoppages and periods

of inappropriate silence. Excess loudness variations accompany the excessive movement. Voice tremor is also found among the dystonic patients.

Phonation in athetosis is often significantly affected. The person often has poor respiratory reserve and respiratory patterns. Both dilator and constrictor spasms have been noted in the study of laryngeal functioning. Voicing is often excessively loud or excessively breathy. It is very unpredictable and frequently poorly coordinated with articulation.

ARTICULATION   As might be predicted, the articulation of patients with these involuntary movement disorders is highly variable, with a range of severity from "slight distortion" to "unintelligible." The dystonic patients of the Mayo Clinic study were found to demonstrate prominent articulation imprecision of consonant production. They also showed vowel distortion and irregular breakdown of articulation. Short phrases were noted with prolonged intervals. Prolongation of phonemes and variability of rate were also observed frequently. Reduction of stress was a relatively prominent characteristic of speech production.

Kent and Netsell (1978) and Platt, Andrews, and Howie (1980) have investigated the articulation of athetoid adults using cinefluorographic and intelligibility measures. The studies found that athetoid speech is frequently reduced in intelligibility as a result of articulation problems. Kent and Netsell found large ranges of jaw movement, inappropriate tongue positioning, prolonged transition time, and retruding of the lower lip. Platt, Andrews, and Howie (1980) found particular difficulty with accuracy of anterior tongue placement, reduced precision of fricatives and affricatives, and inability to achieve extreme positions in vowel formation. They found place and voicing errors to be predominant, particularly in final consonants.

RESONANCE   Of the thirty dystonic patients studied by the Mayo Clinic, eleven were found to show hypernasality. In the Kent and Netsell (1978) cinefluorographic study of athetoid adults, all subjects had trouble achieving velopharyngeal closure. The most severe problem, however, was velar control. Instability of velar position was noted frequently. The velum sometimes moved inappropriately, causing a loss of closure, or, in some cases, the velum showed repetitive movements that were not related to respiration.

Hyperkinetic Dysarthria: Tardive Dyskinesia

Another movement disorder resulting from extrapyramidal damage is tardive dyskinesia, which is attributable to the long-term use of phenothiazine and similar drugs. Symptoms include choreiform, myoclonic, and peculiar rhythmical movements, with a high incidence of abnormal movements in the oral region. Constant random movements of the lips and tongue may be found with a frequent "fly catcher's" movement of the tongue in which the tongue involuntarily moves in and out of the mouth. There also may be palatal involvement. Patients may become dysphagic and intelligibility is affected variably, with some patients becoming unintelligible because of the random movements. Most patients, however, have only a mild speech disorder.

The Cerebellum and the Cerebellar Pathway Lesions: Ataxic Dysarthria

As noted, the cerebellum serves as an important center for the integration or coordination of sensory and motor activities. It receives fibers from the motor and sensory cortex either directly or through intervening nuclei. Damage to the cerebellum and/or its pathways causes a disorder called *ataxia* and the motor speech symptoms yield an *ataxic dysarthria*.

Etiology

Damage may occur as localized to the cerebellum alone or may be part of more generalized damage affecting several systems. Etiologies of localized damage include stroke, trauma, tumors, alcohol toxicity, and multiple sclerosis. Encephalitis, vascular lesions, neuronal degeneration, lung cancer, and multiple sclerosis are some of the causes of generalized damage that may include the cerebellar system.

Associated Neurologic Characteristics

Ataxia is a disruption in the smooth coordination of movement. There is a failure to coordinate sensory data with motor performance. The hand may overshoot its target when reaching for an object. If the outstretched arm is pushed aside, it swings past its former position and overcorrects. Abnormalities like these are shown when the patient is asked to touch his nose or run his heel down his shin. Rapid alternating movements may be affected. Equilibrium is affected and gait may be impaired. Movement is slow to be initiated and slow through the range. Repetitive movements may be irregular and poorly timed, a condition called *dysmetria*. Muscle tone is hypotonic. Intention or kinetic tremor (tremor during purposeful movement) is also present.

Speech Characteristics

The dysarthria with localized damage to the cerebellum has the following characteristics:

Phonation
Voice may be approximately normal or may show excessive loudness variations. Harshness similar to a coarse voice tremor may also be noted.

Resonance
Velopharyngeal functioning is usually intact, with normal resonance characteristics. Occasionally, hypernasal resonance is found. Less frequently, nasal emission is demonstrated.

Articulation
Imprecise consonant production, vowel distortion, and irregular articulatory breakdown mark the speech of ataxic dysarthria. Rate is usually slow, although some patients use normal rate.

Prosody
Prosodic changes are usually readily observable in ataxic dysarthria. A speech prosody characteristic termed "excess and equal stress" by Darley, Aronson, and Brown (1969a) is a predominant feature. This refers to the tendency to emphasize or put stress on usually unstressed syllables and words and to increase the emphasis on stressed syllables and words. Also contributing to the prosodic changes is the prolongation of phonemes and prolongation of normal intervals in speech.

You may read or hear the term *scanning speech* in connection with ataxic dysarthria. This term was originated by Charcot in 1877 to describe the speech of a multiple sclerosis patient. He described the speech as being very slow, with a pause after each syllable as if the words were being measured or scanned. Others have used the term *scanning speech* to describe a different set of characteristics from this; therefore, the term has not been found useful and is not recommended. If used, it should be explained fully. The term *explosive speech* has also been used to describe ataxic production. The Mayo Clinic study noted excess loudness variations with excessive effort in ten of the thirty ataxic speakers. This forceful effort and increase in intensity, especially noted after pauses, gives the impression of explosiveness.

Other Mixed Dysarthrias with Diverse Lesions

Multiple Sclerosis: Mixed Spastic-Ataxic Dysarthria

Etiology
The etiology of MS has not been discovered. It is a complex disease causing demyelination in various tracts of mainly white matter. The lesions involve the

entire central nervous system, but the peripheral nervous system is seldom involved.

Associated Neurologic Characteristics
Early signs are mild or unnoticed until retrospection. They may include transient parathesias of the extremities, transient diplopia or blurring of vision, mild weakness or clumsiness, and mild vertigo. More severe signs of MS include marked difficulty with gait, dysarthria, significant weakness, visual disturbances, nystagmus, bladder disturbance, and personality change due to frontal lobe involvement. During the course of MS there will be frequent remissions and exacerbations of symptoms.

Speech Characteristics
In the Mayo Clinic's study of 168 patients diagnosed with MS (Darley, Aronson, & Brown, 1975), 59 percent were judged as having normal overall speech performance. Twenty-eight percent showed minimal impairments and 13 percent more severe impairment. The primary speech deviations were as follows.

PHONATION   The most frequently encountered deviation was impairment of loudness control. Harsh voice quality was also ranked high. Breathiness did not occur nearly as frequently but was noted in 37 patients. Pitch control and inappropriate pitch levels were also found.

ARTICULATION   About half of the patients were judged to have defective articulation. Although the cerebellar system is frequently involved, only 9 percent showed the irregular articulatory breakdowns characteristic of ataxic dysarthria.

RESONANCE   One-quarter of the MS patients demonstrated some degree of hypernasality.

PROSODY   A characteristic called *impaired emphasis* ranked high in the speech of these subjects. This included judgments of rate, appropriateness of phrasing, pitch and loudness variation for emphasis, and increased stress on usually unstressed words and syllables. Only 14 percent demonstrated the ataxic characteristic called *excess and equal stress*.

Wilson's Disease: Ataxic-Spastic-Hyperkinetic Dysarthria

Etiology
Wilson's disease is a rare metabolic disorder associated with a deficiency of a copper binding protein. It is also known as hepatolenticular degeneration and is genetic, with onset frequently between age 10 and 16. If it is diagnosed early,

dietary and chemical regimens can restore the copper balance and return the patient to normal functioning.

Associated Neurologic Characteristics
If hepatic liver damage has occurred, the patient may appear jaundiced. Neurologic symptoms include muscular rigidity, ataxia, and sometimes involuntary movements. Intention tremor is often present. The patient will usually have a masked facial expression, dysphagia, and drooling, as well as dysarthria.

Speech Characteristics

PHONATION   The characteristics of reduced stress, monoloudness, and monopitch were ranked first among deviant speech dimensions for the Wilson's disease patients in a study by Berry et al. (1974). Inappropriate silences were observed often. A harsh and/or strained voice was also a prominent characteristic for many patients. An inappropriately low pitch was used often.

RESONANCE   Hypernasality occurred frequently among these patients.

ARTICULATION   Imprecise consonants were ranked high. Irregular articulatory breakdown similar to that in ataxic dysarthria was often present. Rate was usually judged too slow. Intelligibility was generally poor.

PROSODY   Prosodic insufficiency was noted in the speech of these patients, with reduced stress, monopitch, and monoloudness being ranked high (as in Parkinson's disease). In many cases, however, prosodic excess was also noted, with the characteristics of equal and excess stress, prolonged phonemes, and slow rate being ranked high.

Shy-Drager Syndrome: Variable Dysarthria

Etiology
This syndrome was first described by Shy and Drager in 1960. It appears usually after the fourth decade of life and affects males more often than females by a ratio of 3 to 2. It is a degenerative disease of the autonomic nervous system and may also affect several components of the central nervous system. Prognosis is usually poor, though progression is slow.

Associated Neurologic Characteristics
With this disease, involvement may include the pyramidal, extrapyramidal, or cerebellar system or some combination of the three systems. Early signs usually involve autonomic nervous system disorders including bowel and bladder incontinence, sexual impotence, reduction of perspiration, and difficulty maintaining blood pressure when standing (known as orthostatic hypotension). Later symptoms include a gait disturbance, weakness, tremor of the limbs, and the dysphagia and dysarthria.

Speech Characteristics

A study of Ludlow and Bassich (1983) comparing acoustic and perceptual analyses of Parkinson's and Shy-Drager documented the following characteristics for the speech of seven patients diagnosed as having Shy-Drager syndrome.

PHONATION   Strained-strangled voice quality as well as breathiness were noted in the voice quality of these patients. A "wet hoarseness" was also identified in many cases. The voice was very often judged too soft, and mean intensity level was below normal.

RESONANCE   Hypernasality may occur if the involvement of the pyramidal system produces elements of a spastic dysarthria.

ARTICULATION   Imprecise consonants are a predominant part of this dysarthria. A variable rate was also ranked high in the deficiency ratings.

PROSODY   Although Shy-Drager patients were shown to have poorer-than-normal ability to change fundamental frequency, their ability was better than that of Parkinson's patients. Acoustic analysis showed, however, that the Shy-Drager patients use their retained ability to change pitch very poorly to effect stress. This is acoustically perceived as monopitch and reduced stress.

Summary

Paralysis, weakness, or incoordination of the oral musculature may result in the clinical entity known as dysarthria. The classic study by Darley, Aronson, and Brown (1969a, b) identified six different types of dysarthria based on perceptual analyses: spastic, flaccid, ataxic, hypokinetic, hyperkinetic, and mixed. Further research using perceptual and acoustic analysis has added to the detailed knowledge about the speech characteristics associated with diseases, trauma, and injuries to the neuromuscular aspect of the speech mechanism. Table 8-1 lists other diseases or syndromes that are usually accompanied by dysarthria.

References and Further Readings

Aronson, A. E., & Hartman, D. E. (1981). Adductor spastic dysphonia as a sign of essential (voice) tremor. *Journal of Speech and Hearing Disorders, 46,* 52–58.

TABLE 8-1
Other Neurological Diseases Associated with Dysarthria

Name	Etiology	Speech Symptoms
Bell's palsy	Inflammation or lesion of the 7th cranial nerve	Slurring due to unilateral weakness of labial muscles
Polyneuritis	Follows infections or may be due to diabetes or alcohol abuse	Flaccid dysarthria
Hemiballismus	Lesions of subthalamic nucleus	Hyperkinetic dysarthria
Palato-pharyngo-laryngeal myoclonus	Brainstem lesions producing rhythmic myoclonic movements of any or all of these structures	Hyperkinetic dysarthria; sometimes only noted on vowel prolongation
Gilles de la Tourette's syndrome	No known etiology	Hyperkinetic dysarthria with spontaneous, uncontrolled vocalizations such as barking, grunting, throat clearing, snorting. Echolalia and coprolalia (obscene language without provocation) may be present.

Bayles, K. (1984). Language and dementia. In A. Holland (Ed.), *Language disorders in adults*. San Diego: College-Hill Press, p. 227.

Berry, W., Darley, F., Aronson, A., and Goldstein, A. (1974). Dysarthria in Wilson's disease. *Journal of Speech and Hearing Research*, 17, 169–183.

Capildeo, R., Haberman, S., & Rose, F. C. (1981). The classification of Parkinsonism. In F. C. Rose and R. Capildeo, (Eds.), *Research progress in Parkinson's disease*. Kent, England: Pitman Medical Limited, p. 19.

Darley, F., Aronson, A., & Brown, J. (1969a). Differential diagnostic patterns of dysarthria. *Journal of Speech and Hearing Research*, 12, 246–269.

Darley, F., Aronson, A., & Brown, J., (1969b). Clusters of deviant speech dimensions in the dysarthrias. *Journal of Speech and Hearing Research*, 12, 462–496.

Darley, F., Aronson, A., & Brown, J. (1975). *Motor speech disorders*. Philadelphia: Saunders.

Golper, L. A. C., Nutt, J. G., Rau, M., and Coleman, R. O. (1983). Focal cranial dystonia. *Journal of Speech and Hearing Disorders*, 48, 128–134.

Hunker, C. J., & Abbs, J. H. (1984). Physiological analyses of parkinsonian tremors in the orofacial system. In M. McNeil, J. Rosenbek, and A. Aronson, (Eds.), *The dysarthrias: Physiology, acoustics, perception, management*. San Diego: College-Hill Press.

Kent, R. & Netsell, R. (1978). Articulatory abnormalities in athetoid cerebral palsy. *Journal of Speech and Hearing Disorders*, 43, 353–374.

Linebaugh, C. W., & Wolfe, V. E. (1984). Relationships between articulatory rate, intelligibility, and naturalness in spastic and ataxic speakers. In M. McNeil, J. Rosenbek, and A. Aronson (Eds.), *The dysarthrias: Physiology, acoustics, perception, management*. San Diego: College Hill Press.

Logemann, J. A. (1983). *Evaluation and treatment of swallowing disorders*. San Diego: College-Hill Press.

Logemann, J. A., & Fisher, H. B. (1981). Vocal tract control in Parkinson's disease: Phonetic feature analysis of misarticulations. *Journal of Speech and Hearing Disorders*, 46, 348–352.

Logemann, J. A., Fisher, H. B., Boshes, B., & Blonsky, E. R. (1978). Frequency and cooccurrence of vocal tract dysfunction in the speech of a large sample of Parkinson patients. *Journal of Speech and Hearing Disorders*, 43, 47–57.

Ludlow, C., & Bassich, C. J. (1983). The results of acoustic and perceptual assessment of two types of dysarthria. In W. R. Berry, (Ed.), *Clinical dysarthria*. San Diego: College Hill Press, 1983, 121–154.

Netsell, R. (1984). A neurobiological view of the dysarthrias. In M. McNeil, J. Rosenbek, and A. Aronson (Eds.), *The dysarthrias: Physiology, acoustics, perception, management*. San Diego: College Hill Press.

Netsell, R., Daniel, G., & Celesia, G. G. (1975). Acceleration and weakness in parkinsonian dysarthria. *Journal of Speech and Hearing Disorders*, 40, 467–480.

Perkins, W. H. (Ed.) (1983). *Current therapy of communication disorders: Dysarthria and apraxia*. New York: Thieme-Stratton.

Platt, L. J., Andrews, G., & Howie, P. M. (1980). Dysarthria of adult cerebral palsy: II. Phonemic analysis of articulation errors. *Journal of Speech and Hearing Disorders*, 23, 41–55.

Portnoy, R. A., & Aronson, A. E. (1982). Diadochokinetic syllable rate and regularity in normal and in spastic and ataxic dysarthric subjects. *Journal of Speech and Hearing Disorders*, 47, 324–328.

Shy, G., & Drager, G. (1960). A neurological syndrome associated with orthostatic hypotension: A clinical pathologic study. *Archives of Neurology*, 2, 511–527.

Weismer, G. (1984). Articulatory characteristics of Parkinsonian dysarthria: segmental and phrase level timing, spriantization, and glottal-supraglottal coordination. In M. McNeil, J. Rosenbek, and A. Aronson, (Eds.), *The dysarthrias: Physiology, acoustics, perception, and management*. San Diego: College Hill Press.

Yorkston, D. M., & Beukelman, D. R. (1981). Ataxic dysarthria: Treatment sequences based on intelligibility and prosodic considerations. *Journal of Speech and Hearing Disorders*, 46, 398–404.

CHAPTER NINE

The Cerebral Control of Speech and Language

"We will assume, but only for the sake of illustration, the correctness of the usual statements that there is a higher centre for 'memory of words' and that subordinate to it is another centre for coordinating the movement of words. But the psychological expression must be rendered into an anatomical one."

—John Hughlings Jackson, "On the Anatomical and
Physiological Localization of Movements," 1875

Cerebral Anatomy

Cerebral Lobes

The mechanisms for the human communicative nervous system are for the most part in the cerebrum. The two cerebral hemispheres are divided traditionally into four lobes: (1) frontal, (2) parietal, (3) temporal, and (4) occipital. The division between the anterior frontal lobe and the posterior parietal lobe is a deep cleft that runs obliquely down the lateral surface of the hemisphere. This is the *central sulcus* or, in older terms, the fissure of Rolando. The *lateral sulcus*, or fissure of Sylvius (Sylvian fissure), enters anteriorly and posteriorly to the place of the central sulcus. It separates the frontal lobe above from the temporal lobe below. Posteriorly, the lateral sulcus divides the temporal lobe below from the parietal lobe. If the hemispheres are separated to expose the medial surface, you can see that the lateral sulcus, here too, separates the temporal and parietal lobes. Deep in the lateral sulcus is an area known as the *insula.*

On the lateral surface of the cerebral hemispheres, the occipital lobe is arbitrarily divided from the parietal lobe by an imaginary line drawn from the superior preoccipital notch to the inferior preoccipital notch. On the medial surface of the cerebral hemisphere, the occipital lobe is divided from the parietal lobe by a natural boundary, the *parietal-occipital sulcus.* Thus the borders of the four lobes can be distinguished on both the outer and inner surfaces of each of the cerebral hemispheres.

Limbic Lobe

A fifth lobe was named by the famous French surgeon, Pierre Paul Broca (1824–1880). This lobe is on the medial surfaces of the two cerebral hemispheres. If you look at the medial surfaces of the hemipheres with the brainstem removed, you will observe an archlike pattern of cortex surrounding the nonconvoluted central portions of the brain. This internal circular arch is called the *limbic lobe* and is formed by several smaller structures (Figure 9-1), including the (1) sub-callosal gyrus, (2) gyrus cinguli, (3) isthmus, (4) hippocampal gyri and (5) uncus.

Some neuroanatomists lump these limbic structures with the olfactory (smell) system and call all of them the *rhinencephalon*, which literally means "smell brain." The concept of the rhinencephalon is very useful in the study of the comparative neuroanatomy of lower animals, whose smell brain is larger and better developed; but in the study of the human communicative nervous system, the limbic lobe, as we defined it, is more helpful.

The exact relationship between limbic lobe and communicative functions is not completely clear. We know, through study of patients with hippocampal lesions, that the limbic lobe structures are related to emotion and recent memory. The structures of limbic lobe are linked to the hypothalamus, which controls vegetative and metabolic functions. Some of the responses attributed to the limbic lobe are found in Table 9-1.

Some of the speculations about the role of the limbic lobe in communi-

TABLE 9-1
Limbic Responses

Pleasure	Wakefulness
Satiety	Alertness
Guilt	Excitement
Punishment	Autonomic
Habituation	activity

FIGURE 9-1 The limbic lobe. Medial view of the left cerebral hemisphere. The circled area is the limbic lobe (Broca's lobe).

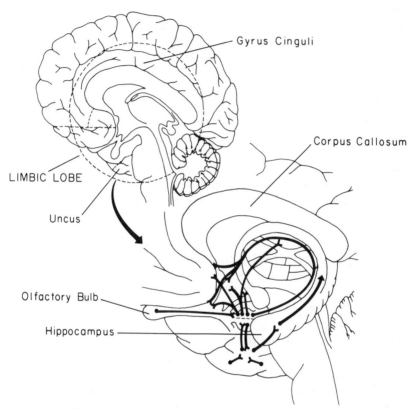

cation suggest that it is involved in automatic signal behavior in both humans and animals, since this behavior is related to basic drives and sensation. In addition, the limbic lobe may participate in the regulation of social communicative behavior through emotion and motivation, which it mediates. Last, the limbic lobe may, through its control of motivation, provide an intentional component to propositional communicative behavior. In brief, the subcortical limbic lobe may drive the cortical speech-language mechanisms. These speculations are reasonable as far as our knowledge goes, but much research is needed to define the exact role of the limbic system in speech and language.

Insula

In the history of neurology some cerebral structures have been singled out because of their supposed relevance to language mechanisms. The *insula*, or island of Reil, is one of these. Since it is deep in the brain, it is initially hard to locate. If we retract or remove the temporal lobe along with the overhanging frontal and parietal lobes, the lateral sulcus will be widened. Peering into the expanded fissure, we will see the area known as the insula. *Heschl's gyri,* crucial areas for communication, are very close to the insula at the posterior end of the upper surface of each temporal lobe. Heschl's gyrus is known as the primary auditory receptive area of the cerebral cortex. It is in these bilateral temporal areas that initial recognition of an auditory stimulus occurs at the cortical level. Heschl's gyri are not recognizable on inspection of the brain because they are buried deep within the lateral sulcus. They are related to the insula as well as to the superior temporal gyrus. The location of the insula is between the auditory recognition area of the temporal lobe and the frontal lobe, in which areas for the motor control of speech expression are located. The insula has long been considered a connective link between the anterior and posterior speech-language areas. Lesions in the insula sometimes have been associated with *conduction aphasia* in current speech-language neurology (see Chapter 10).

Interhemispheric Connections

Corpus Callosum

A pathway called the *corpus callosum* is also crucial to speech-language functions (see Figure 9-2). This pathway serves as the major connection between the hemispheres and conveys neural information from one hemisphere of the brain to the other. The corpus callosum is the largest of the side-to-side interconnections between the two hemispheres. In general, the corpus callosum connects analogous areas in the two hemispheres. The anterior and posterior commissures are small bundles of interhemispheric fibers located anteriorly and posteriorly to the corpus callosum. The anterior commissure connects the temporal lobe with the amygdaloid nucleus, a small subcortical structure. The anterior commissure also connects the occipital lobe in one cerebral hemisphere to the temporal lobe in the other hemisphere. This connection has significance in visual-auditory associations.

Split-Brain Research

The corpus callosum and its role in the transfer of information from one hemisphere to another has attracted wide attention in recent years. The large bundle of tissue may be cleanly and completely severed surgically without damage to other tissue. This operation, called a *commissurotomy,* has been performed on

FIGURE 9-2 The corpus callosum, in the medial view of the right cerebral hemisphere. It is the largest of the commissures connecting the two hemispheres.

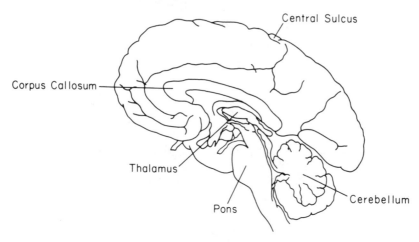

patients who have been plagued by chronic and severe epileptic seizures that could not be controlled by massive doses of anticonvulsive medication. A seizure that begins in one cerebral hemisphere may easily travel across the corpus callosum to the other hemisphere, producing a bilateral generalized seizure. Neurosurgeons reasoned that sectioning the corpus callosum would contain the seizure to one hemisphere.

Results of the early commissurotomies were even more beneficial than had been anticipated. Not only did the surgery contain seizures to a single hemisphere, but they also reduced seizures in the other hemisphere because of apparent reciprocal actions between the hemispheres.

The surgery was not only helpful in seizure control, but also provided information on the differing psychological functions of each hemisphere and on the role of the corpus callosum in the brain mechanisms for speech and language. Roger Sperry, a psychologist, received the Nobel Prize in 1981 for his studies on split-brain patients. One of the most significant observations of these studies was that the brain of split-brain patients clearly showed asymmetry for speech and language functions, and that the corpus callosum played a very decisive role in transmitting language heard in the right ear, and received at the right Heschl's gyrus, to the left hemisphere, where it is processed by the major mechanisms for speech and language (see Figure 9-3).

Experiments on split-brain patients suggested that the right hemisphere was responsible for spatial, tactile, and constructional tasks. These experiments have led to speculations that the two hemispheres function in very different ways, each having its own cognitive style. The left hemisphere is characterized

FIGURE 9-3 A simplified summary of the cerebral specialization based on data from patients whose corpus callosum has been divided and patients with lesions of the corpus callosum.

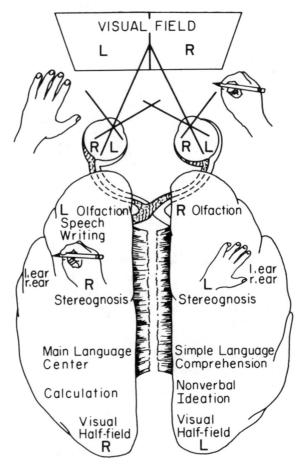

Source: Adapted with permission from E. Gardner, *Fundamentals of Neurology* (Philadelphia: W. B. Saunders, 1975).

as logical, analytical, and verbal, the right as intuitive, holistic, and perceptual-spatial.

There has been a tendency toward excessive elaboration of polar opposites when assigning cognitive tasks to the two halves of the brain. A tempered approach is warranted, in which we realize that both hemispheres are employed to some degree to perform any given cognitive task. It is possible that the right and left hemispheres function alternately depending on the cognitive style chosen by the individual thinker. It is also possible that while one hemisphere is dominant, the other is inhibited. Or it is very likely that both hemispheres are always used in a fully integrated way. In any event, further research into the asymmetrical functions of the two hemispheres will not only clarify aspects of the human communicative nervous system, but will also provide new information about human cognitive functions.

Cerebral Cortex

The cerebral cortex is the gray, rindlike outer covering of the brain. If spread out on a flat surface, the cortex covers a total area of approximately 75 cm² or two and a half square feet, but through its folded surface it becomes very compact. The convolutions of the cortex allow it to be fitted neatly into the small cranium of the human skull. Approximately 30 percent of the cortical surface is devoted to speech-language activity. This thin sheet of tissue, 1.5–4.5 millimeters thick, is most highly developed in the human species and is the primary source of those behaviors that separate humans from lower animals. The cortex is primarily responsible for intellect, judgment, personality, and symbolic behavior, particularly speech, reading, and writing. The cerebral cortex in fact may be considered the highest level of the human communicative nervous system.

Cortical Localization Maps

For over a century, neuroanatomists have divided and classified the human cortex into different areas. These tireless attempts to fractionate the cortex followed in the wake of the unparalleled achievement of Paul Broca in 1861 to demonstrate that different cortical regions were associated with different mental functions, one of which was expression of speech. The localization systems that followed have most frequently been based on cell study of the cortex. These are called *histological* methods. They allow the development of cytoarchitectural diagrams or maps based on the varied cell structures of the cortex. The most popular map, developed by a German neurologist, Korbinian Brodmann (1868–1918), is represented in Figure 9-4. Note that each area of the cortex is numbered, providing a much more convenient way to specify a cortical site than by a complex description of gyri and sulci. Brodmann's map is open to criticism on the grounds that it chops the cortex into innumerable specific centers, implying that cortical areas have sharply defined limits. Although newer studies have argued for a reduced number of areas and have modified their boundaries, this still remains an acceptable shorthand method for designating the numerous cortical areas involved in communicative function.

FIGURE 9-4 Left hemisphere with major architectonic cortical subdivisions of K. Brodmann as indicated by numbers. This numbering system is still in use today.

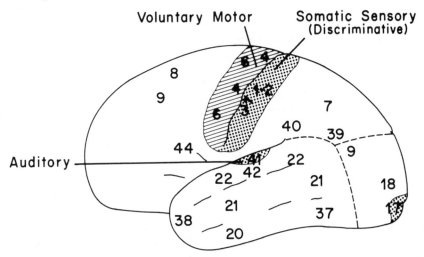

Source: Redrawn and reproduced with permission from W. Penfield and L. Roberts, *Speech and Brain Mechanisms.* Copyright © 1959 by Princeton University Press. Figure II-5 reprinted with permission of the literary executors of the Penfield Papers and Princeton University Press.

Specific Cortical Areas

The cortical areas have been divided into three major divisions: (1) primary motor projection areas, (2) primary sensory reception areas, and (3) secondary association areas.

The primary motor projection area is a bilateral cortical strip in the frontal lobes in which voluntary movement patterns are initiated. It also serves as a source of descending motor pathways, projecting to lower levels of the nervous system.

The primary sensory reception area registers sensory impulses relayed from the periphery to the thalamus and upward to the cortex. The pathway from thalamus to cortex are thalamic radiations. An example of a primary reception area is Heschl's gyrus in the superior temporal lobe.

Association Area Functions

The secondary association areas are generally adjacent to primary motor and sensory areas. The association areas elaborate information received at the primary motor and sensory areas. Motor association areas are sites where motor plans, programs, and commands are formulated. The association area adds meaning and significance to the sensory or motor information received in the primary motor or sensory areas. The matching of present sensory information with past sensory information drawn from memory probably takes place in the association areas. In addition, certain sensory association areas blend and mingle sensory information from several association areas to establish a higher level of cortical sensory information. This results in a complex level of awareness that is above and beyond mere recognition of sensory data. This level of sensory awareness is known as *perception*. For example, if someone places a door key in your hand in the dark of the night, you must recognize its shape and judge its size, weight, texture, and metallic surface in order to match this information with your memories and concepts of keys. Only when you can identify your perception of the key can you name it and relate its function if asked. The everyday sensory recognition of objects is a complex sensory integration of multiple sensations enhanced by memory and conceptual knowledge of objects with similar qualities. This complex activity of knowing is known as *gnosis*.

Cortical Motor Functions

The primary projection cortex is known as the *motor area* or motor strip. In Brodmann's system, it is area 4. It is located on the anterior wall of the central sulcus and the adjacent precentral gyrus. Figure 2-5 shows the areas devoted to the motor control of the different parts of the body. Recall that this area allows contralateral motor control of the limbs. The inverted arrangement of motor control areas on the bilateral motor cortices reveals that cortical control for the muscles and functions of the speech mechanism is represented at the lower end of the motor area on the lateral wall of the cerebrum. The large areas given over to motor control of the oral mechanism contribute to the coordination of its rapid and precise movements during talking, singing, and changes in facial expression.

Anterior to the motor area is the *premotor area* (area 6). The area is considered a supplement to the primary motor projection cortex and is related to the extrapyramidal system. If areas 4 and 6 are ablated, spasticity in the limbs results. There is a third motor area, discovered by Wilder G. Penfield, on the ventral surface of the precentral and postcentral gyri. It is called the *supplementary*, or *secondary*, *motor area* and its function is unclear, but it may be important in all sequential activities including speech.

Cortical Motor Speech Association Areas

Surrounding the foot of the motor and premotor cortices are areas considered motor association areas. These areas are numbered 44, 45, 46, and 47 in the Brodmann system. They have been called the *opercular gyri*. Areas 44 and 45 include (1) the pars opercularis, (2) the pars triangularis, and (3) the pars orbitalis. Areas 44 and 45 in the left hemisphere are sometimes called the *frontal operculum*. Area 44 is known best as Broca's area. Although its function is controversial, it is usually associated with the formation of motor speech plans for oral expression. The cytoarchitecture of the area is similar in both right and left hemispheres, but traditional theory maintains that only the left is involved with speech formulation. Regional cerebral blood flow and metabolic rate studies have suggested that right cortical areas may be activated during some speech and language activities also.

Primary Somatosensory Cortex

This cortical area (Areas 3, 2, and 1) is on the postcentral gyrus and is a primary receptor of general bodily sensation. Thalamic radiations carry sensory data from skin, muscles, tendons, and joints of the body to the primary somatosensory cortex. Lesions of this cortex produce partial sensory loss, or paresthesia; rarely is there complete sensory loss, or anesthesia. Symptoms of a lesion cause numbness and tingling in the opposite side of the body. Widespread destructive lesions produce gross sensory loss with inability to localize sensation.

Primary Auditory Receptor Cortex

Heschl's gyrus (area 41), described earlier, is the primary auditory cortical reception area. The area is found in each temporal lobe, but the left Heschl's area appears to be somewhat larger in most humans. The significance of this neuroanatomic difference is not completely clear, but it may be related to language dominance.

Primary Visual Receptor Cortex

This area is in the occiptal lobe along the calcarine fissure, which can be seen from the medial surface of the hemisphere and is not obvious on the outside of the brain. The area, 17 in the Brodmann scheme, is also known as the striate area. The area receives fibers from the optic tract. Areas 18 and 19, which adjoin area 17, are sensory association areas and are important regions for visual perception and for some visual reflexes, such as visual fixation. Lesions in the area cause visual hallucinatory symptoms. Lesions of the optic pathways cause various degrees of blindness. This partial blindness is considered a visual-field defect.

Primary Olfactory Receptor Cortex

The cortical area that allows you to appreciate the fragrance of a rose is deep in the temporal lobe and is called the olfactory area. It includes an area called the *uncus* and the nearby parts of the *parahippocampal gyri* of the temporal lobe. The olfactory nerves, the end organs for smell, lie in a bony structure in the nose. The nerves end in the olfactory bulb, which is an extension of brain tissue in the nasal area. The bulbs are supported by an olfactory stalk. Destruction of the olfactory system causes *anosomia*, or lack of smell. Irritative lesions produce olfactory hallucinations or *uncinate fits*.

Sensory Association Areas

The sensory association areas, where elaboration of sensation occurs, can best be considered as extensions of the primary sensory receptor areas. Their margins are necessarily vague and it is sometimes controversial as to what the exact functions of certain areas are. The sensory association areas are richly connected to the receptor areas by a host of association fibers but these association fibers are often difficult to follow because of the vast number of relays in the cortical association system. Areas 5 and 7 in the parietal lobe are related to general somesthetic sensation. Areas 42 and 22 (Wernicke's area) are related to language comprehension. Areas 17 and 19 are visual association areas.

Recall that we said that the function of the sensory association areas was that of gnosis or knowing. If the prefix *a* is added to the word, we have a new term, *agnosia*. This describes a perceptual-cognitive deficit presumed to follow a destructive cerebral lesion, meaning lack of recognition. Lesions in auditory association areas affecting the appreciation of incoming sound will produce language disorders. Areas surrounding Heschl's gyrus are involved in adding meaning to sound and providing comprehension of language. Lesions in area 42 destroy the ability to appreciate the meaning of sound, and lesions in area 22 compromise the ability to understand spoken language. The inability to comprehend spoken language can be identified as an *auditory verbal agnosia* if we employ a diagnostic nomenclature that assumes lesions in sensory association areas that produce an agnosia. This defect is sometimes distinguished from an *auditory agnosia*, which refers to the inability to recognize a nonverbal sound like the blare of an automobile horn or the roar of a lawn mower's motor. More commonly, lesions in the left temporal association areas have been identified with classic syndromes of language disorder. Temporal lobe lesions affecting comprehension of language are often labeled *sensory aphasia* because the foremost sign in this well-known aphasic syndrome is the inability to recognize oral language. Bilateral lesions of areas 18 and 19 produce *visual agnosia* in that there is inability to recognize objects visually. *Tactile agnosia* is associated with lesions of the parietal lobe areas 5 and 7.

Another highly significant association area related to language disorder is the *angular gyrus*. This gyrus extends around the posterior end of the superior temporal gyrus. This is usually designated area 39. Lesions in this area have been associated with defects in recognition of the printed word; and reading, writing, and word recall deficits are often present.

Area 40 is the *supramarginal gyrus*, found in the inferior portion of the parietal lobe, which is known as the *inferior parietal lobule*. This gyrus circles the posterior end of the Sylvian fissure. When the supramarginal gyrus and its underlying association pathway in the left hemisphere are damaged, the patient finds it difficult to formulate written language. The disorder is agraphia. A type of aphasia called conduction aphasia and also apraxia are seen (see Chapter 10). Other specific cortical areas have been identified as possible contributors to language mechanisms, but those listed here have received wide acceptance.

Association Pathways

It is obvious that each of the cortical centers involved in speech and language must be interconnected to function fully. Association pathways connect the cerebral lobes and centers within a given lobe. Two distinct patterns of association fibers are found: short fibers and long fibers. Short fibers pass from gyrus to gyrus and are found close to the cortical mantle. Long fibers connect remote regions and make up distinct bundles of fibers.

The uncinate fasciculus is a hooklike configuration of fibers that passes from the frontal lobe to the temporal pole. The occipital-frontal fasciculus is in the white matter and passes from the occipital lobe to the frontal lobe. It travels through the insula and has at times been considered a primary connection in the central mechanism for language. Another long association pathway, the inferior longitudinal fasciculus, passes from temporal to occipital cortex.

The *superior longitudinal fasciculus* makes connections from frontal lobe to parietal, occipital, and temporal lobes in a fanlike fashion. This fasciculus connects the anterior speech mechanism of Broca's area with the posterior region such as Wernicke's area and the angular and supramarginal gyri. A part of the superior longitudinal bundle contains fibers that interconnect the major cortical language regions. These significant fibers make up the *arcuate fasciculus*, which gets its name from its arched appearance (see Figure 2-7).

The cerebral interconnections, like the commissures and fasciculi, are crucial in the theory of human language function and dysfunction. Many of the classic aphasic syndromes appear to be the result of lesions that disconnect one language area from another, or disconnect either hemispheres or the cerebral lobes.

The Clinicopathologic Method

The cortical areas believed to be critical for language function have been established by what is called the clinicopathologic method in neurology. Developed into a powerful technique by the great French neurologist Jean Charcot (1825–1893), it is the method of establishing a relationship between the site of a lesion and the behavioral functions that are lost or modified. The underlying assumption is that the lesioned area is related to the lost or disordered function. This simple logic is very important in clinical neurology: it forms the basis of neurologic diagnosis and is the foundation of the historically traditional neurological examination. Modern technological advances have clarified the actual sites of lesion and made the diagnosis more valid and reliable. Objective neurodiagnostic tests, such as computerized tomographs (CT scans) of the brain, positron emission tomography (PET scans), electroencephalograms, brain scans, cerebral arteriograms, and other tests have established the value of the clinicopathologic method.

Methodological Cautions

Here we had best strike a note of caution about the historical clinicopathologic method of lesion localization and the way this information may be used in speech-language pathology. Without a doubt, the ability to localize a lesion from a deficit in behavioral function has remained an unshakable principle of clinical neurology. The results in diagnosis and treatment of patients have been most impressive. In fact, this information from the disordered brain has been very appealing to those who wish to gather information about brain functions and language in the normal brain. Localizing normal brain function from data from abnormal brains, however, is at best a hazardous enterprise. The great British neurologist John Hughlings Jackson (1835–1911) put it succinctly when he commented on Broca's discovery of a very delimited area for control of articulate speech in the left cerebral hemisphere. When he said, "To localize damage which destroys speech and to localize speech are two different things," he may have uttered one of the most insightful dicta in the neurology of language.

Cerebral Blood Supply

Recall that the brain is supplied by four large arteries (Chapter 3). The two internal carotid arteries enter at small openings in the base of the skull, and the two vertebral arteries enter through the foramen magnum, the large opening at the bottom of the skull. At the base of the brain the three arteries are joined together by one anterior and two posterior communicating arteries, which form a system called the circle of Willis. Sometimes a communicating artery is so small that it does not provide the safety valve of collateral circulation. Under normal conditions, however, the internal carotid arteries easily provide a swift blood supply that irrigates the cerebral hemispheres with no problem.

Middle Cerebral Artery

The internal carotid artery divides into the anterior and middle cerebral arteries. The middle cerebral artery travels far into the lateral or Sylvian fissure and then divides again into several cortical branches that supply the insula and the lateral surfaces of the frontal, parietal, temporal, and occipital lobes. The wide distribution of the branches of the left middle cerebral artery have earned it the title of the *artery of language* or aphasia. Coming from the base of the middle cerebral artery are the lenticulostriate arteries, which supply the internal capsule and part of the basal ganglia. Small hemorrhages or infarcts in the internal capsule may produce a severe and complete contralateral hemiplegia, since many motor projection fibers come together at that point.

Two types of Broca's aphasia are commonly associated with different arterial sites. A vascular occlusion in the branch of the left middle cerebral artery that supplies Broca's area will produce a circumscribed lesion with initial mutism followed by speech apraxia that resolves itself rather quickly. This has been called a *little Broca's aphasia* or *minor Broca's aphasia*.

When a lesion occurs in the upper division of the middle cerebral artery supplying the frontal and parietal lobe, wide areas of brain tissue are affected, including Broca's area. The result is a *big Broca's aphasia* or *major Broca's aphasia*. The classic Broca's syndrome includes speech apraxia, syntactic language disturbances, and often some language comprehension problems, especially at first. Recovery is slower and of a lesser extent than recovery from a little Broca's aphasia.

Anterior Cerebral Artery

This branch of the internal carotid artery enters the median longitudinal fissure between the hemispheres. When it reaches the genu, or bend, of the corpus callosum, it turns and runs backward close to the body of the corpus callosum. The artery supplies the medial surface of the frontal and parietal lobes. It also feeds a small strip of the lateral surface of these lobes. Occlusion of the anterior cerebral artery may produce a transcortical motor aphasia (see Chapter 10) and result in paralysis of the lower limb opposite the site of the lesion.

Posterior Cerebral Artery

The two posterior arteries are a division of the basilar artery. These two arteries supply the medial and inferior aspects of the temporal occipital lobes. A separate branch of the posterior cerebral artery, the calcarine artery, is on the medial surface of the visual cortex; if the artery is compromised, a contralateral half blindness of each eye, called *hemianopsia*, may result. *Alexia* without agraphia, a reading disorder, may be present.

A bilateral occlusion of the posterior cerebral arteries in the medial temporal lobe will often result in a significant disorder of verbal memory. This is common in Karsokoff's syndrome, a memory disorder associated with cerebral vascular problems and alcoholism. A bilateral occlusion of the posterior cerebral arteries may result in cortical blindness and an associated Anton's syndrome. In Anton's syndrome the patient will deny blindness and claim to see objects in the blind field.

Cerebrovascular Disorders

A cerebrovascular accident (CVA) is the most common cause of language disturbance in adults. The terms *stroke* and *cerebral apoplexy* are also used to describe a cerebrovascular accident. Three major types of vascular pathology are classically recognized in cerebrovascular disorders: embolism, thrombosis, and hemorrhage. An *embolism* is a fragment of a blood clot or other material that travels in a blood vessel until it obstructs the blood flow. A *thrombosis* is a fixed clot in a blood vessel that is usually the result of a buildup of atherosclerotic plaque on the vessel wall. Thrombotic and embolic strokes, known as *ischemic* CVAs, are the most common type of stroke. In this condition there is partial or complete occlusion of a blood vessel, so that a portion of the brain tissue is deprived of adequate blood flow. The anemia resulting from this reduced local blood flow is called *ischemia*. Cells in the ischemic area die or *necrose*, forming an *infarct*, or dying area. The tissue involved softens and liquefies within a short time. Necrosis is irreversible in that nerve cells do not regenerate.

In a hemorrhagic CVA, bleeding into the cranium rather than ischemia is the tissue-destroying agent. The blood clot, or *hematoma*, resulting from the bleeding compresses and destroys the local brain tissue. Large intracerebral hematomas are often fatal. If the patient survives the hemorrhage, the blood and necrotic brain tissue are gradually absorbed, but a cavity filled with fluid is left.

A frequent cause of intracranial hemorrhage is bleeding into the subarachnoid space, often caused by cerebral aneurysm. An *aneurysm* is the ballooning out of a thin-walled section of a cerebral artery. Aneurysms are usually situated on major arteries at the base of the brain, particularly at branching points. Rupture of an aneursym causes a rush of blood into the subarachnoid space. The patient may develop narrowed arteries in the vicinity of the aneurysm and may develop a syndrome of delayed ischemic CVA caused by vasospasm.

Arteriovenous malformations also contribute to subarachnoid hemorrhage. These malformations are congenital communications between arteries and veins that have a tendency to bleed. These hemorrhages are less severe then are those of ruptured aneurysms, but result in significant CVAs.

Bleeding may also occur with ischemic infarcts, particularly in cerebral embolism. In cerebral artery occlusion there is likely to be necrosis of both the brain tissue and the blood vessel walls. If the clotting is resolved or if collateral blood flow is established, these necrotic arteries may leak blood through their damaged walls and produce a cerebral infarct.

Summary

The cerebrum contains four lobes on its external surface: the frontal, parietal, temporal, and occipital lobes. A fifth internal lobe, the limbic lobe, plays a role in emotion and recent memory and may also be important in the motivation of communication. The insula historically has been considered a point of confluence of fibers traveling from the posterior portion of the brain to the anterior portion. The corpus callosum and the anterior and posterior commissures connect the two hemispheres and transfer information between them. Split-brain research after commissurotomy has dramatically demonstrated the asymmetrical functions of the two hemispheres. The left hemisphere is verbal, analytic, and logical; the right is perceptual-spatial, intuitive, musical, and holistic.

Cortical localization is a major property of the brain, and the areas contributing to speech and language function may be classified as motor, sensory, and association.

Primary sensory areas receive sensation at the cortex, and primary motor areas initiate movement. Secondary association areas add meaning and significance to motor and sensory information. Deficits in motor association areas produce *apraxia*, or disordered motor programming; deficits in sensory association areas produce *agnosia*, or disordered perception. Left frontal lobe lesions in the motor speech association area (44) result in speech apraxia. Left temporal lobe lesions in the auditory association areas (22, 41) result in Wernicke's aphasia. The supramarginal gyrus (40) and the angular gyrus (39) in the left parietal lobe have been associated with deficits of writing and reading, word recall and the Gerstmann syndrome. The infraparietal area of the angular gyrus is also important in making auditory-visual-spatial associations that support early naming behavior.

A number of the long intercortical association pathways are necessary for higher cortical functions, but certain fibers of the superior longitudinal fasciculus, singled out as the *arcuate fasciculus*, connect the major anterior and posterior language areas.

The language areas originally established by the clinicopathologic method have been confirmed by newer neurodiagnostic methods. These language areas are richly supplied by cerebral arteries. Several arteries join to form the circle of Willis at the base of the brain. The structure of the circle of Willis allows for compensatory circulation in occlusion in the circle of Willis. The middle cerebral branch of the internal carotid artery has been called the *language artery* since its occlusion frequently produces aphasic symptoms. An occlusion of the upper division of the middle cerebral artery produces a classic Broca's aphasia. Occlusions of arteries are produced by an embolism or thrombosis and are the primary causes of cerebrovascular disorder. Hemorrhage is a common third cause of CVAs.

References and Further Readings

Cerebral Anatomy

Geschwind, N. (1979). Specializations of the human brain. *Scientific American*, 241, 180–199.

Snell, R. (1980). *Neuroanatomy for medical students*. Boston: Little, Brown.

Cerebral Asymmetry and Split-Brain Research

Gazzaniga, M. S., & LeDoux, J. E. (1978). *The integrated mind*. New York: Plenum Press.

Springer, S. P., & Deutsch, G. (1981). *Left brain, right brain*. San Francisco: W. H. Freeman.

Young, A. W. (Ed.) (1983). *Functions of the right cerebral hemisphere*. New York: Academic Press.

Cortical Speech-Language Function

Geschwind, N. (1965). Disconnexion syndromes in animals and man. *Brain, 88*, 237–294, 585–644.

Ojemann, G., & Mateer, C. (1979). Human language cortex: Localization of memory, syntax, and sequential motor-phoneme identification systems. *Science, 205*, 1401–1403.

Penfield, W. G., & Roberts, L. (1959). *Speech and brain mechanisms*. Princeton, N.J.: Princeton University Press.

The Clinical-Pathological Method in Speech

Caplan, D. (1981). On the cerebral localization of language functions: Logical and empirical issues surrounding deficit analysis and functional localization. *Brain and Language*, 14, 120–137.

Glassman, R. B. (1978). The logic of lesion experiment and its role in the neural sciences. In S. Finger (Ed.), *Recovery from brain damage: Recovery and theory*. New York: Plenum Press.

Cerebral Arteries

Mohr, J. P., Pressin, M. S., Finkelstein, S., Funkenstine, H. H., Duncan, G. W., & Davis, K. R. (1978). Broca aphasia: Pathologic and clinical aspects. *Neurology 28*, 311–324.

Toole, J., & Patel, A. (1984). *Cerebrovascular disorders* (3rd ed.). Raven Press.

CHAPTER TEN

The Central Language Mechanism and Its Disorders

" . . . it was Wernicke's paper which made the first searching attempt to link the facts of anatomy with the facts of behavior in a way that permitted prediction of syndromes and the organized test of hypothesis. Like Meynert he gave the brain life."

—Norman Geschwind, *Cortex*, 1967

BROCA'S DISCOVERY OF a specific speech-language area in the left hemisphere of the brain had dramatic consequences for neurology. It prompted European neurologists to formulate numerous hypothetical models of the central language mechanism. Several of these models were highly speculative and were based on limited evidence of the correlation between behavioral deficits and brain lesions. Even today the central mechanism for language is not completely understood, and it remains risky to attempt to formulate a model for normal and abnormal communication. However, it is generally conceded that the model formulated by Carl Wernicke (1848–1905) is the most valid and powerful model of the central language mechanism (Buckingham, 1982). The model presented here is based on Wernicke's conception and its modern variations (Eggert, 1977; Geschwind, 1965).

A Model for Language and Its Disorders

Perisylvian Zone

The major neurologic components of language are situated in the area of the dominant hemisphere known as the perisylvian speech area. Table 10-1 summarizes the components of the language model. This zone contains Broca's area, Wernicke's area, the supramarginal gyrus, and the angular gyrus, as well as the major long association tracts that connect the many language centers.

Broca's and Wernicke's Areas

The location and limits of Broca's area in the frontal lobe are well defined by research from several sources, and there is considerable documentation that the area functions primarily as a center for the motor programming of speech articulation movements. Wernicke's area, found in the temporal lobe, rivals Broca's area as a major component in a model of neurologic language functioning. The function of the center is well agreed on, although its borders are sometimes disputed. In contrast to Broca's area, which serves the expressive aspects of motor speech, Wernicke's area is devoted to another major aspect of language—reception of speech. It is assumed that neural structures in Wernicke's area not only allow for comprehension of oral language, but also, in some as-yet-undefined manner, underlie the formulation of internal linguistic concepts. During speaking these are transmitted anteriorly in the brain, traveling forward to Broca's area for the motor programming and expression of language. Little is

TABLE 10-1
Major Components of the Central Language Mechanism Model

Broca's area	Motor programming for articulation
Motor strip	Activates muscles for articulation
Arcuate fasciculus	Transmits linguistic information to anterior areas from posterior areas
Wernicke's area	Comprehension of oral language
Angular gyrus	Integrates visual, auditory, and tactile information Symbolic integration for reading
Supramarginal gyrus	Symbolic integration for writing
Corpus callosum	Transmits information between hemispheres
Subcortical areas	Thalamic naming and memory mechanisms

actually known about the neural correlates of this internal aspect of language, and major advances in knowledge await future research.

Arcuate Fasciculus

Wernicke must be given credit for developing a language model that highlights the connective association pathways between the frontal and temporal speech-language areas. He, in fact, postulated in addition to a motor (Broca's) and a sensory (Wernicke's) aphasia, an aphasia involving these connective association tracts, called *conduction aphasia*. The fiber connections between Broca's area and Wernicke's area are now generally agreed on to be the arcuate fasciculus. The fibers, as described earlier, leave the auditory association area in the temporal lobe, arch around and under the supramarginal gyrus, and pass through the parietal operculum. They travel forward as part of the long association tract known as the superior longitudinal fasciculus, finally ending in Broca's area.

Angular Gyrus

Included as a significant component of the language model is the angular gyrus in the left parietal lobe. Joseph J. Dejerine (1849–1917) suggested that this area was one of two sites associated with the reading disorder called *alexia*. Alexia can also be associated with a lesion of the left occipital lobe accompanied by a lesion of the splenium of the corpus callosum. The left occipital lobe lesion produces a right hemianopsia. The lesion in the splenium prevents the right occipital cortex from transmitting information to the left angular gyrus. The hemianopsia compounded by this disconnection syndrome produces a severe alexia (Dejerine, 1891, 1892).

Inferior Frontal Gyrus

D. Frank Benson has described a third alexia, known as *frontal alexia* (Benson, 1977). The lesion is in the inferior frontal gyrus and extends to the subcortical tissue in the anterior insula of the dominant hemisphere. This third type of alexia is often seen in cases of Broca's aphasia. It may be considered an *aphasic alexia*—an alexia associated with a major aphasic syndrome.

Supramarginal Gyrus

Anterior to the angular gyrus is the supramarginal gyrus, curving around the posterior end of the Sylvian fissure. Together with the angular gyrus, it is known as the *inferior parietal lobule*. Lesions of the supramarginal gyrus are associated with *agraphia*, or writing disorders (see Figure 10-1 and 10-2 for current models of the cortical language mechanisms).

Subcortical Mechanisms

The model displayed in Figure 10-1 suggests that neural mechanisms for language are limited to the cerebral cortex, but evidence from several sources indicates that subcortical mechanisms also play a role. Wilder G. Penfield (1891–1976) and Lamar Roberts (1919–1978) were among the first investigators to present evidence for possible subcortical mechanisms for language and speech (Penfield & Roberts, 1959). They suggested that the pulvinar and ventrolateral nucleus of the thalamus serve as a relay station between Broca's and Wernicke's areas. They demonstrated massive fiber tracts to and from the thalamus and the major cortical speech areas. In addition, direct electrical stimulation of the left pulvinar and ventrolateral nucleus have produced naming problems. Subcortical aphasias have been reported since the last century, but their existence

FIGURE 10-1   A model of the central language mechanism on the dominant cerebral hemisphere. Geschwind (1975) has provided components of the brain mechanisms for language.

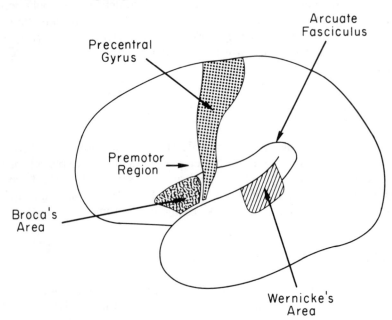

FIGURE 10-2   A superior view of the model of the central language mechanism showing the corpus callosum and the interhemispheric motor pathways that may be involved in apraxia

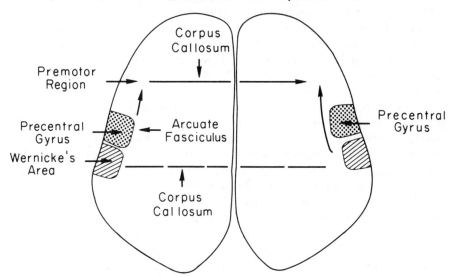

Source: Geschwind "The Apraxias: Neural Mechanisms of Disorders of Learned Movements," *American Scientist*, 63, 188–195, 1975.

has remained controversial. In recent years, however, several cases of thalamic hemorrhage, verified by computerized tomographic brain scan, have indicated that aphasia can result from subcortical lesion alone, without association with cortical damage (Mohr, Watters, & Duncan, 1975). In addition to thalamic aphasia, language disturbance has also been demonstrated in cases with lesions of the internal capsule and the adjacent putamen (Naesar et al., 1982). If patients have capsular/putaminal lesions with anterior-superior white matter extension, they show good auditory comprehension and grammatic use, but slow dysarthric speech with a lasting right hemiplegia. When patients have posterior lesions in the capsule and putamen with white matter extension into the auditory radiations, they show poor comprehension, fluent but defective speech known as Wernicke-type speech, and a lasting right hemiplegia. In patients with capsular/putaminal lesions that show both posterior and anterior-superior extension, a severe receptive-expressive asphasia is found, along with a lasting right hemiplegia. This pattern is clearly different from subcortical thalamic aphasias.

Subcortical language mechanisms are not completely understood, and it is apparent that they play a less significant role than cortical mechanisms do, but their existence appears to be well confirmed. Specific syndromes of subcortical speech and language disturbance will no doubt be described more fully in the future.

Model Functioning

Experts who accept this model describe its function in this manner. Neural motor plans for speech sounds and their sequence in syllables and words are formulated in Broca's area, area 44 (Figure 9-4). Motor commands are projected to the adjacent premotor cortex (6) and to the lower portion of the motor cortex (4), and the actual movement commands for articulation are projected to the muscles of the vocal mechanism via the corticobulbar tracts and the cranial nerves.

Speech perception of oral language is a function of Wernicke's area, which is composed of the superior and middle temporal gyrus. *Neologistic jargon aphasia* results from damage to both these gyri. Neologistic jargon aphasia is characterized by unintelligible fluent speech performance. The neologisms noted in the speech refer to coined words that normally do not appear in the language. Neologistic jargon aphasia with severe semantic and syntactic disturbances is associated with damage at the temporal-parietal juncture, including the supramarginal gyrus and parietal operculum. The disorders suggest that the processing of sentences at the syntactic and semantic levels may involve the auditory association areas of the left temporal lobe (areas 22 and 42), the supramarginal gyrus (area 40), and the parietal operculum in Wernicke's area. The utterance, in a manner as yet unknown, is transmitted via the arcuate fasciculus to Broca's area, where the detailed plans for articulation and vocalization are evoked. A neurolinguistic model such as this, which indicates that Wernicke's area is primarily responsible for auditory comprehension as well as part of the mechanism for initiating the plans for the deep structure of sentences, is found in the work of the linguist Harry Whitaker (1971).

The calling up of words is a critical function in any model of the language mechanism. The angular gyrus is important for word recall as well as for reading and writing. Word recall defects are associated with lesions in the perisylvian zone. Such defects are also present in generalized brain syndromes such as encephalitis. The fact that neurologists view word recall disorders, or *anomia*, as nonlocalizing symptoms has been interpreted to mean that the lexical store required for semantic concepts in sentences has broad representation throughout the brain.

Collosal fibers convey auditory information received at the right Heschl's gyrus to the left hemisphere for processing in the major central language system of the perisylvian zone. Split-brain studies indicate that the right hemisphere participates in language processing to a limited degree only. The right hemisphere comprehends sentences at a low level, recognizing noun and verb categories equally well, but does not process syntax as well as the left hemisphere does (Springer & Deutsch, 1981).

Although the primary cortical brain mechanisms for language are encompassed in the perisylvian zone, disturbances of language can be produced by lesions outside the primary speech-language zones. *Transcortical* or *border zone aphasic syndromes* have been identified as occurring in these zones. These syndromes are associated with lesions falling beyond the perisylvian area (see Figure 10-3). These syndromes, characterized by aphasia without repetition disturbance, are thought to involve cortical areas in a vascular border zone between the territory of the middle cerebral artery and that of the anterior and posterior cerebral arteries. In *transcortical motor aphasia* the lesion is anterior or superior to Broca's area. In *transcortical sensory aphasia* the lesions are at the posterior temporal juncture of the dominant hemisphere. The implication that can be drawn from these clinical data is that language is supported by wide territories in the left hemisphere, with a focus on brain mechanisms in the central portion of the hemisphere devoted to language.

Model Usefulness

The model described had its strongest advocate in a contemporary neurologist, Norman Geschwind (1926–1984). The Geschwind model is a connectionist

FIGURE 10-3   The transcortical border zone. Around the perisylvian speech zone is a large area that is the site of the transcortical aphasias (striped area). B = Broca's area; W = Wernicke's area; AF = arcuate fasciculus; 1 = area of transcortical motor aphasia; 2 = area of transcortical sensory aphasia.

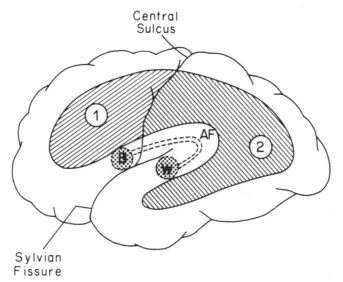

Source: Redrawn and reproduced with permission from M. Espir and F. Rose, *Basic Neurology of Speech and Language* (3rd ed.) (Blackwell Scientific Publications, 1983).

conception of the higher mental functions of speech and language, and as such it gives importance to the classic language and speech centers and highlights the significance of the interconnection of the association fibers between major centers. The model has been of significant use to the clinical neurologist because it allows a high degree of predictability of symptoms associated with specific lesion sites. In addition, the model also predicts possible aphasic syndromes not yet described. It does this by postulating possible lesion sites for these syndromes. In general the model has been confirmed by clinical studies. The classic language centers have been established through computerized tomography and other current objective neurodiagnostic procedures. Geschwind (1969), however, has pointed out that there are some conditions under which the model has not always fulfilled its promise. First, certain features of aphasic syndromes are not readily explained by the model. Second, aphasic cases occasionally occur whose existence is not predicted by the model. Third, in a few cases the expected symptoms do not appear when there is an adequate lesion. Despite these limitations, the model has been extremely useful for neurologists, linguists, and speech-language pathologists.

Whitaker (1971) has correlated the neurologic model with a form of generative transformational grammar. His linguistic analyses of Broca's and Wernicke's aphasia have provided evidence for neurologic sites for several linguistic mechanisms. He also has suggested that the classic linguistic distinction between *competence* and *performance* in language plays a special role in aphasia. Contrary to the belief of many neurolinguists who hold that competence—the tacit knowledge of language—is retained intact in aphasia while only performance is disturbed, Whitaker believes that both competence and performance are compromised after cerebral injury.

Aphasia Classification

The aphasia literature is characterized by a proliferation of clinical classification schemes. The history of aphasia is peopled by students of the disorder who either communicated poorly to each other about the disorder or were in clear disagreement about the nature of the syndromes. Syndromes were often named or classified in terms of personal bias. This has resulted in a number of confusing classification systems. Similar names in two classification systems might be used to describe radically different language syndromes, each with strikingly different lesion sites.

Speech-language pathologists who have devised classification systems have generally disregarded the site of lesion in their systems. They have based their classifications on patterns of performance on standardized language tests. Tests that use classification systems based on performance alone, rather than extensive neurologic data, are Wepman's *Language Modalities Test for Aphasia* (Wepman & Jones, 1961), Schuell's *Minnesota Test for Differential Diagnosis of Aphasia* (Schuell, 1965) and the *Porch Index of Communicative Ability* (Porch, 1967, 1971). The approach to classification based on language performance alone has further complicated the issue of classification.

Dichotomous Classification

It is common to classify patients broadly into one of two categories based on the general locus of the presumed lesion, before specific syndromes are identified. The dichotomous classification of *receptive* and *expressive* aphasia, introduced in 1935 by the neurologist Theodore Weisenburg and the psychologist Katherine McBride, has been one of the most widely used modern divisions. Expressive aphasia is generally associated with anterior lesions and receptive aphasia with posterior lesions.

The *motor* and *sensory* division of aphasia introduced by Wernicke has been widely employed. Motor aphasia usually implies anterior cortical pathology, usually located in the frontal lobe. Sensory aphasia implies a posterior lesion in the temporal lobe. Some experts have done away with the classic terms *motor* and *sensory* and directly classify the aphasias as *anterior* and *posterior*, referring to lesion site.

A recent and widely used dichotomy for spontaneous language in aphasia is *fluent-nonfluent*. All aphasics show some degree of expressive involvement in conversational language. It has been argued that the expressive language of an aphasic can be appropriately described as *fluent* or *nonfluent*. This dichotomy is often considered better than expressive-receptive because it recognizes that practically all aphasics demonstrate some expressive difficulty.

Classification Agreement

Much of the supposed confusion in classification is artificial. There is generally more agreement on the critical features that distinguish various aphasia syndromes than on the names applied to them. The syndromes of the *speech area*, or perisylvian zone, are the most widely accepted of the aphasic syndromes. These include Broca's, Wernicke's, and global aphasia, generally considered the most common aphasic syndromes. Conduction aphasia is a less common perisylvian syndrome. The transcortical aphasias and various alexic syndromes have their lesion sites outside the perisylvian zone.

Broca's Aphasia
This aphasia is marked by nonfluent conversation, decreased verbal output, increased effort in speaking, shortened sentence length, dysprosody, and agram-

matism (reduction of syntactic filler words with retention of nouns, verbs, and adjectives). There are often accompanying motor speech disorders—apraxia of speech and dysarthria. Some neurologists believe that what are called speech apraxic symptoms by speech-language pathologists are merely a form of transient nonfluent aphasia. Lesions limited to Broca's area alone produce speech apraxia or this form of transient aphasia. More widespread lesions produce a chronic and classic clinical picture.

Comprehension of spoken language is always qualitatively better in Broca's aphasia than is production of language. There is much variation, from near normal to clearly abnormal. Often Broca's aphasics have difficulty in understanding syntactic relationships, showing difficulty in comprehending those syntactical items that they have difficulty in expressing. Repetition is always abnormal, and confrontation naming (naming objects and pictures) is poor. Oral reading and reading comprehension are usually poor, although some patients do well. Writing is poor, marked by misspellings and letter omission. In addition, the patient usually has a right hemiparesis and uses the left hand for writing. Some patients cannot write at all because of paresis.

Wernicke's Aphasia

This is a fluent aphasia, characterized by difficulty in understanding language as well as difficulty in repetition of language. The speech is fluent but paraphasic. *Paraphasia* includes the omission of parts of words, incorrect use of correct words, use of neologisms (newly coined words), and substitution of incorrect phonemes in words for correct ones. *Verbal paraphasia* is the incorrect use of words; *literal paraphasia* is the substitution of incorrect phonemes for correct phonemes.

The fluent verbal output may be excessive, a condition called *logorrhea*. Phrase length is normal, and in most cases syntactic structure is acceptable. Articulation and prosody are usually not abnormal. The speech often lacks meaningful and substantive words and is described as *empty speech* clinically. Use of jargon is common, and some cases who are unintelligible because of excessive jargon and neologistic terms are called *neologistic jargon aphasics*.

Comprehension of language is poor, and some patients appear to understand no spoken language at all. Others understand only some words, and certain cases have distinct problems in discriminating phonemes. Repetition of spoken language is poor, and failure and paraphasic errors characterize confrontation naming tasks. Reading is generally disturbed and often parallels the disturbance in the comprehension of spoken language. If written language is intact, the syndrome is sometimes called *pure word deafness*.

Conduction Aphasia

This is a fluent aphasia characterized by intact comprehension and articulation. Repetition is poor and phoneme substitutions are frequent because of the inability to match acoustic information with motor plans for the output of phonemes. Wernicke postulated a lesion in the connection between Broca's and Wernicke's area. Conduction aphasia is less well accepted as a diagnosis than Broca's or Wernicke's aphasia because of questions about the site of lesion. The lesion is not always in the arcuate fasciculus as Wernicke postulated, but the language syndrome has been described repeatedly and can be diagnosed from symptoms alone without neuropathologic evidence. Two distinct locations of pathology have been demonstrated in conduction aphasia. One involves the arcuate fasciculus in the dominant hemisphere, usually deep in the supramarginal gyrus. Some experts argue that the involvement of the supramarginal cortex itself rather than deep white matter is the critical site. The other major site is said to be in the left temporal lobe in the auditory association area.

Conversational speech is fluent and paraphasic, but generally the speech quantity is reduced compared with that of a Wernicke's aphasic. Pauses, hesitation, and incidents of word-finding difficulties are common, so the speech is dysprosodic. Literal paraphasia is often present. Articulation is good. Comprehension of spoken language is also adequate in most cases. If it is disturbed, the diagnosis of conduction aphasia should be questioned.

Repetition of language presents a serious problem to the conduction aphasic, and the dramatic difference between comprehension and repetition is a clue to correct diagnosis. Repetition is much poorer than the ability to produce words in conversational speech. Paraphasic substitutions of words are often present in repetition attempts. Errors are also present in confrontation naming. Reading disturbance is present in conduction aphasia. Oral reading is paraphasic, whereas silent reading for comprehension is adequate. Writing disturbance or *dysgraphia* is present. Spelling is poor, with omissions, reversals, and substitutions of letters. Words in sentences may be reversed, omitted, or misplaced.

Global Aphasia

This aphasic disorder, also known as *total aphasia*, is accepted by many neurologists and speech-language pathologists. Global aphasia is marked by severe impairment of both understanding and expression of language. The person is usually mute or uses repetitive vocalization. This aphasia is usually associated with a large lesion in the perisylvian area. The lesion does not serve as a localizing one for the neurologist, except to the left perisylvian area.

Expressive language is always limited, although true mutism rarely appears other than initially. The patient can often use inflected phonation and sometimes can use simple words like expletives repetitively. Comprehension is often reported to be better than production in the global aphasic. Often the global aphasic becomes adept at interpreting nonverbal communication through gestures and facial and body language. This nonverbal comprehension may be mistaken for comprehension of the spoken word.

The global aphasic does not repeat. If a patient who appears to be global repeats adequately, the speech-language pathologist and neurologist should suspect that one of the transcortical aphasic syndromes, to be described, is present instead of a true global aphasia. Confrontation naming is severely or completely impaired. Reading and writing are also severely or totally impaired. Many of the language functions are not reversible with treatment.

Transcortical Aphasias
These language disturbances are a set of aphasic syndromes whose lesions fall outside the perisylvian area. They have been given various names, but Wernicke identified them as transcortical aphasias, and they are probably identified most commonly by this name. D. Frank Benson (1979) has called them border zone aphasic syndromes since the lesions usually are found in a vascular border zone between the field of the middle cerebral artery and the area supplied by the anterior or posterior cerebral arteries. A hallmark of the transcortical aphasias is the retention of the ability to repeat with good accuracy. In contrast, the aphasias of the perisylvian area present a repetition defect.

Three transcortical aphasias are generally recognized: transcortical motor aphasia, transcortical sensory aphasia, and a mixed transcortical aphasia. This last type has also been called a syndrome of *isolation of the speech area. Transcortical motor aphasia* is a nonfluent aphasia marked by more dysfluency and effort in conversation than is usually seen in Broca's aphasia. Serial speech, repetition, and comprehension appear surprisingly adequate. The lesion is anterior or superior to Broca's area in the dominant hemisphere.

A *transcortical sensory aphasia* is fluent and marked by paraphasias with semantic and neologistic substitutions. The most striking feature is *echolalia*, the repetition of heard phrases. Examples of echolalia are often incorporated into the patient's speech. Comprehension is poor, in sharp contrast to repetition, which is surprisingly good. Reading, writing, and naming are poor. The site of the lesion is controversial. It is usually found in either the temporal or the parietal border zone, or a combination of both these sites. In the best-defined cases, a lesion is found at the posterior junction of the temporal and parietal lobes of the dominant hemisphere.

Mixed transcortical aphasia is rare. The most striking feature is severely disordered language except in one area—repetition. Patients do not speak unless they are spoken to, and answer only in repetition. The articulation of phonemes is good, but the expressive language as a whole is nonfluent. Comprehension is defective, with little or no demonstrable understanding of spoken language. Visual-field defects and other neurologic signs are common. The pathologies are mixed but generally appear to involve the vascular border zones of the left hemisphere.

Anomic Aphasia
Word-finding difficulties, known as *anomia*, are common in many types of aphasia as well as in nonaphasic medical conditions. In fact, many neurologists believe it is inappropriate to consider a diagnosis of aphasia without evidence of some anomia. Further, anomia occurs in most types of dementia and is a clear diagnostic feature of Alzheimer's syndrome, a major dementia. Anomia

often is the only major language residual following recovery from aphasia of any clinical type, and it remains a long-lasting problem in the recovered aphasic. Clearly, anomia is not a good localizing sympton for the neurologist. Rather, it is a common symptom in what is called *nonfocal brain disease*. In those neurologic conditions, where the whole brain is generally affected, anomia is a common language symptom. It occurs in many brain conditions, including encephalitis, increased intracranial pressure, subarachnoid hemmorhage, concussion, and toxic-metabolic encephalopathy.

When anomia is the most prominent symptom in the aphasic syndrome, the condition is called *anomic aphasia*. Expressive speech is often very characteristic in anomic aphasia. Spontaneous speech is fluent but marked by a lack of substantive words. Nonspecific words tend to be substituted for precise lexical items. Syntax is generally preserved except for word recall pauses. The use of vague, indefinite words produces the characteristic of empty speech. Verbal paraphasia results from attempts to make word substitutions for words unavailable to word recall. *Circumlocution*, or the production of a circuitous and wordy description for the unrecalled word, is common.

Comprehension of spoken language in anomic aphasics may range from normal to significantly impaired, but generally is good. Repetition of spoken language is also good. Confrontation naming is impaired but may vary from mild to severe. Reading and writing are often normal but at times show impairment.

Generally the etiology of anomia and anomic aphasia is very variable. Any pathology producing structural changes of the brain in language areas of either hemisphere can result in anomic aphasia. A prominent site is the juncture of the temporal and parietal lobe. A localization scheme for the aphasias is found in Table 10-2.

Testing for Aphasia

Aphasia testing has had a long history in neurology and speech-language pathology. Broca reportedly tested his patients with conversational questions in addition to testing tongue movements, writing, and arithmetic. He also described their gestures. In 1926 the British neurologist Henry Head (1861–1940) published the first systematic aphasia examination in English. The test was not standardized and contained some items that were difficult for normals to perform. Since the appearance of the Head tests, several unstandardized scales as well as many psychometrically sound test batteries have been developed to assess language disturbance in brain injury.

Aphasia tests have been constructed to serve many purposes and have been based on a variety of theoretical biases concerning the nature of the impairment in aphasia. The recent standardized tests generally measure primary language ability while deemphasizing intelligence and educational achievement.

TABLE 10-2
Localization of the Aphasias in the Central Language Mechanism

Aphasias of the Perisylvian Zone
  Broca's aphasia
  Wernicke's aphasia
  Global aphasia
  Conduction aphasia

Transcortical Aphasias of the Borderzone
  Transcortical motor aphasia
  Transcortical sensory aphasia
  Mixed transcortical aphasia
  (Isolation of the speech area)

Aphasias of Subcortical Areas
  Thalamic aphasia
  Capsular/putamenal aphasia syndromes

These tests are capable of separating language performance that is normal from the abnormal, and most allow the experienced speech-language pathologist to determine whether the language disturbance is truly aphasic in nature and not a nonaphasic language disorder. This is accomplished by comparing the pattern of language performance on the test to the language performance of known aphasic patients.

Most standardized aphasia tests assess a wide variety of language functions over a broad range of severity. Some tests yield an overall score of severity, but all tests provide a profile of deficits in the major language modalities. Most tests provided a system of classifying the aphasic performance by clinical type. The majority of tests in use today have not been constructed with the classical neurologic model of Wernicke as their theoretical foundation. Speech pathologists and psychologists have been more concerned about developing aphasia tests that measure precisely the language behavior of aphasias under standardized conditions than they have in providing tests that predict and confirm possible lesions or verify the validity of classical models of neurologic language mechanisms.

Two aphasia tests use a classification based on the classic aphasia syndromes predicted by the Wernicke model. These are the *Boston Diagnostic Aphasia Examination* (BDAE) and the *Western Aphasia Battery* (WAB). The Boston Examination became commercially available in 1972 and was then revised in a second edition (Goodglass & Kaplan, 1983). The Boston Examination yields a diagnosis of the presence of aphasia and clinical type of aphasia. It offers inferences about the possible location of brain damage. It is a comprehensive battery of twenty-seven subtests that may take more than one test session to complete. Statistically derived profiles are available for Broca's, Wernicke's, and anomic aphasia. Case histories are provided to aid in classification of conduction and transcortical sensory aphasia. Statistical data can be used to identify global aphasics with deviations from z-score measures. Information from the Cookie-Theft Picture responses and other data from the Boston Examination will allow diagnosis of language impairment in Alzheimer's disease. Supplementary nonverbal tests from the Boston Examination can be used to assess some of the hemispheric disconnection syndromes.

The *Western Aphasia Battery* (Kertesz, 1983) is a shorter version of the Boston Examination. Its administration time is approximately one hour. It yields a single overall score, the *aphasia quotient* (AQ), which separates normal language performance from abnormal language performance. The AQ is derived from auditory and speech tests. The AQ may also be used as an index of recovery. A *performance quotient* (PQ) is derived from tests for reading, writing, and nonverbal functions. The score derived from subtests is the *cortical quotient* (CQ). Means, standard deviations, and graphic profiles are provided for eight aphasic syndromes: global, Broca's isolation, transcortical motor, Wernicke's, transcortical sensory, conduction, and anomic. Correlations between CT scan data for both the Boston Examination and the *Western Aphasia Battery* suggest that in most cases these two tests generally predict classical lesion sites and tend to verify major elements of the Wernicke central language model.

Speech-language pathologists should be aware of other major aphasia tests in use today which are not based on a classic neurologic model. The description of these tests, not as closely based on a specific neurologic theory as the Boston Examination and the *Western Aphasia Battery*, are beyond the purpose of this book. These aphasia tests include the comprehensive batteries such as Schuell's *Minnesota Test for the Differential Diagnosis of Aphasia* (MTDDA) (1965), the *Porch Index of Communicative Ability* (PICA) (1969, 1971), Wepman's *Language Modalities Test for Aphasia* (LMTA) (1961), and the *Neurosensory Center Comprehensive Examination for Aphasia* (NCCEA) (Spreen and Benton, 1969). Shorter screening tests and scales of aphasia include Eisenson's *Examining for Aphasia* (1954), *Halstead-Wepman-Reitan Aphasia Screening Test* (DeMyer, 1980), Schuell's *Short Examination for Aphasia* (1966), and Keenan and Brassell's *Aphasia Language Performance Scales* (1975).

Clinical neurologists usually assess language and aphasia disturbances as part of the mental-status examination of higher cerebral functions. The mental-status examination is part of the traditional neurologic examination, which is designed to assess major functions of the total nervous system and to lateralize and localize dysfunction when it is present.

Testing for aphasia in the mental-status examination at bedside is one of the oldest areas of examination in the traditional clinical neurologic examination. The techniques are not standardized but vary from one neurologic examiner to another. Generally, the goals of examination are to determine the presence or absence of aphasia, assess its extent in various areas of language function, determine the severity and clinical type of aphasia, and suggest the type and site of the lesion. The neurologist will select language test items that will best achieve these various goals. Commonly employed areas of language assessment include the quantity and quality of conversational speech with the identification of possible dysarthria, repetition of spoken speech, comprehension of spoken speech, word finding or naming, reading, and writing. The language functions tested by the neurologist are found in Table 10-3. An example of a bedside examination of speech and language designed for the clinical neurologist is found in the appendix.

Associated Central Disturbances

Agnosia

The term *agnosia* was introduced into neurology by Sigmund Freud (1856–1939) in 1891. Agnosia is a disorder of recognition due to cerebral injury. Table 10-4 defines the agnosia syndromes. Classic theory places the lesion responsible

TABLE 10-3
Language Functions of Major Aphasias*

	Spontaneous Speech	*Comprehension*	*Repetition*	*Reading*	*Writing*
Broca's	Nonfluent	+	−	±	−
Wernicke's	Fluent	−	−	−	Paragraphic
Conduction	Fluent	+	−	+	−
Global	Mute	−	−	−	−
Anomic	Word recall disorder	+	+	+	+
Transcortical motor	Nonfluent	+	+	+	−
Transcortical sensory	Fluent	−	+	+	−
Mixed transcortical (isolation of speech area)	Nonfluent	−	+	−	Paragraphic

+ Relatively intact
− Impaired

*Developed by H. Kirshner, M.D., Department of Neurology, Vanderbilt University.

TABLE 10-4
The Agnosias

Agnosia: A disorder of recognition due to damage to cortical sensory association areas or pathways.

Visual agnosia: Inability to recognize objects, colors, and pictures.

Auditory agnosia: Inability to comprehend speech and/or nonspeech sounds, also called auditory verbal agnosia or pure word deafness.

Tactile syndrome: Inability to recognize objects by touch. Bilateral parietal lobe lesions.

Gerstmann syndrome: Finger agnosia, right-left disorientation, acalculia, and agraphia. Left parietal lobe lesions usually.

---

for the disorder in the sensory association areas of the cerebral cortex, leaving the primary sensory receptor areas intact. To diagnose the classic disorder correctly certain precautions must be observed. First, one must be certain that the lesion is at the level of the cortical association area rather than at the level of sensory receptor, the sensory pathway, or the primary sensory receptor area in the cortex. Second, one must rule out unfamiliarity with the test item as a reason for failure to recognize the sensory stimuli. To establish basic knowledge of an item, it often is a good procedure to have the patient match items. If an item can be matched or recognized in other modalities, unfamiliarity can be ruled out as a possible cause for the lack of recognition. The concept of agnosia has been highly criticized in modern-day neurology.

Geschwind has argued that most of the agnosias can be best understood in the light of newer disconnection theory. Many of the classical agnosias, he maintains, are really isolated disturbances of the naming function resulting from lesions that isolate the language areas in the left hemisphere from the perceptual recognition areas of the right or both hemispheres (Geschwind, 1965).

Visual Agnosia

Analyzed in disconnection terms, classical visual agnosia is produced when tactile associations are lost because there is a disconnection of the tactile areas from the visual areas in addition to a disconnection of the visual areas from the language areas. This complex series of disconnections is consistent with very large bilateral parietal and occipital lobe lesions. These rare lesions have been demonstrated in the few patients with visual agnosia. Geschwind maintains that since there are no direct connections between the visual and somesthetic cortex, visual-somesthetic connections must be mediated by the intervening association cortex in the parietal lobe. A large parietal-occipital lobe lesion is necessary to destroy the association area connections; a small lesion would not produce an agnosia.

Visual agnosia may also result from unilateral lesions. With destruction of the left visual cortex in addition to a lesion of the splenium of the corpus callosum or extensive involvement of the white matter of the association cortex of the left occipital and parietal lobes, a unilateral left visual agnosia may result.

D. Frank Benson (1979) observes that in the few cases of visual agnosia reported, associated findings are common. These may include hemianopsia and prosopagnosia, a visual agnosia for faces. In addition, other associated disorders are a constructional impairment, alexia without agraphia, amnesia, and some degree of anomia. A color-naming defect may also be present. This inability to match seen colors to their spoken names is called a color agnosia, by Benson (1979) and a color anomia by Geschwind (1965). Lesions in the calcarine fissure and splenium are usually present. These lesions, according to Geschwind, disconnect the right visual cortex from the left language areas.

Auditory Agnosia

Two uses of the term *auditory agnosia* are current. First, the term is used to indicate the inability to recognize nonverbal stimuli even though they are heard; in these cases, language is generally easily and readily understood. This use of the term implies a defect in the ability to recognize nonlinguistic auditory stimuli. Second, the term may be used to indicate that linguistic stimuli cannot be comprehended. This has been called an *auditory verbal agnosia* or *pure word deafness*. Inability to recognize nonlinguistic sound in the face of normal hearing acuity often has been described clinically, but the site of lesion is in dispute. The site is usually presumed to be in the auditory association areas of both hemispheres. Pure word deafness is an uncommon syndrome in which the patient cannot comprehend language, but reads aloud with good comprehension. Both unilateral and bilateral temporal lobe lesions have been described. Unilateral lesions are those deep in the temporal lobe in the fibers projecting to Heschl's gyrus. Bilateral lesions have usually been described as occurring in the midportion of the superior temporal gyri of both hemispheres. Geschwind (1965) notes that in pure word deafness with a unilateral lesion, the lesion must be located subcortically in the left temporal lobe so that the auditory radiations as well as the callosal fibers from the opposite auditory region will be interrupted, preventing Wernicke's area from receiving auditory stimulation. In bilateral pure word deafness the lesions in the temporal lobe spare Heschl's gyrus. It is assumed that the lesions on the left cut off connections between the primary auditory receptor cortex and Wernicke's area. The lesion on the right would cut off the origin of the callosal fibers from the right auditory cortex. It may be that auditory agnosia for nonlinguistic sounds in addition to auditory verbal agnosia (pure word deafness) are the bases of the syndrome known as *cortical deafness*. It is likely associated with bilateral temporal lobe lesions.

Tactile Agnosia

Geschwind (1965) has argued that many instances of classical tactile agnosia should more correctly be called *tactile aphasia*. Tactile aphasia is a disturbance characterized by the inability to name objects tactilely with the preservation of the ability to name on the basis of auditory or visual stimulation and in the presence of intact spontaneous speech. The basis of this disorder is demonstrated by the ability to respond to somesthetic stimulation when the response is demanded from the same hemisphere, but an inability to do so if it is demanded from the opposite hemisphere. A lesion in the somesthetic association area of the left parietal lobe destroys the connection between the left somesthetic cortex and the left language area and produces a tactile naming disorder in association with the right hand. This disconnection syndrome is better called a unilateral tactile aphasia than a tactile agnosia. A lesion in the right somesthetic association area or in the corpus callosum is more likely to produce a true tactile agnosia in the right hand.

Beauvois et al. (1978) have reported a bilaterally damaged case which they have called bilateral tactile aphasia. It is analogous to the auditory and visual agnosia disorders. The patient was unable to name objects on touching them, but could give names when they were heard. The lesion is presumed to be in both parietal lobes.

Gerstmann Syndrome

This well-known syndrome includes an agnosia for the fingers as well as right-left disorientation, acalculia, and agraphia. It has been assumed since Joseph Gerstmann's original description in 1931 that when the four symptoms of the syndrome were present, a left parietal lesion could be found. Critics of the syndrome have pointed out that it is rare, and frequently the syndrome is assumed to be present without all four symptoms being identified. D. Frank Benson has also suggested that the classic Gerstmann syndrome is part of a larger left angular gyrus syndrome including alexia, mild fluent aphasia, and mild constructional impairment.

The procedure for testing for finger agnosia and right-left disorientation clinically is simple. The patient is provided with a method of finger identification by numbering the fingers on each hand from one to five, usually beginning with the thumb. The patient then is asked to close his or her eyes, and the examiner randomly touches a finger on either the right or the left hand. The patient is asked to identify the finger touched by the examiner and to indicate whether the finger in question is on the right or the left hand. Each of the ten digits is systematically assessed. If the patient shows confusion in identifying fingers on the right or left hand, further assessment should be completed by having the patient point to objects to his or her right and left. A quick test to assess the integrity of directional orientation is to ask the patient to touch the right hand to the left ear. The remainder of the symptoms may be tested by having the patient write and print words and sentences from dictation to identify agraphia. Simple arithmetic problems that can be calculated both mentally and on paper are useful in identifying acalculia.

Although finger agnosia and right-left disorientation are associated most commonly with left parietal lesions, they also have been seen with right-hemisphere damage in the parietal lobe. A similar syndrome has been identified in children beyond the age of 5 or 6 years and has been called a *developmental Gerstmann syndrome* (Benson & Geschwind, 1970).

Apraxias

Apraxia is a disorder of learned movement that is not caused by paralysis, weakness, or incoordination and cannot be accounted for by sensory loss, comprehension deficits, or inattention to commands, according to Geschwind (1975). It has also been defined as a disorder of motor planning. It is a high-level motor disturbance that involves integration of the motor components that are necessary to carry out a complex motor act.

Apraxias are important to the speech-language pathologist because certain types of apraxia may affect the motor programs of the speech muscles directly. Other forms of apraxia often accompany the aphasias and the other cerebral language deficits in the cortical motor association areas and the association pathways of the brain. The major apraxias are defined in Table 10-5.

Hugo Liepmann (1863–1925) is credited with elucidating the concept of apraxia around the turn of the century, although John Hughlings Jackson described an apraxic disturbance of the tongue as early as 1866. Liepmann used early disconnection theory to explain apraxia and demonstrated lesion sites to support the variety of apraxias he described.

TABLE 10-5
The Apraxias

Apraxia: A disorder in performing voluntary learned motor acts in which similar automatic gestures are intact. It is due to a lesion in motor association areas and association pathways.

Ideomotor apraxia: Motor plans are intact, but individual motor gestures of a motor act are disturbed.

Ideational apraxia: Disturbance in performing the steps of complex motor plans are disturbed.

Construction disturbance: Disturbance in constructing space.

Apraxia of speech: A disorder of motor programming of speech.

Oral apraxia (Buccofacial apraxia): a disorder of nonspeech movements of the oral muscles. Lesion of Broca's or motor association pathways.

Developmental apraxia of speech: Motor speech programming disturbance in childhood. Lesion site controversial.

Ideomotor Apraxia

Ideomotor apraxia is the most common type of apraxia. In this condition the patient fails to carry out a motor act to the examiner's verbal command. Impairments are found in the oral muscles, the upper and lower limbs, and the trunk muscles. Generally, simple motor gestures are disturbed when attempts are made to elicit them by verbal command, but the level of ideation for the plan of the motor gesture is retained. This can be demonstrated on examination. For example, a patient may be unable to lick his lips with his tongue on command, but may show appropriate licking movements during eating. This deficit in tongue movements involves an apraxia of oral muscles. Difficulty, for instance, in saluting or waving the hand, or difficulty in kicking a ball on command are called *limb apraxias*. Difficulty in bending at the waist in a bow or swinging an imaginary baseball bat are called *trunk apraxias*.

Evaluation of ideomotor praxis is best done in a series of hierarchical steps. The most difficult level requires the patient to carry out a spontaneous motor act alone to a verbal command. The examiner must not provide nonverbal cues for the motor gesture. Assume the examiner says, "Show me how to use a screwdriver." Correct performance involves gesturing to place the tool into a screwhead and twisting the wrist. If the patient fails at the spontaneous level, the examiner asks the patient to imitate him. Imitation of a motor act for a patient with ideomotor apraxia is usually easier, but often the improvement in motor performance is only partial. If the patient fails at the imitative level, an actual object is provided and the verbal command is given again. Use of the actual object is the easiest mode in which to perform the required motor act. Many patients, but not all, who fail at the levels of spontaneous performance and imitation will execute movements markedly better with an actual object. Generally, failure at the spontaneous level, coupled with improvement in motor performance during imitation or in object use, allows a positive diagnosis of ideomotor apraxia.

Since ideomotor apraxia may coexist with aphasia, it is necessary for the examiner to make certain the patient understands the verbal commands given when praxis is tested. This avoids a misdiagnosis of apraxia on two counts. First, a diagnosis of apraxia is avoided when there is actually a verbal-comprehension deficit caused by aphasia. Second, a misdiagnosis of a verbal-comprehension deficit is not made when the actual failure in performance is due to an apraxic disturbance.

The ability to perform learned movements on verbal command is associated with the integrity of the language areas in the dominant left hemisphere. Since adequate verbal comprehension is a prerequisite for testing praxis, Wernicke's area in the left hemisphere must be intact. After the verbal command is recognized and comprehended through the linguistic processing of Wernicke's area, neural impulses are probably transmitted to the left supramarginal gyrus for matching to kinesthetic memories of required motor acts. This information is then transmitted forward by neural impulse along the arcuate fasciculus to the premotor area where a motor plan for the required gesture is evoked. This motor plan is relayed to the motor area of the precentral gyrus. At the precentral gyrus the pyramidal tract is activated to carry out the motor gesture. Presumably, according to disconnection theory, a lesion at any point in this complex pathway will produce an apraxic disturbance on the right side, since motor activities on the right are controlled by motor areas and pathways in the left hemisphere.

A verbal command to the right motor cortex for a learned movement on the left side of the body must be transferred from the left premotor cortex to the right premotor cortex by the anterior fibers of the corpus callosum. Any interruption of the anterior callosal fibers will produce an apraxia of the left side, particularly left-handed apraxia. This has been called a *sympathetic apraxia* in individuals who have a Broca's aphasia and a right hemiplegia. It has been also called a *callosal apraxia*. This disorder was described by Liepmann in 1900 and elaborated on by Geschwind in 1975.

The posterior callosal fibers could theoretically transmit motor information to the right premotor area, but as Geschwind (1975) points out, lesions in the right hemisphere rarely result in a left apraxic hand. Apparently the posterior callosal pathway is rarely used to transmit interhemispheric motor impulses that are affected in such a way that apraxia results.

Another motor disorder, called *limb-kinetic apraxia*, was originally described by Liepmann. Currently the disorder is not considered a true apraxia. This motor disorder, often seen in Broca's aphasia, is a mild motor disturbance in the limb and hand opposite the cerebral lesion. The motor disturbance is thought to be the result of a mild pyramidal tract disorder. It is often characterized by clumsiness of the hand and involuntary grasp reflexes.

Oral Apraxia

Speech-language pathologists recognize a nonspeech ideomotor disorder of the oral muscles called *oral apraxia*, the inability to perform nonspeech movements with the muscles of the larynx, pharynx, tongue, and cheeks although automatic and sometimes imitative movements of the same muscles may be preserved. This disorder is not the result of paralysis, weakness, or incoordination of the oral musculature. The disorder may be an isolated one or may coexist with an apraxia of speech (discussed later). Oral apraxia is usually called *buccofacial apraxia* by neurologists.

Oral praxic disturbance must be differentiated from disorders of the motor pathways involved in upper motor neuron and lower motor neuron systems. A careful cranial nerve examination will usually indicate whether the disturbance is on the higher level of motor planning of praxis as opposed to lower-level motor deficit associated with either supranuclear lesions or cranial nerve lesions. Generally motor involvement affects both voluntary and reflexive oral acts in lower-level motor deficits of the central and peripheral nervous system.

Voluntary oral motor acts will be limited by paralysis, weakness, and incoordination. The effects of the paralysis, weakness, and incoordination will be seen in the more reflexive acts of mastication and deglutition. Supranuclear lesions are associated with typical tongue deviation, hypertonic oral muscles, palatal paresis, hyperactive gag reflex, and lower facial paresis. Lower motor neuron lesions are associated tongue deviation and atrophy, hypotonic oral muscles, palatal paresis, and a hyporeflexive gag reflex. Facial paresis is hypotonic. Extrapyramidal lesions produce involuntary movements of oral muscles, and ataxic movements of oral muscles are found in cerebellar disorders.

Oral apraxia testing is completed on a spontaneous level to verbal command and on an imitative level. Love and Webb (1977) have used a twenty-item test adapted from Moore, Rosenbek, and LaPointe (1976), for assessing oral apraxia in adults with cerebral lesions:

Oral Apraxia Test
1. Open your mouth.
2. Stick out your tongue.
3. Blow.
4. Show me your teeth.
5. Pucker up your lips.
6. Touch your nose with your tongue.
7. Bite your lower lip.
8. Whistle.
9. Lick your lips.
10. Clear your throat.
11. Move your tongue in and out.
12. Click your teeth together.
13. Smile.
14. Click your tongue in top of mouth.
15. Chatter your teeth as if you were cold.
16. Touch your chin with your tongue.
17. Cough.
18. Puff out your cheeks.
19. Wiggle your tongue from side to side.
20. Hum.

Failure to perform appropriately in brain-injured adults suggests a diagnosis of oral apraxia.

Apraxia of Speech
Apraxia of speech is an impaired ability to execute voluntarily the appropriate movements for articulation of speech in the absence of paralysis, weakness, or incoordination of the speech musculature. In 1900 Liepmann discussed a form of ideomotor apraxia that could be localized to the speech muscles; some forty

years earlier, Broca described elements of this disorder as part of *aphemia*. Aphemia, the defect in speech and language that Broca believed to result from damage to the third left frontal convolution of the brain, has become known as Broca's aphasia. The disorder is marked by effortful groping for articulatory movements produced in an apparently trial-and-error manner. There is inconsistent articulation on repeated utterances. The speech is dysprosodic, with great difficulty in initiating utterance.

Oral apraxia and speech apraxia may appear independently or may coexist with each other. Oral apraxia may be the basis of a speech apraxia. Speech apraxia may appear in a pure form or may be accompanied by a language disorder, as seen in a classic Broca's aphasia. Some neurologists and speech-language pathologists deny that what is called apraxia of speech is a pure disorder of praxis. They view the apraxic elements in Broca's aphasia as more of a linguistic problem than a motor problem. Evidence is not yet available to resolve the issue.

Pure apraxia of speech has been traditionally associated with the left frontal lobe, and it is presumed that the lesion is localized specifically to Broca's area or deep to it. Apraxia of speech as an element of a classic Broca's aphasia with linguistic disorder implies a lesion extending beyond Broca's area into regions other than the frontal lobe. The issue of lesion site is not yet settled, since sites beyond Broca's area have also been suggested as contributing to speech apraxic symptoms.

If the speech and language pathologist is presented with a case that appears to be a pure speech apraxia, it is necessary to differentiate it from dysarthria. In speech apraxia, articulation is impaired by inconsistent initiation, selection, and sequencing of articulatory movements; in dysarthria, articulatory movements are more consistent, with distortion errors predominating. Speech apraxics do not display consistent disturbances of phonation, respiration, and resonance, whereas dysarthrics almost always display consistent phonatory, resonance, and respiratory disorders. Dysarthrics show impairment of nonspeech musculature, including paralysis, weakness, involuntary movement, or ataxia. Speech apraxics do not present these neurologic impairments of the oral musculature.

Developmental Apraxia of Speech
Developmental apraxia of speech is a childhood condition reportedly similar to apraxia of speech seen in the adult. The disordered movements of the articulators very frequently appear to contribute to a serious phonologic problem in the school-age child. If an apraxic disorder of the oral muscles is present in the preschool years, it may well delay the development of speech and language and the language developmental milestones of one-word, two-word combinations, and three-word sentences may be disrupted. A clear-cut syndrome has not yet emerged, despite considerable clinical research on the topic. It appears that the prime sign of the disorder is awkward movement of the speech muscles that

cannot be attributed to developmental dysarthria. This single sign appears to be the only clearly reliable and consistent feature for diagnosis of the disorder. There is some question whether the articulation errors of children diagnosed as speech apraxics can reliably and validly be separated from the articulation errors of children with severe functional developmental phonologic disorders.

It is also difficult to accept the disorder in a true apraxic context. Apraxia of adulthood has been unequivocally associated with verified brain lesions. In children, however, this has not been the case. In some instances no brain lesion has been demonstrated at all; in other instances inconsistent "soft" neurologic signs have been found (see Chapter 11), but there has been doubt in these cases about the actuality of cerebral dysfunction because there has been no demonstrable structural lesion or evidence of dysfunction. Issues concerning the validity of this syndrome are discussed in greater length in Love and Fitzgerald (1984). The diagnosis of developmental apraxia of speech remains controversial from the standpoint of both speech pathology and neurology.

Ideational Apraxia

Ideational apraxia, also described by Liepmann, is a higher-order disturbance of complex motor planning than is found in ideomotor apraxia. It is an inability to carry out a hierarchical complex motor plan as the result of cerebral injury. It is the converse of ideomotor apraxia, where individual movements are not available to the patient voluntarily. In ideational apraxia, individual movements can be called up, but a complex motor plan involving all elements of a motor act cannot successfully be executed. For instance, in the simple act of striking a match against a matchbox, the ideational apraxia patient may strike the match on the wrong side of the box, use the wrong end of the match to strike the matchbox, or even strike another object such as a candle on the matchbox. The patient appears to have lost an overall concept of how to proceed to complete the motor task. The patient is able to carry out individual motor acts in a series but cannot complete a hierarchical sequence.

Ideational apraxia is a complex disability that is most often seen with bilateral lesions in brain disease. It is frequently associated with the dementias, but any diffuse cerebral disease, particularly one involving the parietal lobes, may show elements of ideational apraxia. It is likely that failure on series of motor tasks in diffuse brain disease is due to some element of ideational apraxia, but often other cognitive deficits play a role in the failure. Certainly memory is frequently impaired, and verbal-comprehension deficits may be present in persons with this apraxic disorder. Patients with ideational apraxia seem to have particular difficulty in recognizing the use of objects. For instance, the patient who strikes a candle on a matchbox demonstrates this recognition deficit. In addition, the individual is unable to structure a logical series of steps of action. These cognitive losses and confusion have serious consequences. The patient cannot manipulate the environment for survival. The person cannot cook a meal, make a bed, or carry out to completion the normal activities of daily living. Generally, the presence of ideational apraxia serves as a sign of serious generalized intellectual deterioration.

Constructional Disturbances

In 1922 Karl Kleist (1879–1960) described a high-level nonverbal constructional disability that he called *construction apraxia*. He defined it as a cortical deficit in which patients were unable to form a construction in space. For instance, the inability to copy simple geometric designs such as a circle, square, or cross, or to reproduce drawings of more complex items such as a wheel, a wagon, or a bicycle, have been described as disorders of constructional apraxia. Construction disability is commonly tested by reproduction of drawings, drawing to command, or constructing block designs, and by matching stick designs. The advantage of testing for constructional disturbances to the speech-language pathologist and neurologist is that the task provides an excellent method for detecting organic brain disease. Constructional ability is the capacity to draw or construct two- or three-dimensional figures or designs from one and two dimensional models. This high-level nonverbal cognitive function is said to involve integration of much of the brain. Occipital, parietal, and frontal lobe functions are employed. With the extensive cerebral functions involved in constructional performance, it is a highly sensitive objective task to suggest brain disorder in patients with few other signs of possible neurologic impairment. Assessment of constructional ability involves much more than testing the capacity to perform high-level learned movements. The term *constructional disturbance* to describe constructional deficits is preferable to the old term *construction apraxia*. The term *constructional apraxia* is a more limited term than *constructional disturbance*.

The parietal lobes serve as the primary cerebral areas for visual motor integration involved in constructional tasks. Visual receptor areas of the occipital lobe and motor areas of the frontal lobe are used in construction tasks, but it is the parietal lobes that are responsible for the integration of activity in construction tasks. Both right and left parietal lobes contribute to construction performance. Lesions in either parietal lobe will produce a construction deficit. Right-hemisphere lesions tend to produce more deficits than do left-hemisphere lesions. Generally, specific lesions of the right parietal lobe result in more severe constructional deficits than do left parietal lesions. For the speech pathologist, constructional disturbance serves as a good general indicator of adult parietal lobe damage. It may be necessary, however, to have a neuropsychologist or an experienced neurologist interpret constructional errors to determine the possible hemispheric lateralization of the lesion. On occasion, anterior lesions in the frontal lobe may even produce a constructional deficit, so parietal lobe localization is not always reliable.

Certain clinical groups with construction disturbances are of particular interest to the speech-language pathologist. The patient with a right-hemisphere constructional disability may have difficulty in verbal attempts to describe and explain his or her visual-spatial motor performance. Patients with bilateral cerebral lesions, as in dementia, show dramatic constructional disturbances. In fact, the constructional disorder is often seen as an early sign of impending dementia. Language is usually disturbed in these patients as a result of the deficit.

Speech-language pathologists frequently use or have become familiar with common tests of constructional abilities. The *Boston Diagnostic Aphasia Examination* (1983) contains a series of supplementary nonlanguage tests that include tests of drawing to command, stick construction, and construction of three-dimensional block designs. The widely used *Bender-Gestalt* tests, for adults and children (Pascal & Suttel, 1951; Koppitz, 1964) are tests of reproduction of drawings. The tests are very sensitive to parietal lobe involvement. Since many adults and children with speech and language disorders that are not of obvious neurologic origin have been suspected of brain dysfunction, these tests have been routinely employed in some speech and language clinics. Standardized developmental drawing tests and other constructional tests also have been used to assess the maturational level of perceptual motor development in children. Children with delayed language development sometimes show delays in constructional abilities also, so these tests may be part of the assessment battery of the speech-language pathologist. The *Developmental Visual Motor Integration Test* (1967) by Berry and Butenica is an example of a developmental constructional test.

Alexia

Alexia is an inability to comprehend the written or printed word as the result of a cerebral lesion. Terms relating to alexia and agraphia are found in Table 10-6. In current usage, *alexia* is an acquired reading disorder, in contrast to *dyslexia*, an innate or constitutional inability to learn to read. The childhood disorder is often called *developmental dyslexia*. Although this distinction in terms is not universal, it is becoming popular. The classic term *word-blindness* is rarely used in neurology or speech pathology. When employed, it implies difficulty in reading words while letter recognition is more intact. The term *literal alexia* means inability to recognize letters; *verbal alexia* indicates that letters are recognized but words are not. Pure alexia is a reading disorder without a writing disorder *(agraphia)*. A variety of terms and types of alexia have been reported, but a limited number of alexic syndromes are widely accepted. The modern understanding of alexia is attributed to Joseph Dejerine (1849–1917), who in 1891 and 1892 described two classic syndromes, alexia without agraphia and alexia with agraphia.

TABLE 10-6
The Alexias and Agraphia

Alexia: A disorder of reading due to cerebral injury

Agraphia: A disorder of writing due to cerebral injury

Types of Alexia

Alexia with agraphia: The lesion is usually in the dominant parietal-temporal area. Alexia may result from a lesion of the angular gyrus and agraphia may be due to a supramarginal lesion.

Alexia without agraphia: The lesion site is controversial, but there are often two lesions, one in the dominant occipital lobe, the other in the splenium of the corpus callosum, according to Dejerine.

Frontal alexia: The lesion is in the inferior frontal lobe and is associated with a classic Broca's aphasia.

Aphasic alexia: The lesions are the same as in the major aphasias.

Agraphia

Lesions in the left frontal or parietal lobe or in the complex pathways necessary for writing.

Alexia without Agraphia

The cardinal feature of this uncommon syndrome is loss of the ability to read printed material, with retained ability to write both to dictation and sponta- neously. Generally other language functions are intact. The alexia occurs sud- denly as the result of a left posterior cerebral artery occlusion in a right-handed person. A striking clinical feature is the patient's ability to write lengthy mean- ingful messages, but the contrasting inability to read their own writing. The patients generally are able to understand words spelled aloud. Some patients are able to read letters but cannot join them to make syllables, but most pure alexics with this syndrome have difficulties with both letter and word reading. None are completely intact in one function while failing utterly in the other. Sometimes there is a color-naming disorder and a mild anomia. The writing seen in the syndrome is not entirely normal, but retained writing capacity is impressive when compared to the minimal reading ability. Often the patient writes better to dictation or spontaneously than when copying. There is usually a right homonymous hemianopsia. Dejerine (1892) found a cerebral infarct in the left occiptal lobe and involvement in the splenium of the corpus callosum. Since the left visual cortex was damaged, all visual information entered the right hemisphere. The right visual cortex perceived the written material but could not transfer it to the left hemisphere because of the callosal lesion. The inferior parietal lobe in the dominant hemisphere, known as the angular gyrus, combined visual and auditory information necessary in both reading and writing; but in this syndrome the inferior parietal lobule was disconnected from all visual input. Since the lobule and its connections with the language area were intact, the patient was able to write normally.

A common accompaniment to alexia without agraphia is a *deficit in color naming*. The patient presents this deficit despite good object naming. Not all cases of pure alexia show defective color identification. Disconnection theory explains this disorder as a loss of pure verbal association similar to that in the reading disorder. The patient recognizes the color but is unable to call up its name because of a disconnection between visual recognition areas and language areas.

Alexia with Agraphia

This syndrome was classically described as almost total reading disorder, limited writing ability with only minimal aphasia, and a calculation disturbance (acalculia). In clinical practice the language symptoms vary more widely than in alexia without agraphia. The aphasia may be only an anomia but may include a Wernicke's aphasia with paraphasia and comprehension deficit. A Gerstmann syndrome is often present. A right homonymous visual field defect is frequently reported but not consistently present.

Defects in reading letters, words, and musical notes are usually seen. Number reading is disordered, and defects of calculation are frequently observed. Writing disturbance is variable in severity but not severe enough to preclude writing of letters. Patients often cannot copy letters, unlike patients with alexia without agraphia, who copy laboriously and slowly. Also unlike pure alexics, these patients do not comprehend words spelled aloud.

Dejerine localized the neuropathology in alexia with agraphia to the angular gyrus of the dominant parietal lobe, and this localization has been universally confirmed since 1891. He surmised that the angular gyrus in the inferior parietal lobule was essential for the recall of written letters and that its destruction results in disturbances in reading and writing in adults.

Frontal Alexia

In 1977 D. Frank Benson described a third alexia, which he indicated could be clearly separated from the two classic syndromes documented by Dejerine and just described. The alexia is associated with frontal lobe pathology that produces a Broca's aphasia. Frontal alexia differs from the two classic alexias of Dejerine in that the patient understands content lexical items better than syntactical and relational lexical items. In fact, there is an inability to comprehend syntax and difficulty in maintaining verbal sequence in reading. Some patients cannot read letters or nonsense syllables, but do recognize words. This is a literal alexia sign. Frontal alexia usually has an accompanying right hemiparesis and a transitory gaze paresis. The lesion is in the anterior part of the brain in the frontal lobe.

Aphasic Alexia

The most common type of alexia is the reading disturbance that accompanies the major clinical types of aphasia. In most instances significant aphasic symptoms produce so much disturbance of language that reading is secondarily involved. It is generally realized in aphasiology that alexic symptoms in aphasia belong properly in a classification of aphasia, not in an outline of alexia. Reading disturbances in each of the major aphasic syndromes were described earlier in this chapter.

Deep and Surface Dyslexia

In 1973 John Marshall and Freda Newcombe, British psychologists, distinguished three types of paralexic errors: visual, surface, and deep. The concept of deep dyslexia has particularly attracted the attention of speech-language pathologists and neurologists. *Visual dyslexia* is one in which visual confusion of letters predominates. *Surface dyslexia* is characterized by grapheme-to-phoneme conversion errors. In reading aloud a large number of neologisms are produced. *Deep dyslexia* is characterized by semantic errors when reading aloud. Reading errors, such as saying *child* for *girl* or *quiet* for *listen* are common. Derivational errors are also present in *deep dyslexia*. Reading *invitation* for *inviting* is an example. Visual errors are also common in deep dyslexia. Deep dyslexia implies that the dyslexic reader goes directly to the semantic value of a word from its printed form without appreciating the sound of the word. Deep dyslexia has also been called *phonemic, syntactic,* or *semantic dyslexia*. These types of paralexic errors can be found in the traditional alexias.

Agraphia

Writing is a complex learned motor act that involves a conversion of oral language symbols into written symbols. It is assumed that the language symbols to be written originate in the posterior language areas in the dominant hemisphere of the brain. These oral symbols are translated into visual symbols in the inferior parietal lobe. The linguistic message is then sent forward to the frontal lobe for motor processing. Lesions in any of these language areas or pathways may produce the writing disorder called *agraphia*. The most common type of agraphia is one that is secondary to aphasia, known as *aphasic agraphia*. Agraphia also may be seen in the absence of aphasia.

A rare agraphia has been described in which there is a writing disturbance in the left hand only. Patients with lesions of the anterior corpus callosum display this syndrome. The lesion disconnects the right motor cortex in the frontal area from the posterior language areas of the left hemisphere. Writing with the right hand is normal because of intact connections between left motor cortex and the left language areas. The callosal lesion disrupts language messages going to the right motor area, which controls the left hand.

Dementia

Dementia is a brain disease of adult and geriatric populations that affects intellect, memory, personality, and language. The most striking clinical feature is the global or diffuse deterioration of cognitive functions due to bilateral diffuse anatomic disease of the brain. Dementia is called *chronic organic brain syndrome* by psychiatrists. Alzheimer's disease, by far the most common dementing illness, is seen routinely by the neurologist. It is important for the neurologist and the speech-language pathologist specializing in neurogenic communication disorders to recognize the early features of this syndrome so that serious social and vocational embarrassment to the patient and family can be avoided. Language impairment has been recognized as one aspect of the global deterioration in all types of dementia, but it has not traditionally received significant emphasis in early mental examinations of dementing patients. It now is apparent that language disturbance may appear in a high proportion of patients with Alzheimer's disease and other demented patients. Additional symptoms of Alzheimer's disease are memory deficits, abstract reasoning disturbances, constructional impairments, and apathy. As dementia progresses, anomia, significant memory loss, geographic and time disorientations, and ideational apraxic signs appear. These signs may be unrecognized by the family and the physician.

Alzheimer's disease traditionally has been thought to be a devastating *presenile dementia* that leads to total helplessness and custodial care, with death occurring within a few years of onset. The term *senile dementia*, on the other hand, has been applied to those cases of dementia whose age of onset was sixty-five years or beyond. It was assumed that its course was slower and less dramatic, with fewer extensive pathologic changes in brain tissue. Recently it has been recognized that the clinical and pathologic conditions in brain failure in both Alzheimer's disease and senile dementia are identical.

The neurologist's role initially is to rule out any treatable disease that is producing the dementing signs and symptoms or, if necessary, establish a diagnosis of chronic dementia. The speech-language pathologist can assist in establishing this diagnosis through language testing and can provide a profile of individual language functioning in demented patients. Language testing appears to be an effective tool for making a diagnosis and prognosis in dementia. Language tests are among the most effective cognitive measures in separating demented patients from a normal aged population. Further, language deterioration may be used as a predictor of mortality in dementia. Kirshner et al. (1984) have suggested that clinically important language disturbances may be an isolated or prominent early symptom of progressive neurologic impairment even before the patient meets all the criteria for a diagnosis of dementia.

The clinical picture of language impairment in dementia is generally one in which spontaneous speech remains fluent and normal syntax is preserved. The content of the speech loses a degree of abstractness and may be described as *empty speech*. Naming ability shows progressive deterioration with serial naming particularly impaired. Repetition and reading aloud tend to be preserved late into the illness. Reading comprehension and writing are usually affected earlier. In later stages with extreme dementia, the patient may display global mental deterioration and no meaningful use of language.

Testing Language in Dementia

No single language battery has been devised to assess language functions, but standard aphasia batteries may be employed to obtain individual profiles of demented patients. The most widely used aphasia test for this purpose is probably the *Boston Diagnostic Aphasia Examination*. Profiles of demented patients with bilateral brain damage have also been reported on the *Porch Index of Communicative Ability*. The naming function has been studied extensively in dementia to determine the underlying psychological mechanisms of this common symptom. Anomia testing appears helpful because it is an early sign of dementia in most studies. Bayles and Boone (1982) found that naming did not differentiate mild senile dements from elderly normals, but Kirshner et al. (1984) found naming impairment in all their demented subjects, even in those subjects with overall scores in the normal range on the *Boston Diagnostic Aphasia Examination*. It appears that phonology and syntax tend to remain intact longer than semantics in chronic dementia. Bayles and Boone have suggested tests to assess this apparent disassociation of language functions in progressive dementia, which may be helpful diagnostically.

Acute Confusional States

Several etiologies produce confusion, characterized by rapid onset, over a period of hours or days. The cause of confusion includes head trauma, metabolic imbalance, adverse drug reactions, and alcohol and drug withdrawal reactions. Patients generally are inattentive, incoherent, and irrelevant; they demonstrate fluctuating levels of consciousness. Agitation and hallucinations, usually visual, are often present. Acute confusional states generally respond to primary medical treatment. Confusional states are not usually the result of focal brain lesions; there is generally widespread cortical and subcortical neuronal dysfunction. Confusional symptoms are also seen during the period of posttraumatic amnesia (PTA) in traumatic head injury.

Symptomatic language impairment is seen in the confusional states. The language disturbance may be viewed as a secondary symptom of the confusional state. Halpern, Darley, and Brown (1973) reported on the language symptoms of patients with confused language in contrast to other language impairments of cerebral involvement. Lesions in these patients were either bilateral or multifocal. Generally vocabulary and syntax were normal. The most striking feature of the language of these confused patients was its irrelevancy and confabulatory nature. Other investigators have also found irrelevant language response and confabulation in dementia, so it is not a pathognomic feature.

Confabulation is the verbal or written expression of fictitious experiences. It generally fills a gap in memory. It is less marked in the presence of aphasia, since it is a response in which the language areas must be relatively intact. It is more often associated with generalized cerebral deficit or dysfunction rather than with focal lesions. Some instances in which focal lesions are associated with confabulation are in the Wernicke-Korsakoff's amnestic syndrome and in ruptured aneurysms of the anterior communicating artery.

Right-Hemisphere Lesions

The neurology of right-hemisphere lesions is of special interest to speech-language pathologists despite the fact that only a small percentage of the population have right-hemispheric or bilateral representation of language functions. The person who is right-hemispheric dominant for language is usually left-handed or ambidextrous, but not all left-handers or ambidexters have right or bilateral representation for language. Milner (1974), reporting on the results of the Wada test in the left-handed, suggests that 70 percent of left-handers have language represented in the left cerebral hemisphere, 15 percent show bilateral representation, and 15 percent have language represented in the right hemisphere. It appears that in the left-hander there are gradients of hemispheric specialization for language that vary from absolute dominance of one hemisphere to an equal contribution of both hemispheres. For the population as a whole, the left hemisphere is dominant for language regardless of handedness.

If a left-hander becomes aphasic, the language disturbance is usually milder than it is in the right-hander who is left language dominant. Generally, left-handers with presumed lesions in the right hemisphere recover more quickly and thoroughly than do right-handers who are left dominant.

The role of the right hemisphere in recovery of language functions after damage to the left language dominant hemisphere is not completely understood. Neurologists, however, from the era of Wernicke and his contemporaries, have attributed language recovery to the action of the right hemisphere. In 1922 the Scandinavian neurologist Salomon E. Henschen (1847–1930) formulated this principle into a statement that has become known as *Henschen's axiom* in neurology. It asserts that restitution of speech is often due to the activity of the opposite hemisphere. Evidence from hemispherectomies and callosal sections suggest that the right hemisphere can assume some language function. The extent of recovery may be limited. In adult hemispherectomies with no cortical tissue left remaining, language behavior is similar to that of a global aphasic with extensive infarction of the perisylvian area. What language remains appears to be completely the product of the right hemisphere. The mechanisms of right-hemisphere recovery are speculative. Some experts believe that language is relearned by the right hemisphere; others believe that right-hemisphere substitution is the release of already-learned language functions of the right hemisphere. Further, there may be considerable individual variation in hemisphere substitution, and some patients may make more use of commissural connections and right-hemisphere mechanisms than do others. Although the precise mechanism of right-hemisphere language in left-hemisphere aphasia is unknown, it is highly likely that the right hemisphere does play some role in language recovery after cerebral insult to the left hemisphere.

In right-hemisphere lesions of the nondominant hemisphere, a broad spectrum of deficits is seen. The most dramatic deficits are the areas of neglect, inattention, denial, visual, and spatial perceptual disorders, as well as constructional disturbances. Language disorders from right-hemisphere lesions, for the most part, are milder than those resulting from left-hemisphere lesions. Some common right-hemisphere lesion syndromes are:

Neglect, Inattention, and Denial

Neglect is a syndrome in which a patient fails to recognize one side of the body and the environmental space surrounding the neglected side of the body. Patients may use only one sleeve in their clothes and may use only one-half of their body, even though the neglected side of the body is free of paralysis. Neglect of one-half of the environmental space is not the result of a visual-field defect.

The exact neurologic locus of the neglect syndrome with right-hemisphere lesions is not exactly known. Chronic parietal lobe damage shows a high correlation with the syndrome. *Unilateral inattention* may be considered a subtle form of the neglect syndrome. Neurologists test for unilateral inattention through a procedure called *double simultaneous stimulation*. All sensory modalities are tested. In tactile testing, corresponding points on the body are touched at the same time with equal intensity. Visual testing involves having the patient fix her gaze at a point on the neurologic examiner's face. The examiner moves her fingers into both the right and left peripheral visual fields, and the patient reports where she sees the fingers. Auditory testing is performed by having the examiner stand behind the patient and provide a stimulus of equal intensity to both ears.

Extinction is present when the patient suppresses stimuli from one side. Extinction may occur in all modalities or in a single modality. When extinction is elicited, the degree of inattention can be assessed by increasing the strength of the stimulus on the inattentive side.

Anatomically global *attention* is related to the ascending reticular activating system in the pons, the midbrain, and an extension of tegmentum into the diencephalon. The ascending reticular activating system is a nonspecific neuronal system that is coupled with the cerebral cortex to control levels of consciousness and attention. The limbic system also contributes to the focusing attention by adding emotional significance to the object of attention. Unilateral inattention probably results from damage to the brainstem reticular formation or to the cortex. Midbrain lesions of the ascending reticular activating system are rare, but general inattention is commonly seen in bilateral diffuse brain dysfunction caused by metabolic disturbance, drug intoxication, cerebral infection, or postsurgical states of the brain. Extensive bilateral cortical damage also produces inattention. Unilateral inattention to double simultaneous stimulation appears to result from a contralateral lesion to the parietal lobe. Right parietal lobe lesions produce more unilateral inattention than do left-hemisphere lesions. The reason for this asymmetry in unilateral attention defects is unknown.

Denial refers to the observation that many patients develop a dramatic denial of their neurologic illness. The term applies to a symptom that may range from mild to severe denial of an illness. An example of severe denial is the patient's lack of recognition of a hemiplegia. The condition was documented by the Russian neurologist Joseph Babinski (1857–1932). He described a patient with a left-sided hemiplegia and left-sided sensory loss who appeared completely unaware of his neurologic deficit. If the patient's hemiplegic arm was placed on the bed along his left side and the neurologist placed his own arm across the patient's waist, the patient would lift the physician's arm aloft. If he were asked to grasp his left arm with his nonparalyzed right arm, he would grasp the physician's arm. Asked to move his paralyzed arm even though his arm was completely hemiplegic, the patient would emphatically say that he could move his arm. Babinski used the term *anosognosia* to describe this unawareness. Anosognosia is sometimes used to describe symptoms of denial other than the ones described here, but it probably is best to limit it to the specific denial impairment Babinski described. This example of denial is highly common in right-hemispheric lesions, much less so in left-hemispheric lesions. Anosogonia does not appear to be an unawareness or denial based on a psychological mechanism but, rather, the result of a more fundamental neurological mechanism of gnostic loss.

Prosopagnosia

This term refers to the inability to recognize familiar faces and their expressions. The patient recognizes individuals by voice rather than visual perception. The disorder may be a memory disturbance for the category of faces plus a disorder of fine visual discrimination. Bilateral lesions are usually found in the occipital-temporal areas in this disorder. The lesion in the right hemisphere is usually specifically in the right temporal-occipital region. A specific type of *color agnosia* often accompanies prosopagnosia. The lesions that cause the facial recognition deficit also cause the color agnosia.

Agraphagnosia

This is the inability to recognize letters and numbers traced on the skin or fingertips when the eyes are closed. If there is a lack of number and letter recognition or recognition of characters traced on the left hand, a right parietal lobe lesion may be suspected.

Visual-Perceptual and Reading Deficits
Right-hemisphere lesions are associated with meaningful interpretation and recall of complex visual structure. Deficits in the perception and recall of letters, words, and numbers may produce problems in reading.

Spatial Organizational Deficits
As noted earlier in this chapter, constructional disturbances are present when there are either right or left parietal lobe lesions. In most instances, right-hemisphere lesions tend to cause more frequent and severe constructional deficits, but constructional deficits can also indicate a left-hemisphere lesion.

Language Disorders of Visual-Spatial Perception
Rivers and Love (1980) reported on the language performance of patients with right-hemisphere lesions when they were asked to respond to a series of visual spatial processing tasks. Their language was judged poorer than that of normal controls, but not as poor as that of the majority of aphasic controls with left-hemisphere lesions. The right-hemisphere lesion cases showed dysnomia in oral storytelling based on a series of visual stimuli, but showed no differences in naming on confrontation of pictured objects from normal subjects. Other investigators have reported mild agrammatism and telegraphic speech plus anomia in a variety of right-hemispheric conditions.

Paralinguistic and Prosodic Deficits
It has been observed that patients with right-hemisphere lesions have difficulty in appreciating humor, interpreting metaphors, understanding antonyms, grasping the connotative aspects of pictures, and perceiving and producing the appropriate affective quality of linguistic utterances. Elliott Ross (1981) has described the inability to match affective tone with the linguistic utterance as *aprosodia.* The right-hemisphere patient who is able to comprehend emotions but cannot express them appropriately has been diagnosed by Ross as having motor aprosodia. This disorder is characterized by monotone speech and poor ability to repeat sentences, with inappropriate variations of affective and prosodic elements of speech. Ross believes that comprehending emotions in language requires matching language and emotion via the corpus callosum. He speculates, however, that motor aprosodia in the right-hemisphere patient involves a lesion below the cerebral hemisphere.

Dysarthria
A dysarthria involving primarily the articulatory aspects of speech has frequently been reported in right-hemisphere lesion cases. This dysarthria has sometimes been called a pathognomonic sign of nondominant-hemisphere dam-

age. Since dysarthria occurs in lesions of either hemisphere or both hemispheres, it cannot be viewed as an unequivocal sign for the diagnosis of right-hemisphere lesions, but it may be used as a corroborating sign of diagnosis of the syndrome of right-hemisphere lesions.

In summary, the speech and language disturbances of the right hemisphere are not as striking as those of the left hemisphere; but without an intact right hemisphere communication in its broadest sense cannot be fully realized. At present, speech-language pathologists do not have at their disposal a standardized battery of subtests to identify the language dysfunctioning in right-hemisphere lesion syndromes. Until a comprehensive language test battery is developed, informal test items can be adapted from the research literature on right-hemisphere language syndromes to meet diagnostic needs.

Summary

The exact neurophysiology of the central language mechanism is not completely known, but a model developed by Carl Wernicke over a century ago, in 1874, has proved to be the most valid and reliable construct for the explanation of the wide array of aphasic symptoms seen clinically. The model has gained wide acceptance among neuroscientists, linguists, and speech-language pathologists. There is growing support for the model from neurosurgical data, brain and CT scans, and other neurodiagnostic procedures.

Norman Geschwind was an outstanding interpreter of the Wernicke model. The model assumes a large perisylvian speech area on the left cerebral cortex which includes all the major anterior and posterior language areas (Broca's, Wernicke's, angular gyrus, supramarginal gyrus) and the intra- and interhemispheric connective pathways—namely, the arcuate fasciculus and the corpus callosum. Recently, subcortical language mechanisms important in memory and naming have been confirmed at the thalamic level. Thalamic aphasia, without cortical involvement, also has become an accepted aphasic syndrome. Other subcortical aphasic syndromes have recently been reported.

Although aphasic classification systems are abundant, the Wernicke model is the source of the most widely used current classification. Aphasias of the perisylvian zone include Broca's aphasia, Wernicke's aphasia, conduction aphasia, and global aphasia. Aphasia syndromes outside the perisylvian speech zone are called transcortical aphasias. These include transcortical motor aphasia, transcortical sensory aphasia, mixed transcortical aphasia, and the isolated speech-area syndrome. Anomic aphasia is usually associated with bilateral lesions or mild involvement of the perisylvian speech area. Other anomic patients show no demonstrable lesions.

Aphasia syndromes have often been dichotomized into fluent or nonfluent disorders in terms of spontaneous speech performance. Nonfluent aphasia is usually associated with anterior lesions and fluent aphasia with posterior lesions.

There are many associated central disturbances seen alone or with aphasia. Agnosia, or recognition, syndromes are uncommon. Bilateral visual agnosia, auditory agnosia, and its two subtypes—pure word deafness and agnosia for nonspeech sounds—are currently accepted as clinical syndromes. Isolated cases of bilateral tactile agnosia have been described but are uncommon.

The Gerstmann syndrome is controversial. It is said to include finger agnosia, left-right disorientation, acalculia, and agraphia as the result of left parietal lobe lesions; it may be seen independently or may coexist with aphasia. A developmental form of the syndrome has also been described.

Apraxia is a disorder of motor programming due to brain injury. The terminology of apraxia is confusing. The historical classification of Hugo Leipmann, including ideational and ideomotor aphasia, is accepted by many clinical neurologists. Limb apraxia, construction disturbance and buccofacial apraxia (oral apraxia) are syndromes frequently reported in the neurologic and neuropsychologic literature. Apraxia of speech is well accepted by speech-language pathologists. Developmental apraxia of speech remains controversial to both disciplines, neurology and speech-language pathology.

Alexia is a reading disturbance that may exist with aphasia or may be seen independently. Alexia with agraphia, alexia without agraphia, and frontal alexia are reasonably well accepted. Aphasia alexia is the most common disorder of reading in adults. Agraphia is writing disturbance due to brain injury. Dementia, primarily an impairment of intellectual functioning, may present a serious language disturbance. The language of acute confusional states is described, and the right-hemisphere lesion syndrome is outlined.

References and Further Readings

Model of the Central Language Mechanism

Benson, D. F. (1977). The third alexia. *Archives of Neurology*, 34, 327–331.

Buckingham, H. W., Jr. (1982). Neuropsychological models of language. In N. Lass, L. McReynolds, J. Northern, and D. Yoder (Eds.), *Speech, language, and hearing*, vol. I. Philadelphia: W. B. Saunders.

Dejerine, J. (1891). Sur un cas de cécité verbal avec agraphie, suivi d'autopsie. *Mem. Soc. Biol.*, 3, 197–201.

Dejerine, J. (1892). Contributions 'a létude anatomo-pathologique et clinique des differentes variétés de cécité. *Mem. Soc. Biol.*, 4, 61–90.

Eggert, G. (1977). *Wernicke's works on aphasia.* The Hague: Mouton.

Geschwind, N. (1967). Wernicke's contribution to the study of aphasia. *Cortex,* 3, 449–463.

Geschwind, N. (1969). Problems in the anatomical understanding of aphasia. In A. L. Benton (Ed.), *Contributions to clinical neuropsychology.* Chicago: Aldine.

Mohr, J. P., Watters, W. C., & Duncan, G. W. (1975). Thalamic hemorrhage and aphasia. *Brain and Language,* 2, 3–17.

Naesar, M. A., Alexander, M. P., Helm-Estabrook, N., Levine, H. L., Laughlin, S., & Geschwind, N. (1982). Aphasia with predominantly subcortical lesion sites. *Archives of Neurology,* 39, 2–14.

Penfield, W. G., & Roberts, L. (1959). *Speech and brain mechanisms.* Princeton, NJ: Princeton University Press.

Springer, S., & Deutsch, G. (1981). *Left brain, right brain.* San Francisco: W. H. Freeman.

Wernicke, K. (1874). *Der Aphasische Symptomkomplex.* Breslau: Kohn and Neigert.

Whitaker, H. A. (1971). *On the representation of language in the human brain.* Edmonton: Linguistic Research, Inc.

Aphasia Classification and Testing

Benson, D. F. (1979). *Aphasia, alexia, and agraphia.* New York: Churchill Livingstone.

DeMeyer, W. (1980). *The technique of the neurologic examination* (3rd ed.). New York: Mc-Graw-Hill.

Eisenson, J. (1954). *Examining for aphasia.* New York: The Psychological Corporation.

Goodglass, H., & Kaplan, E. (1983). *The assessment of aphasia and related disorders* (2nd ed.). Philadelphia: Lea and Febiger.

Head, H. (1926). *Aphasia and kindred disorders of speech.* Cambridge: Cambridge University Press.

Keenan, J. S., & Brassell, E. G. (1975). *Aphasia language performance scales.* Murfreesboro, TN: Pinnacle Press.

Kertesz, A. (1983). *The Western Aphasia Battery.* New York: Grune and Stratton.

Porch, B. E. (1967). *Porch Index of Communicative Ability, vol. I. Theory and development.* Palo Alto, CA: Consulting Psychologists Press.

Porch, B. E. (1971). *Porch Index of Communicative Ability, vol. II. Administration, scoring and interpretation* (Rev. Ed.). Palo Alto, CA: Consulting Psychologists Press.

Schuell, H. M. (1965). *Minnesota Test for Differential Diagnosis of Aphasia.* Minneapolis: University of Minnesota.

Schuell, H. M. (1966). A reevaluation of the short examination for aphasia. *Journal of Speech and Hearing Disorders,* 31, 137–147.

Spreen, O., & Benton, A. L. (1969). *Neurosensory Center Comprehensive Examination of Aphasia (NCCEA),* 1977 revision. Victoria, BC: Neuropsychology Laboratory, University of Victoria.

Weisenburg, T. H., & McBride, K. E. (1935). *Aphasia.* New York: Commonwealth Fund.

Wepman, J. M., & Jones, L. V. (1961). *Studies in aphasia: An approach to testing.* Chicago: Education Industry Service.

The Central Language Disorders

Bayles, K., & Boone, D. (1982). The potential of language tasks for identifying senile dementia. *Journal of Speech and Hearing Disorders*, 47, 210–217.

Beauvois, M. F., Sailliant, B., Meininger, V. & Lhermitte, F. (1978). Bilateral tactile aphasia: A tacto-verbal dysfunction. *Brain*, 101, 381–402.

Benson, D. F., & Geschwind, N. (1970). Developmental Gerstmann syndrome. *Neurology*, 20, 293–298.

Berry, K. E., & Butenica, N. (1967). *Developmental Test of Visual Motor Integration*. Chicago: Follet.

Gerstmann, J. (1931). Zur symptomatologie der Hirnlasionem im Übergangsgebiet der unteren Parietal und mittern Oppitalwindung. *Nervenarzt* 3, 691–695.

Geschwind, N. (1965). Disconnexion syndromes in animals and man. *Brain*, 88, 237–294, 585–664.

Geschwind, N. (1975). The apraxias: Neural mechanism of disorders of learned movements. *American Scientist*, 63, 188–195.

Halpern, H., Darley, F. L., & Brown, J. R. (1973). Differential language and neurologic characteristics in cerebral involvement. *Journal of Speech and Hearing Disorders*, 32, 162–173.

Henschen, S. E. (1920–1922). *Klinische and Anatomische Beitäge zur Pathologie des Gehirns*, vol. 5–7. Stockholm: Nordiska Bokhandeln.

Kirshner, H. S., Webb. W. G., Kelly, M. P., & Wells, C. E. (1984). Language disturbance: An initial symptom of cortical degenerations and dementia. *Archives of Neurology*, 41, 491–496.

Kliest, K. (1922). In O. Schjernings (Ed.), *Handbuch der argblichen Erfahrugen*. Leipzig: Banth.

Koppitz, E. M. (1964). *The Bender gestalt for young children*. New York: Grune and Stratton.

Liepmann, H. (1900). Daskrankheitshild der Apraxia (motorischen) Asymbolie. *Mtschr. Psychiat.*, 8, 15, 44, 102–132, 182–197.

Love, R. J., & Fitzgerald, M. (1984). Is the diagnosis of developmental apraxia of speech valid? *Australian Journal of Human Communication Disorders*, 12, 71–89.

Love, R. J., & Webb, W. G. (1977). The efficacy of cueing techniques in Broca's aphasia. *Journal of Speech and Hearing Disorders*, 42, 170–178.

Marshall, J., & Newcombe, F. (1973). Patterns of paralexia: A psycholinguistic approach. *Journal of Psycholinguistic Research*, 2, 175–199.

Milner, B. (1974). Hemispheric specializations: Scope and limits. In F. O. Schmidt & F. G. Worden (Eds.), *The Neurosciences: The Third Study Program*. Cambridge, MA: MIT Press.

Moore, W. M., Rosenbek, J. C., & LaPoint, L. L. (1976). Assessment of oral apraxia in brain injured adults. In R. H. Brookshire (Ed.), *Clinical aphasiology: Conference proceedings*. Minneapolis: BRK Publishers.

Pascal, G., & Suttel, B. (1951). *The Bender Gestalt Test*. New York: Grune and Stratton.

Rivers, D. L., & Love, R. J. (1980). Language performance on visual processing tasks in right hemisphere cases. *Brain and Language*, 10, 348–366.

Ross, E. (1981). Aprosodia: Functional-anatomic organization of the affective components of language in the right hemisphere. *Archives of Neurology*, 38, 561–569.

CHAPTER ELEVEN

Language Mechanisms in the Developing Brain

"In a child, speech is a new acquisition, and with most recently evolved faculties it is sensitive. Like an orchard blighted by a late frost, a child loses its speech easily, and he may show a taciturnity or even mutism for a variety of reasons. In such cases there may be no focal lesion of the brain, but only a presumed thinly spread minor cerebral affection. . . . Though vulnerable, speech in the child is also a highly resilient faculty. Hence a considerable restitution of function is always possible and speech may return to normal with little delay."

—Macdonald Critchley, *Aphasiology*, 1970

Brain Growth

Acquisition of speech and language is clearly tied to physical development and maturation in the infant and child. Yet the exact nature of the interaction of growth and development with emerging speech is unknown. It is known, however, that the course of speech and language development is a correlate of cerebral maturation and specialization. Having noted that, a critical question still remains to be answered: What indices of cerebral maturation are of significance to language acquisition? It is clear that there are critical periods in the maturation of the brain as well as growth gradients in different brain structures. Can these critical periods be applied equally to the stages of language acquisition?

Brain Weight

One obvious index of neurologic development is the change in gross brain weight with age. The most rapid period of brain growth is during the first two years of life. The brain more than triples its weight in the first twenty-four months. At birth, the brain is about 25 percent of its adult weight, and at six months it has reached 50 percent of its full weight. At one year, the average age at which the first word appears, the brain is 60 percent of its adult weight. Thus the brain makes its most rapid growth in the first year of life. By two and a half years it has reached about 75 percent of its full growth, and at five years it is within 90 percent of its complete maturation. Table 11-1 illustrates this increase in brain weight. It is not until ten years of age that the brain achieves approximately 95 percent of its ultimate weight. By about twelve years, or puberty, full brain weight is reached. In brief, the brain grows very rapidly during the first two years after birth. It moves at a slower, but still accelerated, pace between two and five years and finally completes its growth at the physical landmark of puberty. The late neurolinguist Eric Lenneberg (1921–1975) argued that the accelerated curve of brain growth in the first years of life matched the course of rapid early acquisition of language of the child. He claimed that primary linguistic skills were achieved by the age of four or five years and that the ability to acquire language diminished sharply after puberty, when accelerating brain growth had reached an asymptote.

Differential Brain Growth

Just as the total brain appears to grow at different rates at different ages, so do its different parts. Various brain structures also reach their peak growth rates at different times. For instance, brainstem divisions, such as the midbrain, pons, and medulla, grow rapidly prenatally and less rapidly postnatally. The cerebellum develops rapidly from before birth to one year. The cerebral hemispheres, important in language development, grow rapidly early, contributing about 85 percent to total brain volume by the sixth fetal month.

The differential growth of the cortex of the cerebral hemispheres is of vital importance for speech and language function because the majority of neural structures for communication are integrated there. Most cortical neurons are in place at birth, but brain growth may be measured through the development of synaptic connections and myelination. One method of establishing a schedule of cortical growth gradients in cerebral maturity is to determine what cortical areas are most developed in myelination at birth. The motor area of the precentral gyrus of the frontal lobe is the first cortical area developed at birth. It

TABLE 11-1
Language and Brain Growth from Birth to Two Years

Age	Language Milestones	Brain Weight in Grams
Birth	Cry	335
3 months	Cooing and crying	516
6 months	Babbling	660
9 months	Intonated jargon	750
12 months	First word approximation	925
18 months	Early naming	1,024
24 months	Two-word combinations	1,064

is soon followed by the somatosensory area of the postcentral gyrus of the parietal lobe. Next, very soon after birth, the primary visual receptor area of the occipital cortex matures. The primary auditory area, Heschl's gyrus in the temporal lobe, matures last. The medial surface of the hemispheres shows the final development of the brain.

The cortical association areas lag behind the development of the cortical receptor areas that are present and active at birth. In fact, the major association areas devoted to speech and language mature well into the preschool years and some even beyond. The progressive development of Broca's area, the frontal motor area for the face area on the motor strip, and the development of Wernicke's area, the posterior auditory association area, are related to progressive stabilization of the phonological system. As the phonemic motor planning system matures, the auditory association system increases its ability to process longer and more complex sequences of connected phonemes. The arcuate fasciculus connecting Broca's and Wernicke's areas apparently begins myelination in the first year, but continues for some time afterwards.

At one year the normal child has a vocabulary of one or more word approximations, usually names for objects that have been seen and sometimes touched. This stage of language development requires the ability to mix neural information from the auditory, somesthetic, and visual association areas. The association area of the inferior parietal lobe is where information from the temporal auditory association areas, the occipital visual association area, and the parietal association area combine to provide the neural bases for the feat of naming that the one-year-old child displays. The rapid growth of vocabulary in the second and third years of life, therefore, may well be a correlate of the maturation of this significant posterior association area in the parietal lobe, which combines information from surrounding association areas. It no doubt is a master association area, rightly named by Norman Geschwind the "association area of association areas."

The left hemisphere is destined to serve as the primary neurologic site for speech and language mechanisms in most infants, children, and adults. The left hemisphere shows early structural differences that will support later language dominance. The Sylvian fissure is longer on the left in fetal brains, and the planum temporale on the left is larger in the majority of fetal and newborn brains. Although the temporal lobe appears well differentiated from early life, Broca's area is not differentiated until eighteen months, and the corpus callosum is not completely myelinated until age ten. The inferior parietal lobe, the master association area, is not fully myelinated until adulthood, often well into the fourth decade.

Myelination for Language

Myelination has been considered one of the more significant indices of brain maturation and often a prime correlate of speech and language, as indicated in Chapter 1. Myelination allows for more rapid transmission of neural information along neural fibers and is particularly critical in a cerebral nervous system that is dependent on several long axon connections between hemispheres, lobes, and cortical and subcortical structures. Lack of maturation of myelin in language association fibers and language centers had frequently been suggested as a cause for developmental delays in language. Immaturity of myelogenesis had not been definitely proved as a demonstrable cause in speech-language delay, but the available data suggest it as a likely factor.

Myelogenesis is a cyclic process in which certain neural regions and systems appear to begin the process early and others much later. In some instances the myelogenetic cycle is short, in other cases much longer. Clear differences in rate of myelogenesis exist between different pathways. Myelination of the cortical end of the auditory projections extends beyond the first year, whereas myelination of the cortical end of the visual projections is complete soon after birth. There is a similar discrepancy between myelination of the auditory geniculotemporal radiations and visual geniculocalcarine radiations. These myelogenetic cycles appear to underlie the early visual maturity and slowly developing auditory maturity of the infant. Myelination cycles can be roughly correlated with the milestones of speech and language development, but since there is no behavioral way of assessing myelogenetic maturation in the living brain of the child with language delay, the concepts have little or no clinical utility for the present-day speech-language pathologist.

Cerebral Plasticity

Children who have begun to develop language normally and then sustain cerebral injury, particularly to the left hemisphere, show a language disturbance of an aphasic nature. The younger the child, however, the more quickly the language disturbance appears to resolve itself and the child appears grossly normal or near normal in language function. This is in relatively sharp contrast to the adult who sustains left cerebral injury. In adult brains, resolution of aphasic difficulty following focal injury to the left hemisphere rarely reaches the level of normality of functioning that is apparent in the child.

One explanation given for this phenomenon is that the child's brain demonstrates considerable plasticity of function, so that nondamaged areas are capable of assuming language function. In terms of language function, cerebral plasticity is defined by a state or stage in which specific cortical areas are not well established because of the brain's immaturity. The brain is more plastic during the most rapid periods of brain growth, and damage to the left hemisphere before the end of the first year of life is often associated with a shift of language function to the right hemisphere. By contrast, injury to the left hemisphere after this critical period is less likely to be associated with a functional reorganization of the brain. Studies from various neurosurgical centers show that approximately one-third of the cases with left-hemisphere damage before one year continue to have speech mediated exclusively by the left hemisphere. In those cases where left-hemisphere dominance for speech continues even in the face of damage, it is dependent primarily on the integrity of the frontal and temporal-parietal language areas. This explanation of cerebral plasticity of speech and language mechanisms rests on the concept of a transfer of functional areas from the left hemisphere to uncommitted areas in the right hemisphere. It has been argued that in certain cases recovery of language is so rapid that transfer and learning by the right hemisphere is unlikely. Another explanation for the rapid recovery of language in children assumes that both hemispheres contain mechanisms for language and that language need not be relearned on the right. If there is a genetic predisposition to develop the mechanisms of the left hemisphere for language, in most normal infants the mechanisms of the right will be inhibited as the left side develops complex language mechanisms. With damage to the left hemisphere there is then assumed to be a release of the mechanisms of the right brain. This explanation also implies that damage to the right hemisphere in the child may be associated with aphasia more frequently than it is in the adult.

Development of Language Dominance

An overriding fact of brain functioning is that the cerebral hemispheres demonstrate asymmetry and that language is dominant in one of them. Cerebral dominance appears to be a developing function because, despite the fact that there are anatomic differences favoring the temporal lobe in the left hemisphere, there is strong evidence suggesting that language is less fixed in the immature brain. Lenneberg advanced the theory that the course of language lateralization follows the course of cerebral maturation. He argued that lateralization is completed by puberty, based on the assumption that at birth the two hemispheres may have equal potential for the development of language mechanisms and that there is gradual lateralization associated with the period of major growth. This theory has been criticized on several grounds. First, current anatomic evidence suggests that the hemispheres may not have equal potentiality for language and that the left hemisphere is organized differently from the right, with speech mechanisms for language in the left. The planum temporale is larger in adults, in newborns, and in fetuses (Figure 11-1). Second, a reexamination of basic data of language recovery following right and left hemiplegia indicates that lateralization may be basically complete at 5 years, rather than 10 to 12 years as Lenneberg suggested. Other interpretation of this data has even suggested that lateralization is present at birth and does not follow a developmental course. It is quite clear that the age at which cerebral dominance for language is established is controversial, and a definitive statement cannot be made from the

FIGURE 11-1 Cerebral asymmetry in the planum temporale. Geschwind and Levitsky (1968) demonstrated a larger left planum temporale in 65 adult subjects, larger in the right in 11 subjects, and equal in 24 subjects. The drawing shows an exposed upper surface of the temporal lobe with a cut made at the plane of the Sylvian fissure. Note a large left planum lying behind the transverse gyrus of Heschl. On the right there are two transverse gyri and a small planum.

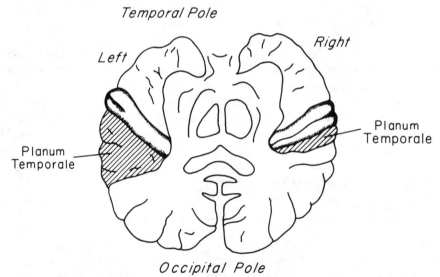

Temporal Pole

Left

Right

Planum Temporale

Planum Temporale

Occipital Pole

Sources: Redrawn from N. Geschwind, in C. Ludlow and M. Doran-Quine (Eds.), *The Neurologic Bases of Language Disorders in Children: Methods and Directions for Research*, NIH Publication 79–440, August, 1979; N. Geschwind and W. Levitsky, Left-right asymmetries in temporal speech region. *Science*, 1968, 161, 186–187.

available evidence; yet recovery of language after damage is usually excellent before the age of five.

Cerebral dominance for language has been long associated with laterality of other functions. As long ago as 1865 Jean Bouillaud (1796–1881) suggested that language dominance and handedness were related in some way. For many years it was believed that the preferred hand was contralateral to the cerebral hemisphere dominant for language. This meant that the left cerebral hemisphere was dominant for language in right-handers and the right hemisphere in left-handers. Primarily through the cortical-stimulation studies of Penfield and Roberts, we now believe that the left hemisphere is almost always language-dominant in right-handers, with approximately 95 percent of this group left-brained for language. In left-handers about 50 to 70 percent also show language dominance in the left hemisphere.

Hand preference is a relevant but not totally reliable index in predicting language dominance. Right-handedness is a relatively universal trait and is usually associated with other preferences in laterality. Human beings also tend consistently to prefer one foot, eye, and ear. There are varying degrees of laterality. Some people are more strongly right-handed than others, but true ambidexters—those who use either hand equally well—are quite rare.

Inconsistency in lateral preferences also is seen often. A person may write with the right hand, throw a ball with the left, and kick a ball with the right foot. This is *mixed laterality* or *mixed dominance*. On occasion mixed laterality has been found to be associated with language retardation or developmental dyslexia in children, but the relationship between mixed laterality and a disorder of cerebral dominance for language is uncertain.

Most right-handed people demonstrate ear preference, which is considered consistent with a contralateral hemisphere laterality for language in the brain. This can be demonstrated through dichotic listening tasks in which simultaneous auditory stimuli are presented to both ears at once. Listeners generally show a consistent lateral preference in recognition of stimuli in one ear over the other ear. This is called an *ear advantage*. Only 80 percent of right-handers show a distinct right-ear advantage, so the relationship to cerebral dominance for language is not always clear.

Childhood Language Disorders

Acquired Childhood Aphasia

Acquired aphasia of childhood is usually defined as present in a child who has begun to develop language normally and then sustains a language disturbance as the result of cerebral insult. In many ways, the language disability is similar to an acquired aphasia of adulthood. The etiology may be classified as infarct, tumor, abscess, infection, or trauma. Lesion sites generally are the same for children and adults. Anterior lesions often are associated with motor speech disorders, whereas posterior lesions usually produce both comprehension problems and related expressive problems. An important distinction, however, is that the child with acquired aphasia less commonly shows a fluent aphasia with a focal posterior lesion than does an adult. In children, nonfluent aphasia is common in both anterior and posterior lesions. Often there is initial muteness followed by slow, sparse, telegraphic expression in the early stages of recovery. This typical nonfluency usually persists and is accompanied by an apparent lack of desire to speak. Neurologists have frequently noted this persistent nonfluency and motivational set in the child as compared to the adult. Occasionally fluent aphasias in children may follow generalized brain damage, as in cases of encephalitis. Initial mutism may be seen in these cases also. Disturbances of reading and writing occur in many children with aquired aphasia. Recovery from alexia and agraphia is usually slower than the more rapid oral language recovery. Generally, the earlier the damage to the child's brain, the better the recovery; but the language performance usually is not as good as that of a normal child of the same age. Although the language reaches a level of practical usefulness in most situations, careful testing usually reveals deficits, particularly in syntactic and semantic comprehension.

Childhood Aphasia with Abnormal EEG Findings

An important subgroup of acquired aphasia is composed of children whose language disturbance is associated with convulsive seizure and electroencephalographic (EEG) abnormalities. The clinical picture is extremely varied. The age of onset of the disorder is generally between eighteen months and thirteen years. The onset of the language disturbance extends from a few hours or days to over six months. The defining sign of the disorder is seizure behavior or abnormal EEG discharges from one or both of the temporal lobes. Seizures may occur before or after the aphasic incident. The children may give the impression of being deaf, because the language disturbance normally includes a comprehension disorder. Both expressive and receptive deficits are present, and total mutism may even occur. The underlying etiology producing the seizure behavior that affects language is often unknown. The long-term course is unclear, with recovery of a minority of cases; many have chronic auditory receptive disorders.

Developmental Language Disability

By far the most prevalent group of childhood language abnormalities are the developmental language disorders rather than the acquired ones. Children with a developmental language disability are those who have never developed language normally. Technically it is inappropriate to call these children aphasic, since their language has not developed normally and then become lost or impaired. Terms used in the past, such as congenital aphasia, developmental aphasia, or dysphasia, are used less commonly today because we realize that the clinical features as well as the neuroanatomical correlates are different for the child with a developmental language disability and an acquired childhood aphasia.

The professional who is confronted with a child who has failed to develop language normally must first decide if the language impairment is the primary disorder or if language failure is secondary to a more generalized condition. Gross failure to develop language has been associated with (1) a peripheral hearing loss; (2) a generalized deficit or cognitive function known as mental retardation; (3) childhood autism, or (4) massive environmental deprivation.

Differential Diagnoses

Hearing Loss

Hearing impairment of any etiology serves to disturb or delay language in children and may be one of the most important causes of language delay in children referred to a speech-language pathologist or pediatric neurologist. It is not uncommon to see a significant hearing loss associated with brain injury. Many disorders that affect hearing also produce cerebral disorder. Intrauterine infection, hyperbilirubinemia with kernicterus, neonatal anoxia, complications of prematurity, and purulent meningitis are among the well-known causes of hearing loss that also severely affect the nervous system.

Hypoxia and kernicterus are accompanied by a typical high-frequency sensorineural loss with a precipitous drop in the primary speech frequencies (500–8000 Hz). These losses have a significant effect on speech if the hearing loss is severe. A profound articulation disorder is present, and in some cases articulatory skills are almost absent.

Mental Retardation

Cognitive deficit limits language development, and the linguistic skills of the retardate are generally poorer than those of the normal child of equivalent chronologic age. Language development in the majority of retarded children proceeds on a slower but normal course until early adolescence, when it reaches an asymptote. It has been argued that, as in the normal child, language development in retardation is paced by cerebral maturation. The lack of development of adequate speech and language in mental retardation often serves as one of the earliest and most sensitive signs of a degenerative disease of the nervous system for the pediatric neurologist and speech-language pathologist.

Childhood Autism
Autism is a relatively uncommon syndrome in which disturbed communication
is often a key sign. The disturbance in communication is often recognized very
early and is found to be profound. Verbal behavior is often severely delayed
and the child is mute or echolalic. Verbal behavior is very stereotyped. The
etiology of autism is controversial. Some experts believe that the syndrome
arises from early affective or environmental deprivation, whereas others view
the disorder as the result of severe cerebral dysfunction. Abnormal electroencephalogram findings have been reported, and there have been findings of
abnormal pneumoencephalograms showing left ventricle and ventricular horn
disorders.

Environmental Deprivation
Deprivation clearly may disturb language development. From the classic cases
of the infrequently totally isolated child, to the more common cases of culturally
deprived children of certain slums and ghettos, it is well known that lack
of appropriate language will delay the course of normal language development. Of course, this type of language problem does not have specific neural
correlates. Table 11-2 provides a classification of the major childhood language
disorders.

Search for Primary Etiologies

Children with developmental language impairment often present serious language delay but are free of hearing loss, generalized cognitive deficits, autism,
or deprivation. It appears that these children may present very subtle and varied
deficits in linguistic function or psychological process—such as cognition, per-

TABLE 11-2
Classification of Neurologic
Childhood Language Disorders

Acquired childhood aphasia
  Childhood aphasia with convulsions

Developmental language disability

Developmental language disability secondary to
  a. peripheral hearing loss
  b. generalized cognitive deficit
  c. autism
  d. environmental deprivation

Minimal cerebral dysfunction

Developmental dyslexia

ception, attention, imagery, or memory—that underlie their language impairment. It has often been assumed that the linguistic and psychological processing deficits are related to a neurologic lesion or dysfunction, but for the most part children with developmental language disorder show no structural lesions or obvious evidence of neurologic dysfunction upon objective neurodiagnostic testing.

Minimal Cerebral Dysfunction

The lack of evidence of obvious neurologic disturbances in many language-disordered children has led the field of speech-language pathology over the past forty years to employ the concept of *minimal cerebral dysfunction* as a possible explanatory etiology in children with developmental language disability. It has been long recognized that some children with language impairment also display behavioral disorders, perceptual and attention deficits, and minor neurological deficits, all of which are suggestive of cerebral disorder. Often, however, the neurological deficits are so mild and subtle that they are said to be overlooked in the routine pediatric neurologic examination. The minor neurologic signs most frequently reported are impairments of fine coordination of hands, clumsiness, and mild choreiform or athetoid movements. These minor signs have been called *soft signs* of possible neurologic damage because they are inconsistent and isolated indications of neurologic disturbance, rarely clustering together to present a classic neurologic syndrome allowing reliable lateralization and location of lesion. The diagnosis, therefore, is often made on the basis of behavioral characteristics rather than neurologic signs. For characteristics implying a diagnosis of minimal cerebral dysfunction (MCD), see Table 11-3.

Soft Signs Questioned

Not only are the so-called soft signs equivocal in many cases, but birth and developmental histories suggestive of possible nervous system damage are absent in many children. Further, both intratest and intertest reliability among neurologic examiners in establishing soft signs has been poor. In addition, many of the behavioral characteristics commonly employed to define minimal cerebral

TABLE 11-3
Signs of Minimal Cerebral Dysfunction

Hyperkinesis	Memory deficits
Attention disorder	Spelling and arithmetic
Perseveration	disorders
Clumsiness	Speech, language, and
Emotional lability	hearing disorders
Perceptual and cognitive	Minor neurologic signs
deficits	Nonspecific EEG
	abnormalities

dysfunction do not always point unequivocally to nervous system impairment. Hyperkinesis, one of the most commonly identified behavioral characteristics of the MCD syndrome, is seen in psychiatric as well as neurologic disease and is a sign associated with disorders of many bodily systems. This holds true for symptoms such as impulsivity, emotional lability, attention disorder, and other often-cited behaviors. Often soft signs are not associated with evidence of a biochemical or structural brain lesion. Geschwind believed that in these cases normal cerebral asymmetry results in lack of a development of certain brain regions, which in turn produces language and learning deficits.

Clearly the concept of minimal cerebral dysfunction as an etiological explanation for all children with developmental language and learning impairments is suspect at this time. It can probably be validly applied to certain subsets of children with speech, language, and learning problems, but certainly not to all, because lesions are not present in the brain. When the diagnosis can be made with some confidence, the neurologist or pediatrician is often able to prescribe medication that will control hyperactivity, impulsivity, and attention disorders. Drug control of these behaviors often enhances speech-language management because it allows the child to direct attention to therapeutic tasks.

Developmental Dyslexia

Reading disorders of childhood are frequently associated with inadequate or inappropriate instruction or emotional disorders. One form of reading disorder, called *developmental dyslexia,* can best be understood in a neurologic context. Known also as congenital word blindness or specific reading disability, developmental dyslexia is the most common disorder of communication found in schoolchildren. It is estimated to occur in 5 to 10 percent of all schoolchildren and is found at all levels of intelligence, from superior to subnormal. The child with dyslexia has great difficulty in attaching sound and meaning to written words. Oral reading is usually very difficult. Words with a similar appearance are often confused, and letters with similar appearance are reversed. Phonemes may be mispronounced in oral reading, and certain phonemes may be omitted or inserted. Reading comprehension is impaired. Disorders of writing are often present, with reversals, poorly formed letters, rotations, repetition, and omission of letters. Written syntax is poor.

The etiology of developmental dyslexia is not established. Frequently, however, left-handedness or ambidexterity, along with mild generalized abnormal patterns, are seen. Often there is a positive family history, with other members of the family having similar problems. Dyslexia predominates in males. Some studies show an autosomal dominant mode of inheritance. Suggestions of focal lesions in the parietal lobe have not been widely supported by neurodiagnostic tests, but it is widely believed that immature development of the parietal lobe may play a role. If there are developmental anomalies of the brain, they are doubtless microscopic and may not be visible on current neurodiagnostic tests. Perceptual impairments, particularly in making visual and auditory associations, have also been found. Usually the problem responds to remedial procedures.

Summary

Development and maturation of the brain paces the emergence of speech and language milestones. Two indices of brain growth—changes in brain weight with advancing age and the differential myelination of cerebral structures— appear to be valid correlates of speech and language development. Neuroanatomic differences, such as larger left temporal planums and longer Sylvian fissures on the left, found in the majority of fetuses and infants, provide some support for an early lateralization of language mechanisms. But infants who sustain damage to the left hemisphere before one year of age demonstrate a degree of early cerebral plasticity for language mechanisms.

Language lateralization and handedness are often associated, but preference is not a totally reliable index of cerebral dominance for language in the developing brain. Language disability in children has not always been unequivocally related to signs of cerebral damage in children. A recognized but relatively uncommon language-disorder syndrome related to clear-cut cerebral injury is acquired traumatic aphasia. Initially it is characterized by muteness and some receptive disorder. Recovery is dependent on the age of onset, with earlier onset offering a better prognosis for almost full language recovery. Epileptic aphasia is also an established syndrome of acquired language disorder. Abnormal EEG activity and transient aphasia are the prime signs in this disorder.

Developmental language disability without evidence of focal brain lesions has long been associated with the primary etiologies of deafness, mental retardation, and massive environmental deprivation. But many children with language delay and disabilities present unknown etiologies but are suspected of cerebral dysfunction. Signs of minimal cerebral dysfunction cannot always be established on neurologic examination, and an idiopathic neurologic disorder is suspected. In the child with unequivocal signs of minimal cerebral damage, speech, language, reading, and writing disorders are often present. Hyperactivity is a major behavioral sign.

A related language disorder in children is called developmental dyslexia. It is a developmental reading impairment. Evidence of an underlying neurological disorder, particularly a focal brain lesion in most cases, is controversial.

References and Further Readings

Brain Growth

Jabbour, J., Duenas, D., Gilmartin, R., & Gottlieb, M. (1976). *Pediatric neurology hand-book* (2nd ed.). New York: Medical Examination Publishing Company.

Lecours, A. R. (1975). Myelogenetic correlates of development of speech and language. In E. Lenneberg & E. Lenneberg (Eds.), *Foundations of language development*, Vol I. New York: Academic Press. Pp. 125–135.

Lenneberg, E. (1967). *Biological foundations of language.* New York: Wiley.

Cerebral Plasticity and Cerebral Dominance

Geschwind, N. (1979). Anatomical foundations of language and dominance. In C. L. Ludlow & M. E. Doran-Quine (Eds.), *The neurologic bases of language in children: Methods and directions for research.* Bethesda, MD: National Institute of Health, Publication No. 79-440, pp. 145–157.

Rasmussen, T., & Milner, B. (1977). The role of early left-brain injury in determining lateralization of cerebral speech functions. *Annals of the New York Academy of Sciences*, 299, 355–369.

Wada, J. A., Clark, R., & Hamm, A. (1975). Cerebral hemispheric asymmetry in humans. *Archives of Neurology* (Chicago), 32, 239–246.

Witleson, S. F. (1977). Early hemispheric specialization and interhemispheric plasticity: An empirical and theoretical review. In S. J. Segalwitz & F. A. Gruber (Eds.), *Language development and neurological theory.* New York: Academic Press. Pp. 213–287.

Neurologic Language Disability in Children

Benton, A. L., & Pearl, D. (1978). *Dyslexia: An appraisal of current knowledge.* New York: Oxford University Press.

Chase, R. A. (1972). Neurologic aspects of language disorders in children. In J. V. Irwin & M. Marge (Eds.), *Principles of childhood language disabilities.* New York: Appleton-Century Crofts. Pp. 99–135.

Critchley, M. (1970). *Developmental dyslexia* (2nd ed.). Springfield, IL: Charles C. Thomas.

Dreifuss, F. (1975). The pathology of central communicative disorders in children. In D. B. Tower (Ed.) *The nervous system*, Vol. 3. *Human communication and its disorders.* New York: Raven Press. Pp. 383–392.

Galaburda, A. M., & Kemper, T. L. (1979). Cytoarchitectonic abnormalities in developmental dyslexia: A case study. *Annals of Neurology*, 6, 94–100.

Geschwind, N. (1972). Disorders of higher cortical function in children. *Clinical Proceedings of the Children's Hospital National Medical Center*, 28, 261–272.

Hécaen, H. (1976). Acquired aphasia in children and the ontogenesis of hemispheric functional specialization. *Brain and Language*, 3, 114–134.

Ludlow, C. L. (1980). Children's language disorders: Recent research advances. *Annals of Neurology*, 7, 497–507.

Miller, J. F., Campbell, T. E., Chapman, R. S., & Weismer, S. (1984). Language behavior in acquired childhood aphasia. In A. Holland (Ed.), *Language disorders in children: Recent advances*. San Diego, CA: College-Hill Press.

Rie, H. E., & Rie, E. (Eds.) (1980). *Handbook of minimal brain dysfunctions: A critical view*. New York: Wiley.

CHAPTER TWELVE

Clinical Speech Syndromes and the Developing Brain

"An examination of infant behavior is an examination of the central nervous system."
    —Arnold Gesell and Catherine S. Amatruda, *Developmental Diagnosis*, 1947

Developmental Motor Speech Disorders

Early cerebral injury to speech mechanisms of the developing brain will result in conditions that may be classified as developmental motor speech disorders. Included in a classification of the motor speech disorders are the *developmental dysarthrias, developmental anarthrias*, and *developmental apraxias of speech*. Developmental dysarthria is a speech disorder resulting from damage to the immature nervous system, characterized by weakness, paralysis, or incoordination of the speech musculature. Developmental anarthria refers to a complete lack of speech due to a profound paralysis, weakness, or incoordination of the speech musculature. Usually the diagnosis implies that useful speech will not develop because of the severity of oral motor involvement. Developmental apraxia of speech is an impaired ability to execute voluntarily the appropriate movements of speech in the absence of paralysis, weakness, and incoordination of the speech muscles. The syndrome of apraxia of speech, in both adults and children, is described in Chapter 10.

Certain types of developmental dysarthria have been well studied; other types have received less attention in the speech pathology literature. The developmental dysarthrias of the cerebral palsies, for instance, have been studied extensively for many years, whereas research on the dysarthrias of childhood muscular dystrophy is much less common. The speech signs commonly observed in the developmental dysarthrias are seen in Table 12-1.

Cerebral Palsy

Developmental dysarthria is most commonly seen in children diagnosed as having cerebral palsy. Cerebral palsy is a neurological condition caused by injury to the immature brain and is characterized by a nonprogressive disturbance of the motor system. There are often many associated problems such as mental retardation, hearing or visual impairments, and perceptual problems produced by infantile cerebral injury. Cerebral palsy is considered a major developmental disability.

The cerebral palsies have been variously classified, but most experts currently accept three major categories of clinical motor disorders: *spasticity*, *dyskinesia*, and *ataxia*. By far the most common type of dyskinesia is *athetosis* (see Chapter

TABLE 12-1
Major Developmental Motor Speech Disorders

Disorder	Speech Signs
Developmental apraxia of speech	Disorder in selection and sequencing of articulatory movements, oral apraxia sometimes present. Comprehension intact, expression poor. Occasionally nonfocal neurologic signs.
Developmental dysarthrias of cerebral palsy	
Spastic dysarthria	Bilateral corticobulbar involvement; dysphagia, articulation disorder, hypernasality, slowed rate, loudness, pitch, and vocal-quality disturbances.
Dyskinetic dysarthria	Usually athetosis; dysphagia; hypernasality; articulation disorder; prevocalizations; loudness, pitch, and vocal-quality disturbances.
Ataxic dysarthria	Articulation disorder; prosodic disorder: unequal stress, loudness, and pitch; explosive, scanning quality.

TABLE 12-2
Classification of the Cerebral Palsies

Lesions	*Clinical Type*	*Limb Involvement*
Pyramidal tracts	Spastic paralysis	Paraplegia—legs only
		Diplegia—legs more than arms
		Quadriplegia—all four limbs
		Hemiparesis—one half of body
		Monoplegia—usually one leg
Extrapyramidal tracts	Atetosis	
	Choreoathetosis	
	Dystonia	—Arms, leg, neck, and trunk
	Tremor	
	Rigidity	
Cerebellum	Ataxia	—Arms, leg, trunk
	sometimes with diplegia	

5). Table 12-2 presents a classification of the cerebral palsies. As in adult disorders, spasticity implies a lesion in the pyramidal system; dyskinesia, a lesion in the extrapyramidal system; and ataxia, a lesion in the cerebellar system. However, syndromes are often not as clear-cut in the child as they are in the adult. Many children with cerebral palsy show a mixed picture. For instance, a child whose clinical picture is primarily that of an athetoid, with typical slow, writhing movements of the limbs, grimaces of the face, and involuntary movements of the tongue and muscles of respiration, may also display hypertonic muscles and the up-turning toes of the classic Babinski sign. The structural closeness of the pathways of the pyramidal and extrapyramidal tracts in the relatively small infant brain no doubt produces such mixed clinical pictures.

Children with cerebral palsy may also be classified according to topological involvement as well as clinical type. Common topological pictures are *hemiplegia*, *diplegia*, and *quadriplegia*. Occasionally a *monoplegia*, *triplegia*, or *paraplegia* will be seen. Children may also be classified by etiology. Common causes are prematurity, anoxia, kernicterus, birth trauma, and infection. Approximately one to two of every 1,000 schoolchildren has some form of cerebral palsy. Of the three major types, spastics are most prevalent, athetoids next, and ataxias least common.

Developmental dysarthria is a major problem in the cerebral palsied population, with 75 to 85 percent of the children showing obvious speech problems. Dysarthria may be complicated by mental retardation, hearing loss, and perceptual disorder in some children. Despite complicating factors, the two major dysarthrias—spastic dysarthria and dyskinetic dysarthria of athetosis—in cerebral palsy can be differentiated. Spastics and athetoids cannot be identified by articulatory errors alone; but when vocal and prosodic features are incorporated into perceptual judgments of speech, the two clinical types become distinct, just as spastic and hyperkinetic types are distinct among adult dysarthrias (Meyer, 1982).

Childhood Suprabulbar Paresis

An isolated paresis or weakness of the oral musculature is sometimes seen in children without major motor signs in the trunk or extremities. This condition results in a form of developmental dysarthria and associated problems. Described by the neurologist C. Worster-Drought (1974), this condition usually affects the corticobulbar fibers that innervate cranial nerves X (vagus) and XII (hypoglossus). The etiology has been attributed to agenesis or hypogenesis of the corticobulbar fibers, but this has not been verified. The muscles of the lips, pharynx, palate, and tongue are involved to varying degrees. The jaw reflex is usually exaggerated. The dysarthria that is present is marked by misarticulations and hypernasality. There may be a history of dysphagia, and occasionally there is laryngeal involvement and drooling. This condition is called congenital childhood suprabulbar palsy because involvement is generally confined to the muscles innervated by the corticobulbar fibers. Paresis of the trunk and limbs is not present as in the child who is obviously cerebral palsied. The condition is brought to the attention of the speech-language pathologist or neurologist because of an isolated dysphagia or dysarthria. Muscles of the oral mechanism are involved, but no other obvious neurologic signs are present in the motor system. Table 12-3 displays neurologic signs seen in the dysarthric syndromes of congenital and acquired suprabulbar paresis of childhood.

TABLE 12-3
Dysarthria in Suprabulbar Paresis
Syndrome of Childhood

Congenital Signs	Acquired Signs
Articulation disorder	Articulation disorder
Hypernasality	Hypernasality
Lip, tongue, palate, pharynx paresis	Lip, tongue, palate, pharynx paresis
May show isolated paresis	Some facial rigidity
Possible agenesis of corticobulbar fibers	Encephalitis
Drooling	Traumatic head injury

Muscular Dystrophy

Next to the condition of cerebral palsy, muscular dystrophy is the childhood neurologic disorder that is most likely to present a developmental dysarthria. The most common type of muscular dystrophy is the *pseudohypertrophic* type, called *Duchenne dystrophy*. It is associated with a sex-linked recessive gene, occurs primarily in males, and usually is manifest by the third year of life. The disorder is marked by a characteristic progression of muscle weakness starting in the pelvis and trunk and eventually involving all the striated muscles, including those of the speech mechanism. The visceral muscles are usually spared. The enlargement of the calf muscles and occasionally of other muscle groups accounts for the name of the disorder. Infiltration of fat and connective tissue produces the pseudohypertrophic effect.

In the later stages of the disease a flaccid dysarthria appears. It is marked by articulation disorder and voice-quality disturbances. Often the articulation disorder is mild, with only one or two phonemes in error. Dystrophic subjects show reduced oral breath pressure and vocal intensity. They do not sustain phonation as well as normals, and they show serious involvement of the muscles of speech. Rate of tongue movement and strength of the tongue are poor. Retracting and pursing the lips as well as pointing and narrowing the tongue are noticeably disordered, and phonemes requiring tongue-lip elevation are often in error. A broadening and flattening of the tongue is sometimes seen in advanced cases. Respiratory and laryngeal muscles are also weakened and affect respiratory and phonatory performance. Despite weakness, labial phonemes are generally produced more accurately than are tongue-tip consonants. Table 12-4 presents the speech and physical signs in the developmental dysarthria of pseudohypertrophic muscular dystrophy.

Diagnosis of Neurologic Disorder with Primitive Reflexes

The neurological examination of the newborn child and infant suspected of cerebral damage has relied heavily on the concept of a primitive reflex profile in recent years. Primitive and postural reflexes follow an orderly sequence of appearance and disappearance, beginning in the fetal period and extending through the first years of life. The reflexes are mediated at a subcortical level. They were first described by Rudolph Magnus (1873–1927), who received a Nobel prize for his efforts. They can provide an accurate method of determining degrees of prematurity of an infant or may suggest neurologic dysfunction. If a normal reflex pattern does not appear on schedule, or if a reflex pattern persists

TABLE 12-4
Developmental Dysarthria in Pseudohypertrophic Muscular Dystrophy

Speech Signs: Flaccid Dysarthria
　Articulation disorder
　Reduced vocal intensity
　Respiratory weakness
　Articulator weakness
　Broad flattened tongue

Physical Signs
　Onset: 3 to 4 years
　Proximal weakness
　Pseudohypertrophic calf muscles
　Proximal atrophy
　Hyporeflexia except ankles
　Mental retardation in one-third of the population

beyond the age at which it normally disappears, the newborn or infant is considered at risk for cerebral injury or other neurologic involvement. Some pediatric neurologists assert that neurological abnormalities at birth predict a diagnosis of minimal cerebral dysfunction at later ages, but other workers have found a limited association between neonatal abnormalities and neurologic signs later on, particularly at one year and beyond. Despite questions about the reliability of prediction for a diagnosis of minimal neurologic abnormality, the careful evaluation of the early primitive reflexes and later evolving postural reflexes provide a basis for diagnosis and therapy of disturbed motor function. They can usually provide a locomotor prognosis, indicating when and how a child with cerebral palsy will walk. Table 12-5 presents a summary of the primitive and postural reflexes of the first year. Although the speech-language pathologist may be more interested in the neurologic status of oral and pharyngeal reflexes, an understanding of the primitive and postural reflexes is essential to assessment of the neurologic maturity of a child suspected of cerebral injury.

There is a notable lack of consensus on the definition of the stimulus and response in the widely tested primitive reflexes. There is also lack of agreement on how the responses change with time and growth. Seven reflexes are reviewed here. They are commonly assessed by neurologists and pediatricians and they are typical of the first year of life, with the peak development at about six months. This peak time period avoids the transitory neurologic signs of the newborn but is sufficiently early to allow a neurologic diagnosis before one year of age. These seven reflexes also appear to be predictive of later motor function

TABLE 12-5
Primitive and Postural Infantile Reflexes of the First Year

Reflex	*Response*
Asymmetric tonic neck reflex (ATNR)	Extension of limbs on chin side and flexion on occiput side on head turning
Symmetric tonic neck reflex (STNR)	Extension of arms and flexion of legs on head extension
`'...e support ..... (PSR)`	Infant bears weight when balls of feet are stimulated.
Tonic labyrinthine reflex (TLR)	Shoulder retraction and neck and trunk extension with neck flexion. Tongue thrust reflex may occur.
Segmental rolling (SR)	Rotation of head or legs elicits segmental rolling of trunk and pelvis.
Galant reflex	Arching of body when skin of back is stimulated near vertebral column
Moro reflex	Adduction and upward arm movement followed by arm flexion and leg extension and flexion

in the child. Of the many infantile reflexes described by neurologists in neurologic literature, they have been the most well studied.

Asymmetrical Tonic Neck Reflex (ATNR)

This infantile reflex pattern is probably the most widely known of the early body reflexes. The reflex has been shown to be universally present in the normal infant by the outstanding child developmentalist Arnold Gesell (1880–1961). When the normal child is supine, he or she may lie with the head turned to one side. There will be an extension of the extremities on that side (the chin side), with a corresponding flexion of the contralateral extremities on the opposite (occiput) side. This position is described as the fencer's position.

To test for the presence of the reflex, the child is placed in a supine position. Observations are made of active head turning and subsequent movement of the extremities. The head is then passively turned through an arc of 180° alternately to each side for 5 seconds. This maneuver is repeated five times on each side. Consistent changes in muscle tone in the extremities generally define the presence of the reflex. A clearly positive response is visible extension of extremities on the chin side and flexion on the occiput side when the head is passively turned. If extension of the extremities on the chin side and flexion on the occiput side lasts more than 30 seconds, the response may be called *obligatory*. If the response is found beyond the eight or ninth month, it is indicative of possible cerebral damage and poor motor development. It suggests that the cortical control of upper motor neurons is not on schedule and that motor behavior is still controlled at subcortical levels. Obligatory tonic neck reflexes persisting into the second year and beyond are usually incompatible with independent standing balance or independent walking; they may disappear later, however, and the child may learn to walk alone. The asymmetrical tonic neck reflex may be seen in various types of cerebral palsy, predicting brain injury, but it is not useful for distinguishing between spastic and dyskinetic types. The ATNR is suggestive of brain injury only, but it is in no way completely diagnostic for cerebral palsy or its subtypes. It can reemerge after a catastrophe such as cardiac arrest and also may be present in progressive disease. The ATNR has little or no effect on the development of speech and shows very little relationship to the oral and pharyngeal reflexes. Elicitation procedures for the ATNR are illustrated in Figure 12-1.

FIGURE 12-1   Asymmetrical tonic neck reflex. This reflex is elicited by turning the head to each side for 5 seconds. This should be repeated five times to each side. The reflex is pathologic if there is obligatory extension and flexion of limbs for more than 60 seconds.

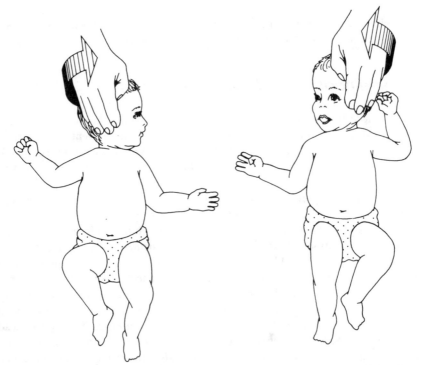

Source: Adapted from A. Capute et al., *Primitive Reflex Profile* (Baltimore: University Park Press, 1978).

Symmetrical Tonic Neck Reflexes (STNR)

This reflex is analogous to the ATNR, but the head is manipulated in flexion and extension in midline rather than turned laterally. The resulting responses are differences between upper and lower extremities, rather than right-left differences in extremities. The normal reflex is an extension of the arms and flexion of the legs if the head is extended in midline. Flexion of the head will have the opposite effect: the arms will flex and the legs will extend.

The technique of eliciting the reflex is first to ask the child to flex and extend his neck. The neck is then passively extended and flexed. This is repeated five times each for extension and flexion. If the reflex sign is absent at five to six months or persists into the second year, it is a symptom of motor abnormality. The reflex does not appear to elicit any associated oral or pharyngeal reflexes (see Figure 12-2).

Positive Support Reflex (PSR)

Magnus saw the positive supporting reaction as necessary for support of erect posture. When the balls of the foot are stimulated, there is co-contraction of

FIGURE 12-2   **Symmetrical tonic neck reflex. This reflex is elicited by passively extending and flexing the neck five times. The reflex is pathologic if there is obligatory arm extension or leg flexion with neck extension for more than 60 seconds.**

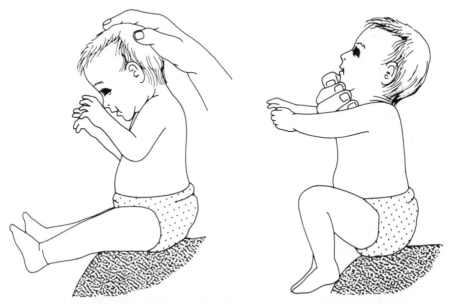

Source: Adapted from A. Capute et al., *Primitive Reflex Profile* (Baltimore: University Park Press, 1978).

opposing muscle groups to fix the joints of the lower extremities so that they bear weight. To test the reflex, the infant is suspended around the trunk below the armpits with the head in midline. He or she is flexed slightly. The child is bounced on the balls of the feet five times. The feet are placed in contact with the floor, and the degree to which the infant can support his or her weight is assessed. The reflex is seen in fetal life and is considered abnormal if it persists beyond four months. A persistent strong response has been associated with spastic quadriparesis. It does not appear to elicit associated oral or pharyngeal reflexes (see Figure 12-3).

Tonic Labyrinthine Reflex (TLR)

This reflex is associated with the changes in tone associated with different postures. The position of the extremities will change with respect to the position of the head in space. This is due to the orientation of the labyrinths of the inner ear. The reflex is tested in both a supine and a prone position. To test in the prone position, the child is held in prone suspension. The head is extended

FIGURE 12-3   Positive support reflex. The reflex is elicited by suspending the child so that the balls of the feet may be bounced on a flat surface. The reflex is pathologic if the child remains on his or her toes and cannot move out of the position for 60 seconds or more.

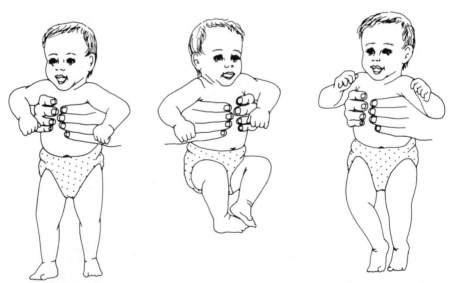

Source: Adapted from A. Capute et al., *Primitive Reflex Profile* (Baltimore: University Park Press, 1978).

about 45° below the horizontal plane. Changes of posture and tone in the extremities are evaluated, with special attention to the shoulder area. When the head is flexed, a normal response involves protraction of the shoulders or flexion of the lower extremities. Consistent tone changes should be present in at least one upper and lower extremity for the reflex to be considered present (see Figure 12-4a).

In testing the reflex in the supine position, support is placed between the

FIGURE 12-4 (a) Tonic labyrinthine reflex. The reflex is elicited by putting support between the shoulders to extend the head 45 degrees. The head is flexed 45 degrees and the child is asked to grasp in midline. The reflex is pathologic if there is severe extensor trust or opisthotonous. (b) shows child in extension and flexion.

(a)

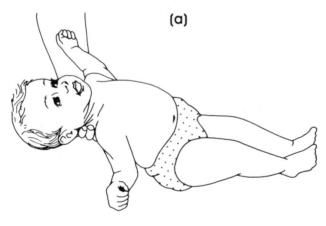

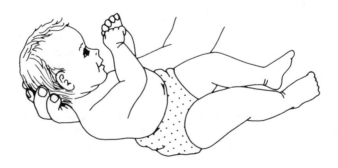

FIGURE 12-4 *(continued)*

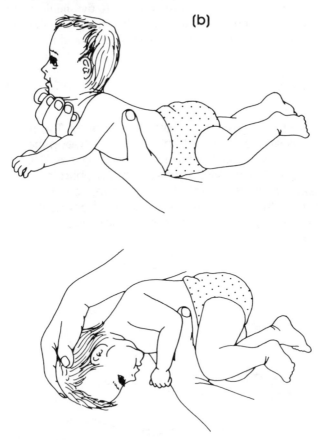

(b)

Source: Adapted from A. Capute et al., *Primitive Reflex Profile* (Baltimore: University Park Press, 1978).

shoulders so that the head is extended at 45°. Position and tone of the shoulders are assessed. Active neck flexion and grasp in midline are elicited. If the flexion and grasp responses are not noted, the head is flexed with the back supported and the midline grasp is sought again (see Figure 12-4b).

The normal response is shoulder retraction if the head is in extension. Trunk and leg extension accompanies shoulder retraction. Neck flexion results in shoulder protraction in 5 seconds and the disappearance of an extension posture.

An abnormal tonic labyrinthine response may be accompanied by extensor hypertonia, and a persistent abnormal response may prevent the infant from rolling over normally. A pathologic response may make the legs so rigid that when the child is pulled to a sitting position, he or she will stand instead. The reflex is not always present in normal children, but is more common in children with pathologic conditions. Of the reflexes reviewed, it is the only one that may be routinely associated with oral reflexes. With the head extended 45°, a tongue reflex or tongue thrust may occur in the cerebral palsied child.

Segmental Rolling (SR)

The normal newborn baby will show a log-rolling response in turning that is a reflex associated with the activity of turning over. It is primary neck-righting reflex action. This early rolling response develops into a segmental rolling response, in which turning of the head produces a reaction in which the infant attempts to undo the applied rotation by twisting the body at the waist, allowing one segment of the body to turn at a time. This corkscrew reaction allows the infant to roll over with a minimum of effort because only one segment of the body moves at a time. Abnormal responses are indicated by perseveration of a simple log-rolling response in which head rotation produces the simultaneous turning of the upper and lower extremities with no segmental control. The response is seen in motor-handicapped children with cerebral palsy.

To test the response, the child is placed in a supine position. The response is tested in two maneuvers: first, the child is rotated from the head; second, the child is rotated from the legs. For head rotation, the child's head is first flexed to approximately 45° and slowly rotated so that the shoulders are turned. Rotation is observed. The child's head is usually rotated with one hand on the side of the face near the chin and the other hand on the occiput of the head. When the child is rolled to the right, the examiner's left hand is the face hand and the right the occiput hand. When the child is rolled to the left, the position of the examiner hands are reversed (see Figure 12-5).

To test the second response using the leg, one leg of the child is flexed at the hip and knee. The examiner holds the flexed leg below the knee, and the child is rotated to turn the pelvis toward midline. Rotation patterns are then observed. Rotation responses have not been associated with oral and pharyngeal reflexes (see Figure 12-6).

The Galant Reflex

This is an arching of the infant's body when the skin of the back near the vertebral column is stroked. The arching is usually forward, toward the stimulation. Arching in the other direction indicates the child is attempting to evade the stimulus. The responses may vary from total absence of response to an exaggerated hip flexion. In the majority of newborns, the response is present bilaterally; unilateral responses have been reported in athetoid cerebral palsy. The response normally disappears by two months of age but persists in athetoids

FIGURE 12-5 Segmental rolling reflex: rotation of the head. This reflex is elicited by rotating the head to turn the shoulders and by rotating the legs (see figure 12-6) to turn the pelvis. The reflex is pathological if the child is obliged to roll in a log-rolling manner and cannot inhibit the reflex.

Source: Adapted from A. Capute et al., *Primitive Reflex Profile* (Baltimore: University Park Press, 1978).

beyond that time. It is thought to be associated with delay of trunk stabilization and head control in this group. It is assumed that persistence of the response beyond six months may interfere with sitting balance. No association with oral or pharyngeal reflexes has been reported (see Figure 12-7).

The Moro Reflex

The Moro reflex, along with asymmetrical tonic neck reflex, is one of the best-known and best-studied reflexes of child neurology. It is present in almost all newborns except for small premature babies. With sudden head extension, there is a rapid and symmetrical adduction and upward movement of the arms. The hands open, and there is a gradual adduction and flexion of the arms. The lower limbs also show extension and flexion. There has been some debate about

FIGURE 12-6 Segmental rolling reflex: Rotation of the legs.

Source: Adapted from A. Capute et al., *Primitive Reflex Profile* (Baltimore: University Park Press, 1978).

whether the Moro response and the startle response are continuous patterns. Both responses appear in the newborn, so they are thought to be discontinuous. The Moro usually reaches a peak at two months and diminishes by four months. A persistent reflex has been associated with cerebral palsy and mental retardation. To test for the reflex, the child is placed supine. Several stimuli may be used. The head may be raised about 3 centimeters from a padded surface and allowed to drop back suddenly. Another stimulus option is to strike the pad on both sides of the child (see Figure 12-8).

The most significant aspect of the stimulus is the quality of suddenness, in either head drop or noise. It is known that primitive and postural reflexes sometimes reinforce more circumscribed reflexes, but there is no evidence that the primitive Moro reflex tends to reinforce oral and pharyngeal reflexes in children with cerebral palsy. The persisting Moro reflex is much less valuable to the neurologist as a sign of cerebral injury than is the ATNR.

In summary, persisting infantile primitive and postural reflexes have been a classic sign of central nervous system dysfunction. In particular, they have been extremely useful in the early diagnoses of cerebral palsy. Infantile reflex behavior also has been incorporated in motor treatment programs for children with cerebral palsy. An important fact for the speech-language pathologist is that the primitive and postural body reflexes, with some exceptions, appear to

FIGURE 12-7   Galant reflex. This reflex is elicited by stroking the back in the lumbar region with a blunt object. The reflex is pathologic if there is persistent curvature of the back and elevation of the hips.

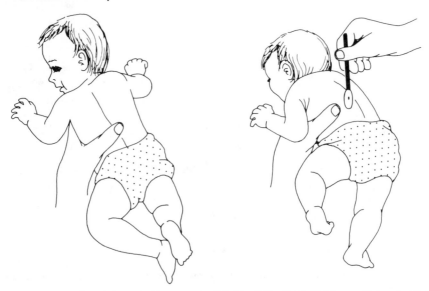

Source: Adapted from A. Capute et al., *Primitive Reflex Profile* (Baltimore: University Park Press, 1978).

FIGURE 12-8   Moro reflex. This reflex is elicited by dropping the head or producing a loud noise. The reflex is pathologic if there is a persistent symmetrical adduction and upward movement of the arms with fingers splayed followed by a flexion of the arms in clasp manner. The back arches.

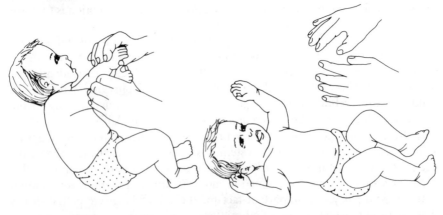

Source: Adapted from A. Capute et al., *Primitive Reflex Profile* (Baltimore: University Park Press, 1978).

have limited influence on oral and pharyngeal reflexes. It should be made clear that these neonatal and early reflexes are important in assessing delayed development of motor function before twelve to eighteen months. They are, however, only a limited aspect of the pediatric neurologic examination for the older child. The more conventional neurologic signs of alteration of muscle tone, abnormal muscle stretch reflexes, superficial reflexes, and the results of objective neurodiagnostic tests are of equal value in making a diagnosis for the examining pediatric neurologist.

Oral and Pharyngeal Reflexes

Over the past half century, study of the normal infant body reflexes and their relation to brain disease has prompted speech-language pathologists and others interested in the management of cerebral palsy to consider another set of reflexes—the oral and pharyngeal reflexes. See Table 12-6 for a summary of major oral reflexes. Some speech specialists have assumed that abnormal oral and pharyngeal reflexes will play a significant role in the speech development of the child with cerebral palsy who is dysarthric or is likely to develop dysarthria with the onset of speech. Absent or persisting reflexes, they argue, are predictive of dysarthria. Neurologists are more likely to argue that when the oral and pharyngeal reflexes are integrated into a spontaneous feeding pattern, they become more diagnostically and prognostically significant in neurologic disease. Similarly, speech-language pathologists are beginning to question whether the isolated artificially elicited reflexes of the first few months of life have as much diagnostic and prognostic importance in speech performance as do the dysphagic symptoms commonly seen in many children with cerebral palsy.

The type, number, and reliability of abnormal oral and pharyngeal reflexes found in cerebral palsied subjects varies from research study to study. Current

TABLE 12-6
Infantile Oral Reflexes

Reflex	Stimulus	Age of Appearance	Age of Disappearance
Rooting	Touch oral area	Birth	3–6 months
Suckling	Nipple in mouth	Birth	6–12 months
Swallowing	Bolus of food in pharynx	Birth	Persists
Tongue	Touch tongue or lips	Birth	12–18 months
Bite	Pressure on gums	Birth	9–12 months
Gag	Touch tongue or pharynx	Birth	Persists

data (Love, Hagerman and Tiami, 1980) strongly suggest that there is little or no correlation between the presence and number of abnormal oral and pharyngeal reflexes and the severity of dysarthria in cerebral palsy as defined by a measure of articulation proficiency. In fact, the number of dysphagic symptoms—disordered biting, sucking, swallowing, and chewing a hard and soft food bolus—are slightly better predictors of articulation proficiency than are an elicited set of neonatal oral and pharyngeal automatisms. The correlation, however, between speech impairment and dysphagic symptoms is not particularly strong either. This limited relation between speech and dysphagia strongly implies that motor control for speech and the feeding reflexes may be mediated at different levels in the nervous system. Evidence indicates that the feeding reflexes are mediated at the brainstem level and that voluntary speech is controlled at the cortical, subcortical, and cerebellar levels, with the prime voluntary pathways for speech being the corticobulbar fibers. Brainstem reflex pathways apparently subserve only vegetative and reflex functions and are inactive during the execution of normal speech. Therefore, early motor speech gestures probably are not directly related to the development of motor reactions in feeding during infancy and childhood, even though some of the motor coordinations and refinements in speech acquisition are analogous to some of the biting and chewing gestures in feeding.

Even though early oral motor behavior in feeding may only have a limited resemblance to actual motor patterns for speech, management programs to improve muscle function and coordination in eating have been initiated as a possible prophylactic measure for future dysarthria. The assumption of these programs is that any improvement in motor activity of the oral musculature gained through feeding therapy might conceivably result in improvement in speech performance, since the parallel activities of speech and feeding do have the same muscles in common. At the very least feeding therapy will probably make eating faster and easier. This, of course, is an important consideration in the total management of the child with cerebral palsy, one that should not be overlooked by speech-language pathologists and neurologists. In fact, dysphagia may be just as disturbing as dysarthria in the young cerebral palsied person. Direct motor training of the muscles during speech, rather than feeding training, appears to be the most effective method for improving the dysarthria, since cortically mediated speech activities drive the muscles at a more rapid and coordinated rate than do brainstem-mediated reflex feeding activities.

The feeding reflexes have sometimes been used diagnostically by speech-language pathologists in planning management programs in cerebral palsied children. Persistent feeding reflexes have been also employed as one of several possible factors in coming to the decision to elect an augmentative communicative system with a nonspeaking motor-handicapped child. One pair of experts have asserted that " . . . of all factors investigated, obligatory persistence of oral reflexes can in isolation lead to a decision to elect an augmentative communication system" (Shane & Bashir, 1980). Their assumption is that retained oral reflexes indicate a very poor prognosis for oral speech development. This claim may have to be reevaluated in the light of the aforementioned findings concerning the poor correlation between articulatory proficiency and the number of retained oral reflexes in a cerebral palsied population (Love, Hagerman, & Tiami, 1980).

Despite the controversy about oral reflexes and speech in diagnosis, management, and prognosis, a description of six commonly tested oral pharyngeal reflexes is offered for the speech-language pathologist who may wish to consider this aspect of disturbed oral motor functions in the cerebrally injured infant and child. In the typical infantile oral motor evaluation, it is probably best to elicit each of these infantile automatisms artificially one by one first, to determine whether they are absent or abnormally persisting. Next it is appropriate to assess the spontaneous functions of mastication and deglutition in the feeding act to determine how these neonatal reflex behaviors have become integrated into a more complex and voluntary oral-pharyngeal pattern of feeding. Infantile mastication and deglutition utilize the five cranial nerves (V, VII, IX–X, XII) important for future speech, so evaluation of early feeding allows cranial nerve assessment for the child who is too immature to cooperate in standard cranial nerve testing (see Table 12-7).

Rooting Reflexes

If the perioral face region is touched, two responses in combination make up the rooting reflex. The side-to-side head turning reflex is usually elicited by gently tapping on the corners of the mouth or cheek. The response is alternate head turning toward and away from the stimulus, ending with the lips brushing

TABLE 12-7
Cranial Nerve Function in Infantile Chewing and Swallowing

Cranial Nerve	*Functions*
VII	Closes lips.
V, XII	Bites and chews.
X	Pulverizes bolus; propels bolus to pharynx; peristaltic action of tongue.
V, VII, IX–X, XI, XII	Reflex swallow; velopharyngeal closure; supra- and infrahyoid movement, glottal closure; increased peristalsis.

the stimulus. Occasionally the response will occur without the stimulus when the infant is hungry. This activity usually precedes any actual suckling. The side-to-side head-turning response is present in the full-term baby and premature infant. The reflex usually disappears by one month of age and is replaced by the direct head-turning response, a simple movement of the head toward the source of stimulation. The source is grasped with the lips and sucked. If the stimulus is applied to the corners of the mouth, the bottom lip usually lowers and the head and tongue orient toward the stimulus. The direct head-turning response is established at one month and disappears by the end of the sixth month of life. Persistence beyond a year usually may suggest cerebral injury, and asymmetry of response indicates damage to one side of the brain and facial paresis. The cranial nerves involved in the reflex are V, VII, XI, and XII. The reflex is mediated by the pons, medulla, and cervical spinal cord (see Figure 12-9).

Suckling Reflex

If a finger or nipple is placed in the infant's mouth, bursts of suckling behavior will occur, interspersed with periods of rest. The suckling reflex is integrated at birth, but within two or three months the action develops more purpose and jaw activity is incorporated into the pattern. Involuntary suckling may disappear between six months and a year. Persistent suckling beyond a year suggests brain injury. The reverse, inability to suckle, may also be an early sign of cerebral

FIGURE 12-9   The rooting reflex. The reflex is elicited by stimulating the cheek lateral to the mouth. From birth the infant normally will turn the head toward the stimulus and then grasp the stimulus in the mouth. The reflex is pathologic if it is absent in infants from any cause or if it persists beyond the fourth month.

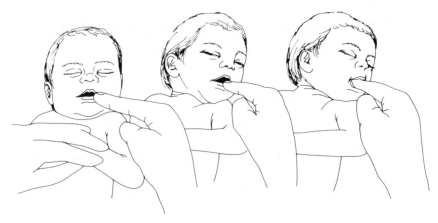

injury. The cranial nerves involved in suckling are V, VII, IX, and XII. The reflex is mediated at the pons and medulla (see Figure 12-10).

Swallowing Reflex

The swallowing reflex develops after the sucking reflex and is integrated into a total feeding pattern. Suckling activities produce saliva, which accumulates in the reflexogenic area of the pharynx. The swallowing reflex is triggered, and swallowing may be observed by visible upward movement of the hyoid bone and thyroid cartilage of the larynx. The upward movement of the thyroid cartilage of the larynx may also be felt through palpation during the swallow. It is sometimes difficult to separate suckle and swallow, since swallow may precede

FIGURE 12-10 The sucking reflex. The reflex is elicited by putting the index finger 3 to 4 cm into the mouth of the infant. From birth, the infant will normally engage in rhythmic sucking of the finger. The reflex is pathologic if it is absent or exaggerated or if it persists beyond the fourth month.

a suck or follow a first or second swallow. The act of deglutition involves muscles of the mouth, tongue, palate, and pharynx and is dependent on a highly co-ordinated movement pattern. Cranial nerves V, VII, IX, X, and XII are involved in the act of swallowing. An immature swallow with tongue thrusting is sometimes seen until about eighteen months. A mature swallow is present afterwards. The reflex is mediated at the level of the brainstem in the medullary reticular formation. Disturbances in swallowing are frequent manifestations of neurologic deficits in the infant and child, and the most important sign of neurologic disorder among the feeding reflexes.

Tongue Reflex

This reflex may be considered part of a suckle-swallow reaction in which the tongue thrusts between the lips. If lips or tongue are touched, cranial nerve XII predominates. Excessive thrusts beyond eighteen months are abnormal. The reflex is mediated at the medulla.

Bite Reflex

Moderate pressure on the gums elicits jaw closure and a bite response. This reflex is present at birth and in the normal infant disappears by the ninth to the twelfth month, when it is replaced by a more mature chewing pattern. The reflex may show exaggeration in the brain-injured child and may interfere with feeding and dental care. Its persistence inhibits the lateral jaw movements of chewing seen in the spontaneous mastication pattern. A weak response is seen with brainstem lesion. Corticobulbar lesions exaggerate the response. Cranial nerve V innervates the reflex. It is mediated at the low midbrain and pons.

Gag Reflex

A stimulus applied to the posterior half of the infant tongue or a stimulus on the posterior wall of the pharynx stimulates a rapid velopharyngeal closure. This primary action is accompanied by mouth opening, head extension, depression of the floor of the mouth with an elevation of the larynx and diaphragm. This reflex is present at birth and continues throughout life. The gag serves as a protective mechanism for the esophagus. Brain-damaged children often show a hyperactive gag. In the severely motor-involved child, the gag may be difficult to elicit. In the ataxic child, the gag is sometimes hypoactive. Cranial nerves IX and X innervate the gag, and the reflex is mediated at the level of the pons and medulla (see Figure 12-11).

FIGURE 12-11 The gag reflex. The reflex is elicited by stimulating the posterior half of the infant's tongue with a tongue
blade or stimulating the posterior pharyngeal wall. The reflex
is present from birth. The reflex is pathologic if it is absent or
exaggerated.

Assessing Mastication and Deglutition

In the infant and child at risk for neurologic injury, the clinical evaluation of
neural control of the oral and pharyngeal activities involved in chewing and
swallowing allows the speech-language pathologist to estimate the motor potential of those muscles that ultimately will fall under the control of higher
nervous centers devoted to the production of speech. The fact that speech and

feeding are mediated at different levels within the nervous system implies that evaluation of chewing and swallowing will predict future muscle activity in speech in only a very limited manner. Probably mere gross estimates of muscle potential for speech can be derived from any nonspeech examination because of the semiautonomous control of the muscles for the dual function.

In addition to gross estimation of muscle function in mastication and deglutition, the infantile oral motor examination of the cranial nerves for speech permits the speech-language pathologist and neurologist to observe signs of possible neurologic disorder that may not be readily apparent in other motor behaviors. Mastication and deglutition, as relatively complex motor behaviors in the repertoire of infant motor activity, are highly sensitive to neurologic dysfunction. Dysphagia may be an early and even sometimes an isolated sign of brain injury.

Modified Feeding

Examination of chewing and swallowing is best accomplished through the technique of modified feeding. In the prespeaking child, this technique can replace the more traditional procedures of the adult speech cranial nerve test, which requires a level of maturity not yet developed in the infant and very young child. By selectively placing small morsels of solid food in different locations in the oral cavity of the child, an examiner can judge the integrity of the bulbar muscles and the brainstem neural pathways innervating these muscles. Normal children from birth to thirty-six months respond well to the technique. It may be used with motor-handicapped children with oral motor involvement well beyond three years of age. In the normal child, spontaneous feeding emerges out of the neonatal oral and pharyngeal reflexes and reaches its full maturity at about the age of three. Experiences with solid foods provide a gradual refinement and integration of movements of the lips, tongue, palate, and pharynx for chewing and swallowing.

When testing the infant or motor-handicapped child without sitting balance, it is usually best to place the child in a supine position with the head resting on a small pillow. In the child with some sitting balance, placement in a relaxed sitting position with adequate head support is preferred for the examination. Usually the mere presence of food will intrigue the child into opening the mouth for examination. In the rare child who is resistant, compression of the nostrils will force the mouth open for breathing and allow some observation of muscle action of the lips and tongue if morsels of food are placed in the mouth.

Cranial Nerve VII

Placing a small food bolus first on the lower lip in midline and observing the child's oral reaction to it will provide evidence of the ability to use the muscles of the lip and lower face purposefully. Pursing the lips during rooting and sucking indicates intact facial movement. Lack of a smiling response may be suggestive of severe bilateral facial muscle involvement. The normal baby smiles to a human face at two to four months of age. A sober expression and sluggish grin must be carefully evaluated as a possible neurologic sign of a bilateral corticobulbar system involvement ultimately affecting the paired nerves of cranial nerve VII. An asymmetrical smile with a unilateral flattening of the nasal fold on one side of the face may be associated with unilateral paresis. This sign is not as obvious in the infant and young child as it is in the adult. Lack of lip tonicity may be present, and lip seal may not be maintained. In the brain-damaged child, drooling may result from the poor lip seal.

Cranial Nerve XII

The child with cerebral injury often is unable to shape, point, and protrude the tongue in retrieving food from the lower lip by licking. The lack of tongue protrusion is common in both spastic and athetoid children. In the brain-injured infant, the tongue often will not cup, even during crying. Neither will the tongue thin, nor will the tip elevate with precision. This inability to produce any fine tongue movements suggests motor involvement of both the intrinsic and the extrinsic tongue musculature.

Unilateral or bilateral atrophy of the tongue may be seen in young children, and this loss of muscle bulk suggests lower motor neuron disease. However, fasciculations are rarely seen in the tongue muscles of infants.

Excessive tongue thrust, sometimes called the tongue reflex, is common in children with severe brain damage. It is particularly common in athetosis. It may be associated with orthodontic problems and excessive drooling. In addition, occasional wavelike involuntary movements are seen in the body of the tongue mimicking the involuntary movements of limb and trunk in extrapyramidal athetosis.

Cranial Nerve V

When confronted with a small food bolus on the lips or tongue, the young child begins the total act of deglutition by initiating voluntary mastication. The aim of the evaluation at this point is to determine whether the bolus of food can be pulverized and whether the particles of food can be selectively manipulated to transport the food to the back of the oral cavity. With a large food bolus the tongue is usually elevated, so the bolus is placed between the tongue surface and the anterior hard palate and crushed. Smaller boluses of food are crushed between the hard palate and tongue, and the tongue directly begins a wavelike, peristaltic movement, carrying the food to the pharynx. If the food bolus is large, the tongue often acts in a whiplike fashion to propel the food laterally between the molars for grinding and pulverization. Observation of the vigorous tongue actions will confirm the integrity of the neural control of the tongue.

Disorders involving neurologic integrity of the tongue and jaw innervation often force cerebrally damaged children to eat only diced or liquified food.

Adequate biting and vigorous anterior-posterior movements of the mandible plus lateral grinding action of the jaws assures the speech-language pathologist that cranial nerve V innervation is intact and that muscles innervated from the pons are functional. On the other hand, an exaggerated and too powerful bite may be a manifestation of an abnormal jaw reflex, suggesting an upper motor neuron lesion above the level of the pons. In older children with brain damage, a firm tap on the lower jaw may elicit a clonus, suggesting a hyperactive jaw reflex. If the lower jaw deviates to one side on jaw opening or during mastication, it suggests pterygoid muscle weakness on the side of deviation. In athetosis the jaw may become a major articulator, producing the motor power for elevating a poorly controlled tongue in achieving tongue-tip-alveolar ridge contacts and other tongue-elevation gestures.

Integration of V, VII, IX–X, and XII

When the food bolus is well masticated, the final, involuntary stage of deglutition is initiated. The nasopharynx is closed by the action of the muscles of the soft palate and the pharyngeal constrictors. Cranial nerves IX and X produce this closure. Saliva or the food bolus is pushed through the palatal fauces, into the pharynx, and on to the esophagus in a peristaltic wave. Muscles of the soft palate, the pharyngeal constrictors, and the muscles of the tongue and larynx work in intricate coordination to propel the food bolus to the esophagus. In one sense, swallowing becomes the penultimate integration of the nervous mechanisms to be used later in motor expression of speech.

Speech, however, requires more intricate coordination of muscles than do chewing and swallowing. This fine coordination is accomplished through increasing cortical and cerebellar control of the pontine and bulbar muscles. Certain other complex motor adjustments are seen in speech that are not seen in chewing or swallowing. As an example, the grooved fricative /s/ requires finer motor control than is seen in mastication. To produce an adequate /s/, a central groove in the lip and blade of the tongue must be formed, with the sides of the tongue firmly anchored between the lateral dentition. This specific tongue configuration, common to speech, is not seen in brainstem-mediated functions. Intricate coordination of intrinsic and extrinsic tongue muscles is needed for the grooved fricatives. These fine motor configurations are not present in feeding. Thus an assessment of mastication and deglutition in a prespeaking child suspected of neurologic impairment is most appropriate, but when speech emerges, the evaluation of motor control should be based on the motor control for phonemes, syllables, words, and sentences assessed in the traditional articulation test format, and the results of a standard oral examination that includes assessment of the speech cranial nerves (see Chapter 7).

The action of all the cranial nerves for speech and of the corticobulbar system, which activates the cranial nerve nuclei, can be assessed in infancy through observation of chewing and swallowing. All the nervous action of the bulbar muscles are integrated into the single act of feeding in infancy.

Summary

The developmental motor speech disorders include developmental dysarthria, developmental anarthria, and developmental apraxia of speech. Developmental dysarthria is by far the most common of the motor speech disorders and is most frequently seen in children with cerebral palsy. Cerebral palsy is primarily a movement disorder due to damage to the immature brain. The three major clinical syndromes of cerebral palsy are spasticity, athetosis, and ataxia. Most cerebral palsied children present multiple disabilities in addition to their motor disorder.

Next to cerebral palsy, childhood muscular dystrophy is the most common motor disorder in children. Pseudohypertropic muscular dystrophy is the largest subgroup of the childhood dystrophies. Flaccid dysarthria may appear in the later stages of this progressive degenerative disease. An uncommon syndrome is an isolated motor involvement of the oral muscles. This disorder has been called congenital suprabulbar paresis.

The diagnosis of early neurologic injury is dependent on a total pediatric neurologic examination that usually includes an assessment of the primitive reflexes of the first year of life. Absent or highly persistent reflexes are usually indicative of abnormality. Among the best-studied reflexes are the: (1) asymmetrical tonic neck reflex, (2) symmetrical tonic neck reflex, (3) positive support reflex, (4) tonic labyrinthine reflex, (5) segmental rolling reflex, (6) Galant reflex, and (7) Moro reflex. Only the tonic labyrinthine reflex may activate an oral response of tongue thrusting.

The influence of persistent oral reflexes or dysphagic symptoms on later speech production in developmental dysarthria is controversial, but speech-language pathologists and pediatric neurologists usually recognize the following oral reflexes as often disturbed by early cerebral injury: the rooting reflex, suckling reflex, swallowing reflex, bite reflex, tongue-thrust reflex, and gag reflex. These infantile oral reactions are mediated at a brainstem level, whereas speech movements are initiated and carried out through the corticobulbar system and influenced by other motor systems.

In the infant and older prespeaking child, a gross estimate of the movement potential of the oral muscles can be obtained by observing the muscle action in mastication and deglutition in modified feeding activities. Chewing and swallowing involves the integration of the action of the cranial nerves V, VII, IX–X, and XII, those nerves that are critical for normal speech production. In the older child, a standard cranial nerve examination suggests the degree of motor involvement on speech production.

References and Further Readings

Cerebral Palsy

Hardy, J. C. (1983). *Cerebral palsy*. Englewood Cliffs, NJ: Prentice-Hall.

Meyer, L. A. (1982). A study of vocal, prosodic and articulatory parameters of the speech of spastic and athetotic cerebral palsied individuals. Ph.D dissertation, Vanderbilt University.

Neilson, P. D., & O'Dwyer, N. J. (1981). Physiopathology of dysarthria in cerebral palsy. *Journal of Neurology, Neurosurgery and Psychiatry*, 44, 1013–1019.

Scherzer, A. I., & Tscharnuter, I. (1982). *Early diagnosis and therapy in cerebral palsy*. New York: Marcel Dekker.

Thompson, G. H., Rubin, I. L., & Bilenker, R. H. (1983). *Comprehensive management of cerebral palsy*. New York: Grune and Stratton.

Childhood Suprabulbar Paresis

Worster-Drought, C. (1974). Suprabulbar paresis. *Developmental Medicine and Child Neurology*, 16 Supplement 30, 1–30.

Muscular Dystrophy

Sanders, L. J., & Perlstein, M. A. (1965). Speech mechanism in pseudohypertrophic muscular dystrophy. *American Journal of Diseases of Children*, 109, 538–543.

Walton, J. N. (1981). *Disorders of voluntary muscle* (4th ed.). London: Churchill-Livingstone.

Primitive Reflexes

Capute, A. J., Accardo, P. J., Vining, E. P. G., & Rubenstein, J. E. (1978). *Primitive reflex profile*. Baltimore: University Park Press.

Oral and Pharyngeal Reflexes

Anderson, D. J., & Mathews, B. (1976). *Mastication*. Bristol: Wright.

Dubner, R., Sessle, B. J., & Storey, A. T. (1978). *The neural basis of oral and facial function*. New York: Plenum.

Love, R. J., Hagerman, E. L., & Tiami, E. G. (1980). Speech performance, dysphagia and oral reflexes in cerebral palsy. *Journal of Speech and Hearing Disorders*, 45, 59–75.

Shane, H. C., & Bashir, A. S. (1980). Election criteria for adoption of an augmentive communication system: Preliminary considerations. *Journal of Speech and Hearing Disorders*, 45, 408–414.

Synopsis of Medical Conditions Related to Communication Disorders

I. Congenital Disorders
    A. *Cerebral palsy:* Defect of motor power and coordination related to damage of the immature brain.
    B. *Congenital hydrocephalus:* A condition marked by excessive accumulation of fluid, dilating the cerebral ventricles, thinning the brain, and causing a separation of cranial bones; caused by developmental defect of the brain.
    C. *Craniostenosis:* A contraction of the cranial capacity or narrowing of the sutures by bony overgrowth.
    D. *Down's syndrome:* A syndrome of mental retardation associated with many and variable abnormalities, caused by representation of at least a critical portion of chromosome 21 three times instead of twice in some or all cells.
    E. *Idiopathic mental retardation:* Mental retardation of unknown cause.
    F. *Minimal cerebral dysfunction:* A syndrome of neurologic dysfunction in children usually marked by impairments of fine coordination,

clumsiness, and choreiform or athetoid movements. Learning disorders are often associated with the diagnosis of MCD.

G. *Neurofibromatosis:* Small, discrete, pigmented skin lesions that develop in infancy or early childhood, followed by the development of multiple subcutaneous neurofibromas that may slowly increase in number and size over many years.

II. Vascular Disorders

A. *Cerebral embolism:* Obstruction or occlusion of a vessel in the cerebrum by a transported clot or vegetation, a mass of bacteria, or other foreign material.

B. *Cerebral hemorrhage:* Bleeding; a flow of blood, especially if it is very profuse into the substance of the cerebrum, usually in the region of the internal capsule by the rupture of the lenticulostriate artery.

C. *Cerebral thrombosis:* Obstruction or occlusion of a vessel in the cerebrum by a fixed clot developing on the arterial wall.

D. *Pseudobulbar palsy:* Muscular paralysis from UMN lesions of the cranial nerves. Often accompanied by signs of dysarthria, dysphagia, and emotional liability with outbursts of uncontrolled crying and laughing.

E. *Recurrent cerebral ischemia or transient ischemic attacks:* Temporary disruptions of the blood supply that produce specific neurological signs; experienced as sudden, transient blurring of vision; weakness; numbness of one side, difficulty with speech; vertigo or diplopia; or any combination of these.

F. *Subdural hemorrhage:* Extravascularization of blood between the dural and arachnoid membranes.

III. Infections

A. *Acute anterior poliomyelitis:* Inflammation of the anterior cornu of the spinal cord; an acute infectious disease marked by fever, pains, and gastroenteric disturbances; followed by flaccid paralysis of one or more muscular groups and later by atrophy.

B. *Cerebral abscess:* Intracranial abscess; abscess of the brain, specifically of the cerebrum; a collection of pus in a localized area.

C. *Encephalitis:* Inflammation of the brain.

D. *Jacob-Creutzfeldt disease:* Spastic pseudosclerosis with cortico-striatal-spinal degeneration, subacute presenile dementia; characterized by slowly progressive dementia, myoclonic fasciculations, ataxia, and somnolence; gradual onset; usually fatal within a few months to years.

E. *Meningitis:* Inflammation of the membranes of the brain or spinal cord.

F. *Neurosyphilis:* Syphilis affecting the nervous system; an infectious venereal disease caused by a microorganism.

G. *Sydenham's chorea:* An acute toxic or infective disorder of the nervous system, usually associated with acute rheumatism occurring in young persons and characterized by involuntary semipurposeful but ineffective movements; these involve the facial muscles and muscles of the neck and limbs, intensified by voluntary effort but disappearing in sleep.

IV. Trauma

A. *Penetrating head injury:* Open head injury; causes altered consciousness, can produce fairly definitive and chronic aphasias.

B. *Closed head injury:* An injury to the head in which there is no injury to the skull or in which injury is limited to an undisplaced fracture; also known as nonpenetrating head injury; can produce loss of consciousness; often produces diffuse effects.

V. Tumors

A. *Astrocytomas grades 1–2 and oligodendrogliomas:* Less common of the glial cell tumors, with a better prognosis than glioblastoma multiforme. Slow growing, usually treated with surgery and radiation therapy, with an average survival rate of five to six years after surgery.

B. *Glioblastoma multiforme:* Also known as malignant glioma or astrocytoma grades 3–4. Most common primary brain tumor in adults. Most frequent sites are frontal and temporal lobes, although they may occur anywhere in the brain. Infiltrative and rapidly growing, with an average survival rate of about one year.

C. *Meningioma:* Benign tumor arising from the arachnoid cells of the brain. Slow growing and usually occurring at the lateral areas and base of the brain; generally does not invade the cerebral cortex; favorable prognosis.

VI. Degenerative Diseases

A. *Presenile dementia:* General mental deterioration due to organic or psychological factors, developing before age 65.

B. *Senile dementia:* Progressive mental deterioration in the aged, with loss of memory, especially for recent events.

C. *Parkinson's disease:* A degenerative disease resulting from damage to the dopamine-producing nerve cells of the striatum and the substantia nigra; characterized by rest tremor, rigidity of muscles, paucity of movement, slowness of movement, limited range, limited force of contraction, and failure of gestural expression.

D. *Wilson's disease:* A genetic metabolic disorder caused by inadequate processing of dietary intake of copper. The disorder is characterized by motor symptoms, with a significant dysarthria.

E. *Huntington's chorea:* A chronic progressive hereditary disease, characterized by irregular, spasmodic, involuntary movements of the limbs or facial muscles; sometimes accompanied by dementia and dysarthria.

F.   *Friedreich's ataxia:* A hereditary disease characterized by degeneration principally of the cerebellum and dorsal half of the spinal cord. Ataxic dysarthria is often an accompanying sign.

G.   *Dystonia musculorum deformans:* A hereditary disease occurring especially in children; characterized by muscular contractions producing peculiar distentions of the spine and hip; bizarre postures.

H.   *Multiple sclerosis:* An inflammatory disease involving mainly the white matter of the central nervous system in which there are scattered areas of demyelination causing impairment of transmission of nerve impulses. May cause a variety of symptoms, including paralysis, nystagmus, and dysarthria, depending on the lesion sites.

VII. Metabolic and Toxic Disorders

A.   *Reye's syndrome:* Sudden loss of consciousness in children following the initial stage of an infection, usually resulting in death with cerebral edema (swelling) and marked fatty change in the liver and renal system. Surviving children often have motor, cognitive, and speech problems.

VIII. Neuromuscular Disorders

A.   Progressive muscular atrophies

1.   *True bulbar palsy:* Disorder caused by involvement of nuclei of the last four or five cranial nerves, characterized by twitching and atrophy of the tongue, palate, and larynx; drooling; dysarthria; dysphagia; and finally respiratory paralysis. Usually a manifestation of amyotropic lateral sclerosis (ALS).

2.   *Amyotrophic lateral sclerosis (ALS):* A disease of the motor tracts of the lateral columns of the spinal cord causing progressive muscular atrophy, increased reflexes, fibrillary twitching, and spastic irritability of muscles.

B.   Muscular dystrophy

1.   *Pseudohypertrophic (Duchenne) type:* A type of muscular dystrophy characterized by bulky calf and forearm muscles and progressive atrophy and weakness of the thigh, hip, and back muscles and shoulder girdle; occurs in the first three years of life, usually in males and rarely in females.

2.   *Facio-scapulohumeral type:* Muscular dystrophy causing atrophy of the muscles of the face, shoulder, girdle, and upper arms; occurs in either sex, with onset at any age from childhood to late adult life, characterized by prolonged periods of apparent arrest.

3.   *Ocular myopathy:* Muscular dystrophy affecting external ocular muscles, causing ptosis, diplopia, and possibly total external ophthalmoplegia; sometimes there is associated upper facial

   muscle weakness; dysphagia; and atrophy and weakness of neck, trunk, and limb muscles.

C. *Myasthenia gravis:* A disorder characterized by marked weakness and fatigue of muscles, especially those muscles innervated by bulbar nuclei.

D. Congenital neuromuscular disorders

  1. *Mobius syndrome:* A congenital disorder characterized by paresis or paralysis of both lateral rectus muscles and all face muscles; sometimes associated with other musculoskeletal anomalies.

IX. Other

A. *Epilepsy:* A chronic disorder characterized by paroxysmal attacks of brain dysfunction (seizures) usually associated with some alteration of consciousness. The seizures may remain confined to elementary or complex impairment of behavior or may progress to a generalized convulsion.

B. *Wernicke-Korsakoff syndrome:* A cerebral disorder characterized by confusion and severe impairment of memory, especially for recent events. The patient compensates for the memory loss by confabulation. The syndrome is often seen in chronic alcoholics and is associated with severe nutritional deficiency.

Bedside Neurological Examination

I. Mental Status
    A. Orientation: person, place, time
    B. Memory and information
        1. 3 objects at 5 minutes
        2. Presidents back to Kennedy
    C. Language
        1. Spontaneous speech characterization
        2. Confrontation naming
        3. Auditory comprehension (commands, yes/no questions)
        4. Repetition (words, phrases)
        5. Reading (printed commands)
        6. Writing (signature, words, and sentences to dictation)
    D. Calculations
        1. Serial 7s (count by 7s to 100)
        2. $0.43 from $1.00
    E. Visuospatial ability
        1. Clock drawing
        2. Copying of figures
    F. Insight, judgment
II. Cranial Nerves
    A. I   Smell
    B. II Visual fields, pupillary reactions, optic fundi
    C. III, IV, V   Extraocular movements

Source: Developed by Howard Kirshner, M.D., Department of Neurology, Vanderbilt University School of Medicine.

    D.   V   Facial sensation
    E.   VII   Facial symmetry
    F.   VIII   Hearing
    G.   IX, X   Articulation, palatal movement, gag reflex
    H.   XI   Sternomastoid, trapezius strength
    I.   XII   Tongue movement

III. Motor Examination
    A.   Bulk
    B.   Spontaneous movements (fasciculations, tremor, movement disorders)
    C.   Strength
        1.   Evaluation of strength on right and left
            a.   deltoid
            b.   biceps
            c.   triceps
            d.   hip flexion
            e.   knee flexion
            f.   ankle dorsiflexion
            g.   ankle plantar flexion
    D.   Reflexes
        1.   Evaluation of reflexes on right and left
            a.   biceps
            b.   triceps
            c.   brachioradialis
            d.   ankle
            e.   plantar
            f.   jaw
    E.   Stance and Romberg
    F.   Gait
        1.   Spontaneous gait
        2.   Tandem gait
        3.   Tiptoe gait
        4.   Heel gait
    G.   Sensory examination
        1.   Pinprick
        2.   Touch
        3.   Vibration
        4.   Position
        5.   Stereognosis, graphesthesia ("cortical" sensory modalities)
    H.   Cerebellar
        1.   Finger–nose–finger
        2.   Rapid alternating hand movements
        3.   Fine finger movements
        4.   Heel–knee–shin

Screening Neurologic Examination for Speech-Language Pathology

I. Mental Status
   A. *General behavior and appearance:* Is the patient normal, hyperactive, agitated, quiet, immobile? Is he neat, slovenly? Is he dressed in accordance with his peers, background, and sex?
   B. *Stream of talk:* Does he respond to conversation normally? Is his speech rapid, incessant, under great pressure? Is he very slow and difficult to draw into spontaneous talk? Is he discursive, able to reach the conversational goal?
   C. *Mood and affective responses:* Is the patient euphoric, agitated, inappropriately gay, giggling; or is he silent, weeping, angry? Does his mood swing in a direction appropriate to the subject matter of the conversation? Is he emotionally labile?
   D. *Content of thought:* Does the patient have illusions, hallucinations or delusions, and misinterpretations? Is he preoccupied with bodily complaints, fears of cancer or heart disease, and other phobias? Does he feel that society is maliciously organized to cause him difficulty?

Source: Adapted with permission from W. DeMyer, *Technique of the Neurologic Examination* (New York: McGraw-Hill, 1980).

E. *Intellectual capacity:* Is he bright, average, dull, obviously demented, mentally retarded?

F. *Sensorium*

    1. Consciousness: Is patient alert, drowsy, or stuporous?

    2. Attention span: Note response in cerebral function test.

    3. Orientation: Can he answer questions about his person, location, and time?

    4. Memory: Recent and remote, as disclosed during history taking.

    5. Fund of information: Note in history-taking.

    6. Insight, judgment, and planning: Note in history-taking.

    7. Calculation: Note performance on cerebral function test.

II. Speech, Language, and Voice

A. *Dysphonia:* Neuromotor difficulty in producing voice (X).

B. *Dysarthria:* Neuromotor disorder of articulation and voice

    1. Labials (VII)

    2. Velars and velopharyngeal closure (IX-X)

    3. Linguals (XII)

C. *Dysphasia:* Cerebral disorder of understanding and expressing language

    1. Fluent
    2. Nonfluent   } (Give screening aphasia test.)

D. *Dyspraxia:* Cerebral disorder of articulation and prosody and/or disorder of oral movement

    1. Dyspraxia of speech

    2. Oral dyspraxia

E. *Dementia:* Cerebral disorder of language of intellectual deficit

    1. Presenile

    2. Senile

F. *Disorganized Language:* Cerebral disorder of language of confusion.

G. *Dysphagia:* Neuromotor disorder of chewing and swallowing (V, IX–X, XII).

III. Cranial Nerves for Speech and Hearing

A. *Speech* (V, VII, IX–X, XII, and XI)

    1. V: Inspect masseter and temporalis muscle bulk, and palpate masseter when the patient bites.

    2. VII: Forehead wrinkling, eyelid closure, mouth retraction, whistling, or puffed out cheeks, wrinkled skin over neck (platysma), and labial articulation.

    3. IX–X: Phonation, hypernasality, swallowing, gag reflex, palatal elevation.

    4. XII: Lingual articulation, midline and lateral tongue protrusion, inspect for atrophy, and fasciculations.

    5. XI: Inspect sternocleidomastoid and trapezius contours, and test strength of head movements and shoulder shrugging.

      6.   Test for pathologic fatigability by requesting 100 repetitive movements (eye blink, etc.) if the history suggests myopathic or myoneural disorder.

  B. *Hearing* (VIII)

      1.   Threshold and acuity: Adequacy of hearing for conversational speech.

      2.   If history or preceding observation suggests a deficit, do air-bone conduction audiometric screening.

IV. Motor System

  A. *Inspection*

      1.   Initial appraisal of the motor system occurs when you take the history. Inspect the patient for postures, general activity level, tremors, and involuntary movements.

      2.   Observe the size and contour of the muscles, looking for atrophy, hypertrophy, body asymmetry, joint misalignments, fasciculations, tremors, and involuntary movements.

      3.   *Gait testing:* Free walking, tandem walking, deep knee bend.

  B. *Palpation:* Palpate muscles if they seem atrophic or hypertrophic, or if the history suggests that they may be tender or in spasm.

  C. *Strength*

      1.   *Upper extremities:* Test biceps.

      2.   *Lower extremities:* Test knee flexors and foot dorsiflexors, if necessary and feasible.

      3.   Discern whether any weakness follows a distributional pattern, such as proximal-distal, right-left, or upper extremity–lower extremity.

  D. *Muscle tone:* Make passive movements of joints to test for spasticity, clonus, or rigidity.

  E. *Muscle stretch (deep) reflexes:* Jaw jerk (V afferent, V efferent) as well as other MSRs, if necessary and feasible.

  F. *Cerebellar system* (gait tested previously)

      1.   Finger-to-nose, rebound, alternating motion rates

      2.   Heel-to-knee

V. Sensory Examination

  A. Test superficial sensation by light touch with cotton wisp and pin prick on face.

  B. Ask if the face feels numb.

  C. Test superficial sensation on the tongue surface with swab stick unilaterally and bilaterally, both anteriorly and posteriorly.

VI. Cerebral Function

  A. When the history of antecedent examination suggests a cerebral lesion, test for finger agnosia and right-left disorientation.

  B. Have the patient do the cognitive, constructional, and performance tasks from standard aphasia or neuropsychological tests.

Glossary of Terms

abduction: movement of a body part away from the midline.

acalculia: inability to do simple arithmetical calculation due to brain injury.

action potential: a buildup of electrical current in the neuron.

acuity: sharpness or acuteness.

adduction: movement of a body part toward midline.

afferent: traveling toward a center.

agnosia: a lack of sensory recognition as the result of a lesion in the sensory association areas or association pathways of the brain.

alexia: an acquired disturbance of reading due to brain injury.

alexia with agraphia: a classic neurologic syndrome of reading disorder in which there is damage to the angular gyrus and the surrounding areas.

alexia without agraphia: a classic neurologic syndrome of reading disorder, usually caused by a left posterior cerebral artery occlusion in a right-handed person. The resulting infarct produces lesions in the splenium of the corpus callosum and the left occipital lobe.

alpha motor neurons: neurons allowing contraction of extrafusal fibers. They are neurons that have their final common path in cranial and spinal nerves.

Alzheimer's disease: the most common type of dementia. The most striking feature is progressive deterioration of cognitive functions. Language disturbance is a major symptom in Alzheimer's and Alzheimer-like dementia.

angular gyrus: a convolution in the left parietal lobe that is critical for language processing.

anomia: loss of the power to name objects or recognize and recall their names.

anoxia: absence of oxygen in inspired gases, arterial blood, or tissue.

anterior horn cell: a cell in the ventral portion in an H-shaped body of gray matter in the spinal cord associated with efferent pathways.

apex: the extremity of a conical or pyramidal structure.

apraxia: a disorder of learned movement distinct from paralysis, weakness, and incoordination, that results in a disturbance of motor planning.

apraxia of speech: a disorder of programming the muscles of articulation in the absence of paralysis, weakness, and incoordination.

arcuate fasciculus: a long subcortical association tract connecting posterior and anterior speech-language areas in the cerebrum.

association area of association areas: the area of the inferior parietal lobe where the visual, auditory, and tactile association fibers converge.

asymmetry: disproportion or inequality between two corresponding parts around the center of an axis.

asynergy: a lack of coordination of agonistic and antagnostic muscles, particularly associated with cerebellar disorders.

ataxia: defect of posture and gait associated with a disorder of the nervous system. Sensory ataxia, associated with dorsal column dysfunction, is distinguished from cerebellar or cerebellar pathway ataxia.

autism: a major developmental disability marked by disturbed stereotyped behavior and language patterns. Echolalic verbal behavior is often present, as are neurologic signs.

axon: literally, "the axis"—a straight, relatively unbranched process of a nerve cell.

basal ganglia: a group of subcortical structures, part of the extrapyramidal system, which are associated with motor control of tone and posture.

bilateral: related to or having two sides.

border zone: the limit of the cerebral area served by either the anterior, middle, or posterior cerebral arteries.

bouton: from the French, meaning "button"—a synaptic knob.

brain scan: a neurodiagnostic tool utilizing a radioisotope to detect damaged brain tissue.

Broca's aphasia: a common adult language disorder characterized by nonfluent speech and language, usually accompanied by hemiplegia and an anterior lesion of the brain.

Broca's area: a major speech-language center in the dominant frontal lobe, important for expression of language.

capsular: referring to the internal capsule.

cerebral arteriogram: an X-ray picture of the arteries of the brain after injection of a contrast medium.

cerebrum: the major portion of the brain, consisting of two hemispheres, which contain the cortex and its underlying white matter as well as the basal ganglia and other basal structures.

chorea: a disorder characterized by irregular, spasmodic, involuntary movements of the limbs or facial muscles.

choreiform: resembling chorea.

circumlocution: a wordy and circuitous description of an unrecalled word.

clonus: a form of movement marked by contractions and relaxations of a muscle, occurring in rapid succession.

colliculi: little hills or mounds within the brain. The superior and inferior colliculi are two examples found in the midbrain.

competence/performance: *Competence* refers to the innate rules of language that are presumably stored in brain tissue. *Performance* refers to the overt use of the rules of language in speaking, writing, and gesturing.

computerized tomography (CT): an X-ray imaging technique in which the brain is viewed at different depths and these various views are correlated by computer to show structural lesions of the brain.

conduction aphasia: an adult language disorder in which auditory comprehension is good, but exact repetition is poor. The site of lesion producing the syndrome is in debate, but it may interrupt the arcuate fasciculus.

confabulation: the verbal or written expression of fictitious experiences.

confusional state: acute symptoms of mental disorganization and agitation that may accompany head trauma or other medical conditions. The language is often marked by irrelevancy and confabulation.

connectionism: theory of brain function that gives prominence to the interconnection of the association fibers between brain centers.

construction disturbance: the inability to form a construction in space because of a cerebral deficit.

contralateral: related to the opposite side, as when pain is felt or paralysis occurs on the side opposite to the site of the lesion.

corpus callosum: the largest transversal commissure between the hemispheres; it is about 4 inches long.

corpus quadragemia: the two pairs of colliculi (superior and inferior) of the midbrain.

decussate: crossing over or intersection of parts.

deglutition: the act of swallowing.

dendrite: literally, "treelike"—the short branching processes of a nerve cell.

denervation: a cutting of the nerve supply by excision, incision, or blocking.

dentate nucleus: the largest and most lateral of the deep nuclei of the cerebellum.

dichotic listening: a test situation in which simultaneous auditory stimuli are presented to both ears at the same time. Ear preference (right or left) refers to the ear in which auditory stimulus is first recognized in a dichotic listening situation.

diplegia: paralysis of corresponding parts on both sides of the body.

diplopia: double vision.

distal: away from the center of the body.

dysdiadochokinesia: the inability to perform and sustain rapid alternating movements. Speech-language pathologists in particular have applied this term to a motor deficit in the oral muscles. The measure is also called alternate motion rate. Dysdiadochokinesia has been a neurologic sign associated with cerebellar disorder syndromes.

dyskinesia: a disorder of movement usually associated with a lesion of the extrapyramidal system.

dysmetria: the inability to gauge the distance, speed, and power of a movement.

dysphagia: difficulty with swallowing.

dysprosody: disturbance of stress, timing, and melody of speech.

efferent: conducting (fluid or nerve impulses) outward from a given organ or part.

electroencephalogram: a graphic record of electrical activity of the brain as recorded by an electroencephalograph.

encephalitis: inflammation of the brain.

encephalopathy: pathology of the brain.

equilibrium: equally balanced.

etiology: the cause of disease or damage.

extensor: a muscle, the contraction of which tends to shorten a limb; antagonist to flexors.

extraocular: adjacent to but outside the eyeball.

facilitation: process of making the nerve impulses easier by repeated use of certain axons.

fasciculation: involuntary contractions or twitches in a group of muscle fibers.

fissure: a groove on the surface of the brain or spinal cord.

flaccid: flabby; without tone.

fluent/nonfluent: a dichotomous classification of aphasic language on the basis of the type of conversational speech.

foramen: an aperture or perforation through a bone or a membranous structure.

frontal alexia: a reading disorder, known as the "third alexia," associated with a lesion in the left frontal lobe, often accompanying a Broca's aphasia.

gamma motor neuron: neurons innervating the muscle spindle, allowing contraction of intrafusal fibers and increase in the sensitivity of the fibers to the muscle stretch reflex.

genu: any structure of angular shape resembling a flexed knee.

Gerstmann syndrome: a cluster of left parietal lobe lesion signs including finger agnosia, left-right disorientation, acalculia, and agraphia. A developmental form of the syndrome has been described.

gyrus: an elevation or ridge on the surface of the cerebrum.

hemianopsia: a visual-field defect of one-half of the eye field.

hemiplegia: paralysis of one side of the body.

hemorrhage: bleeding; a flow of blood, especially if it is very profuse.

Henschen's axiom: restitution of speech is due to the opposite hemisphere.

homunculus: literally, "little man." A caricature mapping the connections between the area of the motor or sensory cortex and the innervated body part.

hyperreflexia: a condition in which the deep tendon reflexes are exaggerated.

hypertonia: extreme tension of the muscles.

hypotonia: muscle flaccidity, defined as a decrease in normal muscle tone when passive movement is performed.

ideational apraxia: disorder of motor planning in which complex motor plans cannot be executed, although individual motor components of the plan can be performed.

ideomotor apraxia: a motor disturbance in which there is inability to carry out motor acts on command, but some evidence is present that these motor acts can be carried out imitatively or automatically.

innervate: to supply with efferent nerve impulses.

internuncial: a neuron functionally imposed between two or more other neurons.

intervertebral foramina: the openings between the vertebrae of the spinal cord through which the motor and sensory roots exit and unite to form the spinal nerves.

ipsilateral: on the same side.

island of Reil: (also insula) part of the cerebral cortex forming the floor of the lateral fissure.

kernicterus: a form of infantile jaundice in which a yellow pigment and degenerative lesions are found in areas of the intracranial gray matter.

lacrimal: related to the tears, their secretion, and the organs concerned with them.

language dominance: refers to the hemisphere that is the site for the major language areas and connections.

lesion: an area of damage in the body.

magnum foramen: opening in the base of the skull through which the spinal cord is continuous with the brain.

mamillary bodies: two nipple-shaped protuberances on the ventral surface of the hypothalamus. The mamillary nuclei inside have connections that are important to hypothalamic function.

masking: the "drowning" of a weak sound by a louder one.

mastication: the chewing of food.

minimal cerebral dysfunction (MCD): a syndrome of neurologic dysfunction in children usually marked by impairments of fine coordination, clumsiness, and choreiform or athetoid movements. Learning disorders are often associated with the diagnosis of MCD.

mixed dominance: the inconsistency in laterality of speech and related motor functions such as handedness, footedness, and eyedness in some individuals. Sometimes associated with language and learning disorders.

monoplegia: paralysis of one limb.

motor integration: a complete and harmonious combining of muscular elements of the nervous system.

myelin: the fatty substance surrounding some axons that speeds neural transmission.

myelogenesis: the cyclic process of laying down of myelin on certain fiber tracts. The myelin-covered areas are the white matter of the brain.

neologistic jargon: utterances that include meaningless, newly coined words.

neologistic jargon aphasia: a temporal lobe syndrome marked by newly coined words and unintelligible utterances.

neuron: nerve cell.

neural integration: a complete and harmonious combining of components of the nervous system.

nystagmus: rhythmical oscillation of the eyeballs, either horizontal, rotary, or vertical.

obligatory: without an alternate path.

olfaction: the sense of smell.

olivary nucleus: oval elevations in the medulla that are way-stations in the auditory pathways.

operculum: a lid or covering structure.

optic chiasm: the structure located on the floor of the third ventricle composed of the crossing optic nerve fibers from the medial (nasal) half of each retina and fibers from the lateral (temporal) half of each retina that do not cross midline.

oral apraxia: buccofacial apraxia; inability to program nonspeech oral movements.

organic brain syndrome: a psychiatric term used to describe deterioration of intellect and related functions due to brain dysfunction. The term *dementia* is the neurologic equivalent for the same condition.

palpate: to examine by feeling and pressing with the palms of the hands and fingers.

paraplegia: paralysis of both lower extremities and generally the lower trunk.

paraphasia: to substitute words or sounds in words in such a way as to decrease intelligibility or obscure meaning.

parasympathetic: that division of the autonomic nervous system concerned with the maintenance of the body. Its fibers arise from the brain and the sacral part of the spinal cord.

perisylvian zone: an area on the lateral wall of the dominant hemisphere for language that includes the major centers and pathways for language reception and production.

PET scan (positron emission tomography): an imaging technique that visualizes the functioning brain, showing its activity through blood flow and glucose metabolism.

phrenic nerves: nerves arising from the cervical spinal cord that supply the diaphragm.

plantar: relating to the sole of the foot.

plasticity: the concept that in the immature brain some functional areas are not established and that unestablished areas may assume any one of a variety of functions.

postganglionic: pertaining to those nerve fibers in the autonomic nervous system that are exiting the ganglion.

praxis: the normal performance of a motor act.

preganglionic: pertaining to those nerve fibers in the autonomic nervous system that are going toward a synapse at a ganglion but have not reached it.

prematurity: a state of being premature, denoting an infant born after less than thirty-seven weeks of gestation; birth weight is no longer considered a critical criterion.

prone: the body position when lying face down.

prosopagnosia: a variety of visual agnosia characterized by inability to recognize the faces of other people, or even one's own face in a mirror; associated with agnosia also for color, objects, and place.

proximal: toward the midline or center of the body.

pseudohypertrophy: increase in the size of an organ or part, due not to increase in size or number or the specific functional elements but to that of some other tissue, fatty or fibrous.

pulvinar: the posterior end of the thalamus.

putamen: a part of the lenticular nucleus, a structure of the basal ganglia.

quadriplegia: paralysis of all four limbs.

reflex arc: a pathway leading from a receptor of a sensory stimulus to a motor response, which is known as an automatic reflex action.

refractory period: a momentary state of reduced irritation after a neural response.

secretamotory: stimulating secretion.

servomechanism: a control device for maintaining the operation of another system.

soft signs: minor and inconsistent neurologic signs often said to be associated with a diagnosis of minimal cerebral dysfunction. These signs may indicate possible neurologic lesion or immaturity.

somesthesia: the consciousness of having a body.

somesthetic: pertaining to the senses of pain, temperature, taction, vibration, and position.

spasticity: the syndrome of hypertonus with exaggeration of stretch reflexes following certain neural lesions.

splenium: the thickened posterior part of the corpus callosum.

split brain: refers to the conditions in which the corpus callosum has been surgically divided so that there is no information flow between hemispheres.

sublingual: below the tongue.

substantia nigra: a mass of gray matter extending from the upper border of the pons into the subthalamic region.

sulcus: (also fissure) a groove on the surface of the brain or spinal cord.

summation: the product of the neural impulses acting on a given synapse.

supine: the body position when lying on the back.

supramarginal gyrus: a convolution in the inferior parietal lobe, surrounding the posterior end of the Sylvian fissure.

sympathetic: that division of the autonomic nervous system concerned with preparing the body for "fight or flight." Its neurons arise in the thoracic and upper lumbar segments of the spinal cord.

synapse: a juncture or connection. The functional contact of one neuron with another.

tectum: roof of the midbrain. It is composed of the superior and inferior colliculi.

transcortical aphasia: several types of language disturbances whose causes are lesions outside the perisylvian area.

transitory: related to or marked by a transition.

tremor: a purposeless involuntary movement that is oscillatory and rhythmic.

triplegia: paralysis of an upper and a lower extremity and of the face, or of both extremities on one side and one on the other.

uncus: the hooked extremity of the hippocampal gyrus.

vermis: the medial portion of the cerebellum between the two hemispheres.

vesicle: a blister or bladder. Intracellular bladder believed to be filled with neurotransmitter substances.

volitional: voluntary.

Wernicke's aphasia: a common adult language disorder characterized by fluent, paraphasic speech and language. The patient is free of hemiplegia, and the lesion is usually in the temporal lobe.

Wernicke's area: a major speech-language center in the dominant temporal lobe, important for comprehension of language.

Index